Which executive programme?

A critical guide to the world's best management development courses

Third edition

Stuart Crainer

FINANCIAL TIMES
MANAGEMENT

E·I·U

The Economist
Intelligence Unit

Financial Times Management
128 Long Acre, London WC2E 9AN   Tel: +44 (0) 171 447 2000   Fax: +44 (0) 171 240 5771
Website: http://www.ftmanagement.com
A Division of Financial Times Professional Limited

The Economist Intelligence Unit

The Economist Intelligence Unit is a specialist publisher serving companies establishing and managing operations across national borders. For over 50 years it has been a source of information on business developments, economic and political trends, government regulations and corporate practice worldwide.

The EIU delivers its information in four ways: through subscription products ranging from newsletters to annual reference works; through specific research reports, whether for general release or for particular clients; through electronic publishing; and by organising conferences and roundtables. The firm is a member of The Economist Group.

London	New York	Hong Kong
The Economist Intelligence Unit	The Economist Intelligence Unit	The Economist Intelligence Unit
15 Regent Street	The Economist Building	25/F, Dah Sing Financial Centre
London	111 West 57th Street	108 Gloucester Road
SW1Y 4LR	New York	Wanchai
United Kingdom	NY 10019, US	Hong Kong
Tel: (44.171) 830 1000	Tel: (1.212) 554 0600	Tel: (852) 2802 7288
Fax: (44.171) 499 9767	Fax: (1.212) 586 1181/2	Fax: (852) 2802 7638
e-mail: london@eiu.com	e-mail: newyork@eiu.com	e-mail: hongkong@eiu.com

Website: http://www.eiu.com

Electronic delivery
EIU Electronic
New York: Lou Celi or Lisa Hennessey   Tel: (1.212) 554 0600   Fax: (1.212) 586 0248
London: Jeremy Eagle Tel: (44.171) 830 1007   Fax: (44.171) 830 1023

© The Economist Intelligence Unit Limited 1998

Published 1998

ISBN 0 273 63566 2

British Library Cataloguing in Publication Data
A catalogue record of this book is available from the British Library

Library of Congress Cataloging in Publication Data applied for.

The authors of EIU Research Reports are drawn from a wide range of professional and academic disciplines. All the information in the reports is verified to the best of the authors' and the publisher's ability, but neither can accept responsibility for loss arising from decisions based on these reports. Where opinion is expressed, it is that of the authors, which does not necessarily coincide with the editorial views of The Economist Intelligence Unit Limited or of The Economist Newspaper Limited.

10 9 8 7 6 5 4 3 2 1

Typeset by the Economist Intelligence Unit
Printed by Bell and Bain Ltd., Glasgow

The Bradford Executive Development Programme

A strategic resource for business development

The Bradford Management Centre is far more than a provider of education for key executives. For more than thirty years we have proved to be a valued strategic resource for many national and international blue-chip companies - making tangible improvements to their business performances through people development.

We achieve this not by providing packaged solutions to unique requirements, but by developing co-operative programmes that are tailor-made for individual clients. We put the emphasis on fostering long-term relationships. It's our policy to get to know our clients and listen carefully to their particular needs. And then we respond with business and management educational programmes which are practical, relevant and underpin company-specific knowledge.

It's an approach that has enhanced our global reputation for excellence in management development, education and research. But like many of the organisations with whom we work in partnership, we are continually innovating to remain at the forefront of new educational developments which are relevant to the current - and increasingly international - business environment.

No other UK Business School can match our wealth of experience in designing and delivering single-company programmes. Isn't it time that you found out how we can help improve your business performance?

Please contact Stuart Sanderson, Chairman, Executive Development Programme, at the University of Bradford Management Centre, Heaton Mount, Keighley Road, Bradford, West Yorkshire BD9 4JU. Tel: 01274 234440. Fax: 01274 234444.

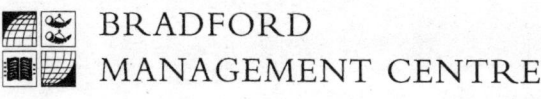

BRADFORD
MANAGEMENT CENTRE

UNIVERSITY OF BRADFORD
Making knowledge work.

Contents

Preface

The executive education market continues to flourish throughout the world, with an increasing number of providers offering a widening variety of executive programmes. Although business schools dominate the market, they face intense competition from consulting firms and from the fast-developing corporate university sector.

The market for tailored or customised programmes is growing rapidly, and in many schools open programmes are being squeezed as tailored programmes expand. However, open programmes retain a central role in executive education and tailored programmes can be seen as a niche market existing alongside open programmes. In response, business schools have had to clarify the role and exact objectives of open programmes. As a means of delivering functionally based knowledge or of passing on leading-edge business concepts, open programmes remain critical tools.

Amid such significant changes in the marketplace, selecting the most appropriate programmes is becoming ever more difficult. *Which executive programme?* aims to remove some of the mystery from the selection process. It is designed to help executives make an informed choice on the programmes which best suit their personal needs and those of their organisations.

Which executive programme? contains comprehensive details of a selection of the open programmes available from leading business schools throughout the world. The selected programmes have been offered for more than one year by established providers with a proven track record. Their content is aimed at middle and senior managers and only those lasting three days or longer have been included in the programme directory. The programmes are all delivered in English or a major European language. (Where the latter is the case, the language is specified in the directory entry.)

This book is divided into three parts. Part 1, Global trends in executive education, is an overview of the market. It describes the latest trends and gives advice on choosing a provider. Parts 2 and 3 are directories, the first of programmes and the second of providers.

In Part 2 open programmes are classified by subject matter. There are sections on finance, general management, human resources, international management, leadership, marketing and personal development. Each is preceded by a brief introduction outlining the key issues in that particular subject area.

Part 3 is the providers' directory with an alphabetical list of leading business schools offering executive programmes. Each entry includes contact details, a brief description of the business school and the types of programmes that are available. Some schools offer only tailored (or customised) courses. The growing importance of these programmes deserves special attention and they are examined in detail in Chapter 4.

Other providers are excluded for a number of reasons. Business schools remain the dominant force in the marketplace. Their resources are substantial and their expertise is generally, although not uniformly, high. They are usually better placed to meet the broad executive development needs of international organisations. The profusion of alternative, smaller providers makes it difficult to reach conclusions about the quality of their programmes or their resources. Nevertheless, specialised or local programmes can sometimes be better delivered by consulting or training companies.

MBA programmes are not included in this book. The provision of these has become an enormous industry that merits its own in-depth coverage. This is provided in another publication, *Which MBA? A critical guide to the world's best programmes*, published annually by the EIU and Financial Times Management.

Although *Which executive programme?* is comprehensive it is not exhaustive. In such a fast-changing, global market programmes are continually developing and new providers are emerging. It is, therefore, a snapshot of the programmes and providers in spring 1998 and the exclusion of a provider from the directory is not necessarily a reflection of the quality of its services. Any provider that believes it merits inclusion in future editions should contact the EIU.

Which executive programme? © The Economist Intelligence Unit Limited 1998

The author

Stuart Crainer is a business and management writer. He is the author of numerous books, including *The Ultimate Business Guru Book*, 1998; *From Corporate Man to Corporate Skunk*, 1997; *The Ultimate Book of Business Quotations*, 1997; *The Ultimate Business Library*, 1996 (all published by Capstone Publishing, Oxford); with Randall White and Philip Hodgson, *The Future of Leadership*, 1996; *Key Management Ideas*, 1995 (both published by Pitman, London). He is also editor of *The Financial Times Handbook of Management*, Pitman, London, 1995, and contributes to a wide variety of newspapers and magazines throughout the world, including the *Financial Times*, *The Times*, *Across the Board*, *Management Today* and *Strategy & Business*.

Part 1

Global trends in executive education

Rotterdam School of Management
Erasmus Graduate School of Business

The Rotterdam School of Management is a leading international business school, operating as a self-financing and independent foundation of Erasmus University. Consistently ranked among the top five in Europe and top ten in the world, the RSM is renowned for its international character and innovative programs. The RSM combines Erasmus University's excellence with visiting faculty from prestigious international universities and managers from different industries.

The RSM offers in-company executive programs that are tailored to fit the company's needs. Programs may cover one specific functional area or may focus on change management. An in-company executive MBA Program is also conceivable.

Additionally, the RSM offers open executive courses, and full-time and part-time International MBA Programs.

For more information please contact the Rotterdam School of Management.

Rotterdam School of Management
Erasmus Graduate School of Business

Chapter 1
The emergence of a global business

Fuelling the growth

In 1960 the average person needed to learn one new skill every year to prosper in the workplace. Today the average person needs to learn one new skill every day.
From *The 500 year Delta**

Corporate change requires further education

Executive education is one of the great business success stories of recent years. Over the last decade the number of programmes and providers has mushroomed, servicing what has become an estimated $12bn global market for executive education.** The most important stimulus to this growth is intensifying competition and accelerating change in business. As a result, corporate strategies are constantly changing and evolving to keep ahead of the competition. This requires changing skills, and changing skills require education and development. The basis of the executive education industry is to ensure that companies have the management expertise in place to support their business strategies.

"Huge changes are occurring at a rapidly increasing rate. Companies want methods by which their people can become attuned to managing change," says Jean Hauser, head of the Center for Custom Programs at the University of North Carolina's Kenan-Flagler Business School. This point is continually reinforced by people in business schools and in industry. "The world has changed and so has the role of business schools. The market is now multifaceted and there are all manner of competitive challenges," notes Ian Tanner, director of the executive centre at Manchester Business School. "We are in a time of change and transformation. That is not an academic invention. It is what our clients are saying. They are dealing with uncertainty and we are giving people the tools to understand this new context."

---

* Jim Taylor and Watts Wacker with Howard Means, Capstone Publishing, 1997.
** Figure taken from Albert A Vicere and Robert M Fulmer, *Leadership by Design*, Harvard Business School Press, 1998.

Closer to the heart of the business

Change and competition mean that instead of being somewhat peripheral, executive education is now commonly seen as a means by which companies can gain a competitive edge. At the same time, exploration of emergent issues such as intellectual capital and knowledge management means that developing people has never been higher on the list of corporate priorities.

In her book *World Class**, Rosabeth Moss Kanter of Harvard Business School sets out three criteria for thriving in the global economy.

- Concepts: knowing what the leading-edge ideas are.

- Competence: implementation of these ideas to the highest standards.

- Connections: access to a worldwide network of movers and shakers with whom you can exchange information and experiences.

Executive education has a clear role to play in these criteria. It is fundamental to the dissemination of innovative ideas, spreads knowledge of best practice and helps in the creation of managerial networks.

It is therefore not surprising that education in general, and job-related learning in particular, is now a much sought-after commodity. Peter Drucker confidently predicts that "the fastest-growing industry in the US will soon be the continuing education of adults because things are changing so fast in every field and occupation".

The expansion of choice

More providers—

In executive education things are undoubtedly changing fast. Growth can be seen in two broad areas. First, there has been rapid expansion in the number of providers. As well as business schools (whose numbers continue to grow every year), there are numerous consulting and training companies. There are also increasing numbers of corporate universities, where companies have cut out the middleman and established their own executive education centres (see Chapter 3).

—and more programmes

Second, there has been a large increase in the choice of programmes. Ten years ago programme content was dominated by traditional business functions. Although the basics are still on offer, consumers can now choose from an array of different subjects and a range of delivery mechanisms, including distance learning and programmes via the Internet. This demonstrates the greater degree of flexibility now offered by providers. Nowhere is this more evident than in the growth of tailored and consortium programmes, which enable client organisations to exercise far greater control than would have previously been contemplated.

---

* Simon & Schuster, New York, 1995.

Demand-led growth

This is symptomatic of a fundamental change in the executive education marketplace: it has moved from being product-led to being demand-led. Given that schools and other providers are only now beginning to understand the nature of the demand, the potential for further growth appears significant. "As appreciation of the link between organisational learning and competitiveness increases, so too will the market for executive education," predicts Randall White of RPW Executive Development, based in North Carolina.

The role of open programmes

The core of executive development

Amid this maelstrom of change (and opportunity), the core product remains the open (or public) programme. The scope of these programmes is now immense, and few subjects or permutations are not covered somewhere in the world. There has been talk recently of the demise of open programmes in favour of the tailored approach. But they are not disappearing, and the range and number of programmes featured in this book demonstrate that such talk is seemingly premature.

"There is still demand for open programmes and that will continue to be the case," says Wanda Wallace, managing director of executive programmes at Duke University's Fuqua Business School. "In some subjects, such as mergers and acquisitions, only a few key people require knowledge. Open programmes provide them with that knowledge. More generally, advanced management programmes offer an important means of revitalising managers."

The benefits of open programmes

Open programmes offer a number of important benefits compared with tailored and alternative solutions.

- **Time for reflection.** They allow executives time for reflection away from the daily demands of work. This may appear to be self-indulgent, but for harassed modern managers fresh thinking is as difficult as it is important.

- **Networking and outside perspective.** They provide exposure to other corporate cultures and networking opportunities. This is the principal advantage of open as opposed to tailored programmes. Executives are constantly told by management thinkers that looking inwards is dangerous. It is only by looking outside their own company, learning from elsewhere, that innovation will occur.

- **Benchmarking skills.** They are a useful means of expanding skills and broadening horizons. Executives can benchmark their competencies against managers in other companies, and aspects of their company's performance against best practice. Open programmes open eyes as well as minds.

- **Generalising specialists and vice versa.** From an educational point of view, open programmes are a good way to introduce functional experts to general management issues, or to enhance functional knowledge among general managers.

- **Latest management thinking.** Executives can also be introduced to the latest management ideas and best practice through open programmes. Leading management thinkers, such as strategy gurus Gary Hamel and Andrew Campbell, take part in them.

- **Cost-effectiveness.** The range of open programmes now on offer means that they remain off-the-shelf, cost-effective solutions to many development needs. They can be used to top up skills and knowledge and to augment or add depth to in-house programmes.

Open programmes remain central to executive development even though they are now supplemented by a growing number of alternatives (see Chapter 4). The aversion once expressed by precious academics to executive education seems largely to have disappeared.

Chapter 2
New corporate and personal imperatives

Great expectations

Development was once something "done" to executives. Their skills were developed so that they were best equipped to perform successfully for their employers. The needs of the individual were not usually considered. Indeed, the development needs of organisation and individual were regarded as mutually exclusive.

Now, however, attitudes towards executive development, as well as the corporate and executive agenda, are more complex and often more confusing. "The mantra for the millennium is faster, cheaper and better," says Jean Hauser, head of the Center for Custom Programs at Kenan-Flagler Business School. "Success or failure has to do with the quality of decisions people make over time. How do people make better, faster, more robust decisions?"

Companies are indeed taking a more hard-headed, business-led approach to training in all its manifestations. "The early 1980s was a boom time for executive development and management training," says Dena Michelli, business development director for executive programmes at London Business School. "But programmes were often seen as a bit of a perk; the approach was not focused enough on what the organisation was getting out of it. Then, as companies started feeling the pinch, they began to ask what benefits they actually received from their investment and learned that you do not just throw this sort of learning at people. Executive programmes are expensive. As a result, there is now a much tighter fit between programmes and the needs of the business. It is a much more exacting market, which makes demands on business schools that were not there before."

Indeed, according to a 1997 survey by Albert Vicere, a professor and director of the Institute for the Study of Organisational Effectiveness at Penn State University, annual corporate expenditure on executive education has reached a median figure of $1m, with over 2,400 people in each company being involved. Although they are drawn from large organisations, such figures give some idea of the growth now being experienced in executive education.

With growing recognition of the importance of executive education and sizeable budgets, it is not surprising that the role of human resource (HR) professionals is now given greater significance in many organisations. HR management has taken on a strategic role which gives it far greater influence on the direction and development of people and organisations.

Corporate expectations are simple: companies want their executives to acquire practical skills in a timely and cost-effective way. They then want to see those skills speedily applied to deal with real problems. Executive education has to deliver business results.

The personal perspective

At the same time, the perspective of executives has changed. In the media over recent years the fashionable topics have been employability, the rise of the disaffected Generation X and the demise of the psychological contract between employer and employee. Corporate man—the blindly loyal executive—has been exposed as an illusion as his job security has eroded. The burden of career development is increasingly seized by individual executives who recognise the need for continual development.

This catalogue of change appears to be overwhelming. But when media over-enthusiasm is removed the truth is usually a little different. Ambitious, forward-thinking, professional executives have always made their own developmental decisions whenever they could. They have always looked to the future and managed their careers when possible or been prepared to move with the times and the circumstances.

Undoubtedly, in companies and business schools there is greater emphasis on the development of individuals. In the past, development was often regarded as mass production. Now there is growing awareness of individual developmental needs. There are increasing numbers of executives with personal development plans, career plans, competency targets and so on. These vary in thoroughness, although the general aim is the laudable one of bringing some clarity to what has traditionally been a grey area. In some cases development has become central to the entire system of performance appraisal.

At Rothmans International a comprehensive Career Development Programme has been developed for the company's senior managers, which includes a detailed psychological assessment and a two-and-a-half day workshop in which participants receive one-to-one tuition from occupational psychologists. The finale is a "personal self-managed career system" which provides a monthly schedule of career objectives, job opportunities and aspirations, as well as competency requirements.

Achieving a balance

John Evans, chairman of London-based CPI Career Management, which developed the programme with Rothmans International, believes that a broader approach to encompass both corporate and personal goals is now essential. "The Rothmans programme is built around a holistic and highly personalised approach which recognises that appraisal is linked to a wide range of issues. It is naive and short-termist to think otherwise," he says. "There are, and have to be, mutual benefits. From the organisation's point of view, the programme gives it the opportunity to liberate the potential of its employees. And the employees gain insights into what they can and cannot do, where their career can go and how they can direct it. People are rarely aware of their full potential and to make them aware is good for everyone."

The message is that the needs of company and executive do not have to be mutually exclusive. "People are sent on executive programmes to acquire new skills and competencies, to benchmark themselves against others, to learn from the experience of others," notes Colin Carnall, director of programmes at Henley Management College. "A key use of programmes is the accelerated development of individuals, but increasingly, too, they want participants to feed that learning back to the organisation."

In practice, such a balanced view of corporate and individual needs is often difficult to establish. In some companies there is still a suspicion that investing in executive education is potentially dangerous as it makes executives more likely to find a job elsewhere. Alternatively, some executives may feel uncomfortable about accepting increased responsibility for their own development. Changing such views will clearly take time.

"Although there is still a lot of womb-to-tomb mentality, the psychological contract has changed. Organisations must now provide the environment and the resources for people to grow," says Dena Michelli of London Business School, adding the observation: "Very often the lexicon develops before behaviour changes."

The managing director of executive programmes at Fuqua Business School, Wanda Wallace, believes the bottom line is that developing people makes good business sense. "The companies which will win in the next century will be the ones which pay attention to their intellectual capital and to their people," she says. "Ultimately, if a group of people are your intellectual assets, your competitive advantage of the future, you need to keep them loyal. Some companies say that employability is not the right approach. But they still have to think of how to create new opportunities for people to maintain their loyalty. A lot of companies are recognising this. The opportunity for business schools is that companies need good partners."

Seize the Chicago advantage

Advance your career while you work by earning a world-renowned M.B.A. degree

- in 11 one- and two-week modules spread over 18 months (ten in Barcelona, one in Chicago)
- taught by the distinguished Chicago business school faculty, a group that includes several Nobel Prize winners
- with an elite group of international managers. (More than 30 countries are represented in our most recent class.)

Places are limited. So get one step ahead—request an application now. The next class starts in July.

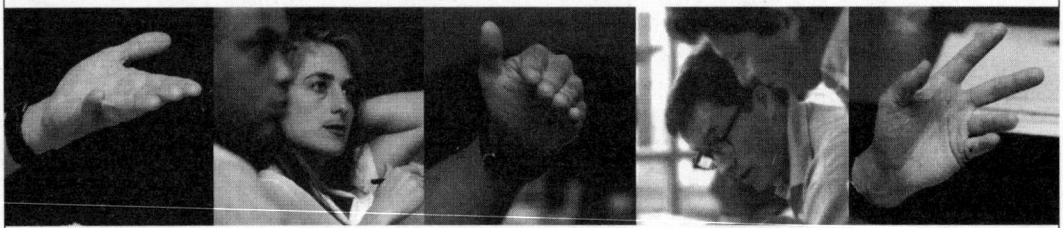

The University of Chicago International Executive M.B.A. Program at Barcelona

Chapter 3
The providers

Competition for business schools

Business schools
Business schools as providers of executive education have a number of advantages. The best are large, well-resourced institutions with lengthy track records and international recognition. Smaller, newer business schools often have the advantage of being part of a university with extensive resources. (See Chapter 5 for more information about business schools.) However, executive education is not the sole preserve of business schools. They face competition on two broad fronts.

Consultants
First, there is competition from consultants. In practice, this term covers a multitude of diverse organisations. These can be divided into four main groups:

- offshoots of global management consultancies;
- general providers of management development and training across a wide spectrum of issues and disciplines;
- niche organisations which address defined issues, such as mentoring and coaching;
- providers of a particular proprietary brand of management development, often based on original research or a particular philosophy of management. (These are now frequently vehicles for an individual thinker or management guru.)

Corporate universities
The second source of competition, which is growing in size and stature, is corporate universities. Companies such as Disney and Motorola have established their own training organisations chiefly intended to supply training to company employees.

Other sources

Competition also comes from a number of other organisations, hybrids whose roots are part academic, part consultant and part business. Typical of these is the Covey Institute, a corporate giant which emerged from Stephen Covey's self-improvement books and now has a revenue of some $90m. An interesting example is Body Shop's New Academy of Business. This was established by the former chief executive of Body Shop International, Anita Roddick, in 1995 and aims "to bring together the best in values-led business practice with progressive management thinking". There are also various technology-led bodies such as Pentacle The Virtual Business School, which use the immediacy of technology to cover its lack of traditional resources.

The blurred divide with consulting

As disseminators of best practice consultants are highly effective. They are masters of the media and communication, and they are gaining increasing renown as originators of innovative thinking. (The big business ideas of recent years have usually come from consultants rather than academics.)

Business schools and consultants have different roles. As one commentator explains: "The sole purpose of universities is the creation and dissemination of new knowledge. In contrast, consulting firms help companies to implement. Consulting firms are hired hands; they cannot do the thinking. Companies often tell us they wish they had debated the issues with us before they hired consulting firms."

Yet in some respects, the divide between business schools and consultancies is increasingly blurred. "The big consultancies have not been slow to move into areas such as leadership and organisational transformation where we work and where we would like to work," concedes Ian Tanner, director of the executive centre at Manchester Business School. A number of business school deans have consulting links. In the US alone there is Thomas Gerrity of the University of Pennsylvania, who is president of CSC Consulting; F David Fowler of George Washington University and KPMG; William Hasler of the University of California and KPMG; and Tom Sarowski of the University of Kansas and Andersen Consulting.

Consultants as thought leaders and educators

Consulting firms are keen to establish themselves as intellectual thought leaders. They have invested heavily in positioning themselves as being in the knowledge business. McKinsey & Co, for example, now spends $50m-100m per year on "knowledge building" (research, publishing and related activities) and claims to spend more on research than Harvard, Wharton and Stanford combined. Even if this claim is only partially true, it is a startling statistic. Early in 1998 Andersen Consulting launched The Third Millennium Forum, which it trumpeted as "a new-generation business school designed to assist multinationals to identify the key business capabilities their organisations must possess in order to survive into the next millennium". The consulting company Arthur D Little established its own school of management as long ago as 1964, and the UK's Ashridge Management College has its own consulting company.

Traditional roles are being questioned. "In the new business world the environment is moving faster than we can learn so being a consultant in the traditional sense is a nonsense. Companies need educators," says Eddie Obeng of Pentacle The Virtual Business School. "Instead of selling companies a method, they need to identify the problems, invent an appropriate method and help them to learn the new skills required to implement it. They have to leave the learning with their clients rather than abandoning them with a weighty report and a weightier invoice."

Alliances with business schools

Greater co-operation between business schools and large consulting firms is already under way and is likely to spread further. The consulting firm Booz-Allen & Hamilton, for example, has recently made a research alliance with INSEAD in France. As part of this alliance, Booz-Allen will sponsor a major research programme through the Centre for Integrated Manufacturing and Service Operations at INSEAD. There will also be closer recruitment ties between the two organisations. "It is very natural that there is a close relationship between a top management consulting firm and a top business school," says Brian Dickie, president of Booz-Allen's worldwide commercial business. "We share a mission to help shape the ideas and practice of business on a global basis, and we share a mission to educate and place future generations of business leaders."

Such alliances break down the barriers between business schools and management consultants. More barriers are likely to fall.

Corporate universities

The second major source of competition for business schools comes from the fast-emerging corporate universities. When they were first established corporate universities raised a few academic eyebrows. There were sniggers at the thought of McDonald's Hamburger University or Disney University in Florida (which sports a coat of arms featuring Mickey's eponymous ears rather than rampant lions and the obligatory Latin motto). The mirth has subsided and suspicion has taken over. If corporations can train their own executives, the market for business schools is reduced.

Strongest growth in the US

The trend towards do-it-yourself management development is strongest in the US where over 1,000 corporate colleges are now operating. They come in all shapes and sizes, and cover virtually every industry. Dana Corporation, an Ohio automotive-parts manufacturer, has Dana University; Ford has a Heavy Truck University in Detroit; Intel runs a university in Santa Clara; Sun Microsystems has Sun U; and Apple has its own university in Cupertino, California.

Corporate universities are not solely an American phenomenon. IBM has a business school in the UK, and one of the leaders in the field is GEC's Dunchurch College in

Rugby, UK, which first opened its courses to outsiders in the 1960s. After decades of honing the skills of civil servants, the UK's Civil Service College now offers over 500 courses, attracting managers from the public and private sectors.

Closer ties to the business world

The growth in corporate universities can largely be attributed to three things. First, critics of traditional business schools have accused them repeatedly of being too far from the pulse of the business world. This is a widely perceived weakness on which corporate universities are keen to capitalise. In response, many business schools have attempted to bring more reality into their programmes, through project-based work, and have developed tailored programmes. (To a large extent the debate about business schools being distanced from reality is now a spurious one, but stereotypes linger.)

Emphasis on development

Second is the realisation in many organisations that developing people is crucial to their future survival. It is too important to be delegated to an external organisation. Research in the US revealed that companies with their own universities spent 2.5% of their payroll on learning, double the US national average.

Increasing use of technology

The third impetus is technology. It is notable that many of the corporate universities are based around Silicon Valley. Through utilising the latest technology, companies can economically and effectively deliver distance learning and "virtual" learning. Crucially, learning can become both continuous and immediate.

A high price tag

Corporate universities are not for the faint-hearted; they are extremely expensive to run. Research in the US by Jeanne Meister of Corporate University Exchange, a New York consultancy, calculated that the average operating budget for a corporate university was $12.4m (although 60% reported budgets of $5m or less). Typically, National Semiconductor University in Silicon valley, opened in 1994, occupies a 22,000 sq ft premises with nine classrooms and space for 430 students. Such facilities, as business schools have been pointing out for years, are costly. Running Intel University, also in Silicon valley, cost the company $150m in 1996. Intel offers 2,600 courses, which had 40,000 participants in 1996. It is hardly surprising that corporate universities are largely the domain of multinationals.

They want to be more like traditional universities—

The chief disadvantage of corporate universities has been that they often do not offer anything other than an internal qualification. In an effort to broaden their appeal, corporate universities are establishing partnerships with a wide range of organisations. Courses are increasingly affiliated to those of more traditional academic institutions. At National Semiconductor University, for example, participants can earn associate's, bachelor's or master's degrees from other universities.

"There is a difference between training and development. Corporate universities should handle training. Universities are not good at training. It is skill-based while development is really giving you the knowledge. You don't know when you will need that knowledge. It is an investment in tomorrow while training is about today," says Jean Hauser, head of the Center for Custom Programs at Kenan-Flagler Business School. "The danger of developing yourself is that you end up talking to yourself."

—but they need to maintain their uniqueness

Whether the growth in corporate universities will continue is a matter of some debate, most obviously within business schools. If corporate universities are to succeed they must maintain their difference from alternative training providers. Seeking out affiliations and partnerships may be attractive but, in the long term, could be self-defeating. Hamburger and Harvard would be wise to discard any notions of an unlikely alliance. The more corporate universities resemble traditional universities and business schools, the less their appeal is likely to be.

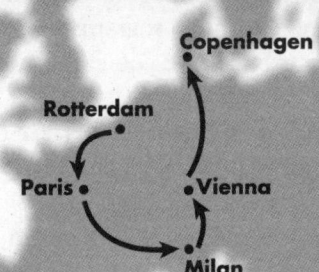

Chapter 4
The rise of tailored programmes

Continuing expansion

New growth is from tailored programmes

The rise of tailored programmes is a truly global phenomenon. An increasing number of schools now generate the majority of their executive programmes' revenue from tailored programmes. For example, at Duke University's Fuqua School of Business tailored programmes now account for 70% of total revenue, compared with 65% in 1995. It is expected that this proportion will rise to around 75% in the next few years. At Columbia University tailored programmes made up 48% of total revenue in 1997, compared with 22% in 1992.

Business schools report that growth in executive education is coming primarily from tailored courses. Companies with increasingly higher expectations are demanding that such programmes support their business goals. Tailored programmes can undoubtedly offer some economies of scale. Large numbers of managers can be put through a programme simultaneously, with cost benefits and the opportunity to create momentum for change initiatives.

Nevertheless, tailored programmes are labour intensive and, consequently, represent a substantial investment. Typically, a programme is preceded by extensive field research (focus groups, questionnaires, studies) to calibrate the issues, before the design process gets under way. Prices vary greatly. The degree of flexibility available in tailored programmes adds to the complexity. As a rough estimate, a one-week programme may cost about $3,500 per participant, although it can easily be $5,000 or more.

Control and flexibility

Companies can influence the content—

The chief attractions of tailored programmes are the paradoxical combination of control and flexibility. Companies have an input into the design of the programme, ensuring the content is relevant to their business needs. Clearly, this gives them far greater control. Materials, project work and case studies can reflect the context of the business.

—the timing and the delivery

At the same time, the delivery of tailored programmes is more flexible. Timing can be geared to work schedules and sessions can be held at company sites or elsewhere. Tailored programmes can involve a broad range of activities and delivery methods. London Business School, for example, has designed a programme for middle managers at 3M which is delivered in five modules. Academic input is followed by learning assignments. There are also facilitated learning groups which "provide support to a personal learning agenda, review on-the-job learning that has taken place and provide ideas for experimentation". In addition, the programme uses peer assessment instruments.

The World Bank has an innovative tailored programme that is led by Harvard in the US but also draws on prominent faculty members from a number of other business schools, including Stanford in the US and IESE in Spain.

Partnerships and consortium programmes

Such partnerships are increasingly common, as are consortium programmes. London Business School is also involved in the Global Business Consortium which brings together executives from a host of corporate giants including ABB, BT (British Telecom), Lufthansa, SKF and Standard Chartered Bank. The companies nominate five senior participants for the three-week programme, which includes modules in Asia and Australasia, India and Europe.

Tailoring for an industry

Creativity and marketing awareness are also seen in programmes which are tailored for particular industries. Wharton, for example, offers industry-specific programmes, including an executive management programme for ophthalmic administrators and one on leadership skills for professors of gynaecology and obstetrics. An increasing number of such niches are being developed by business schools in an effort to fuse the best of open programmes with the advantages of tailored programmes.

The holistic approach

In addition to offering control and flexibility, tailored programmes provide a more holistic approach to executive education. Companies are demanding total delivery of a comprehensive and carefully thought through response to their business situation and developmental needs. Tailored programmes are, as a result, characterised by the following.

- **Faculty involvement.** Providers require a clearer understanding of the business goals and the corporate culture of their client. This requires the close, long-term involvement of faculty. Professors can no longer walk into a seminar room, give their lecture on globalisation and then disappear. Companies demand multidisciplined faculty to lead their programmes and they require faculty commitment.

- **Greater commitment.** As well as greater commitment from faculty, tailored programmes require substantial involvement from senior management. In some programmes senior managers are used as additional teaching resources. Some companies go one stage further and involve their own customers in their programmes.

- **Encouraging reflection.** Programmes are often designed not so much to teach as to encourage participants to reflect, recognise and draw on existing knowledge. "It is very effective to get 50 people in a room and to then debate the issues. Tailored programmes give companies an opportunity to huddle," says Jean Hauser, head of the Center for Custom Programs at Kenan-Flagler Business School. "It's a debate among smart people. As outsiders we can raise tough questions. We provoke debate." This level of debate clearly contrasts with the normal experience. "On an open programme you probably don't get more than two people from the same company in the room. They can't talk openly about their problems and concerns," says Fuqua's Wanda Wallace. "On tailored programmes you get smart faculty who understand your company and understand your company's twist on a subject like marketing. You have all the people in the room you need to actually solve the problem."

- **Solving real problems.** Increasingly, tailored programmes are concerned with genuine business problems. Programme design is often driven by the key issues faced by the business. At the centre of most tailored programmes is a business problem. The content is resolutely focused on reality, especially through the use of projects (often undertaken by participants between modules).

In many cases, tailored programmes play a central role in enabling corporate transformation or, at least, a substantial change in the business. According to Dena Michelli, business development director for executive programmes at London Business School, one reason for the growing popularity of tailored programmes is that they enable companies going through a major transformation to develop a critical mass in terms of the number of managers on courses. This, she says, can offer both economies of scale and a shared vocabulary and vision.

"If you want to transform an organisation and you get people going through a programme together that creates a shared experience: it can help build momentum. It's more cost effective, too, which is also advantageous," says Ms Michelli. "Companies are looking for greater commitment, energy and imagination on relevant issues in their employees, and managers who are more decisive, more comfortable with risk and who will devote less time to non-value creativity. This is what programmes must deliver."

Chapter 5
Making the choice

What do you want?

The sophistication of buyers of executive programmes is developing rapidly. "Executive education is a growth area and companies are becoming increasingly selective. They have clearer ideas about what they need and business schools are seeking to meet their needs with greater flexibility," says Jonathan Slack, chief executive of the UK Association of Business Schools.

There is a wide choice of suppliers—

Consequently, the expectations of consumers are high. They can afford to compare two, three or even more suppliers before making a decision. As Ian Tanner, director of the executive centre at Manchester Business School, has found: "There is no doubt that HR professionals have become a lot more knowledgeable and are more likely to compare what different schools are offering. There's an element of beauty contests going on that wasn't there before."

—but first determine your requirements

Beauty is in the eye of the beholder and the starting point for selecting programmes should be a clear understanding of the business or career development issues to be addressed. The initial step of needs analysis is now better understood than previously owing to the use of competency-based approaches to management development, career development plans, proactive forward thinking and appraisal processes. In particular, the appraisal process plays an important role in identifying the development needs of individuals and in gaining support from line managers. Many companies are also moving to 360-degree appraisal processes which allow them more accurately to identify the development needs of individuals at all levels, including senior management.

Who can deliver it?

Picking an appropriate provider

As discussed in Chapter 3, there are many types of provider. This complicates any purchasing decision and it is important to try to correlate your requirements to the appropriate type of provider. Programmes on basic or specialised skills may often be better sourced from smaller consulting or training firms. For some functionally based training (such as managing sales accounts) it can also be worth considering local training providers.

Larger consulting firms are best equipped to deal with discrete business problems where the onus is on short-term problem resolution and implementation. If the problem requires the long-term assimilation of knowledge and skills, tailored programmes may be more appropriate than the broader brush of open programmes.

Business schools' breadth can be persuasive

The chief attraction of business schools is that they offer a broad range of expertise. France's INSEAD, for example, boasts 90 permanent faculty with a further 45 visiting professors. During the last year 4,500 people attended its open programmes and it delivered 72 weeks of programmes related to the Asia and Australasia region alone. This combination of specialist and generalist knowledge, backed by considerable resources, remains highly persuasive.

How much will it cost?

An important element in any competitive battle is that of price. Executive education is no exception.

When making price comparisons it is important to consider whether you are comparing like with like in terms of quality. The standing of schools is reflected in the price although, with increased competition, there may be room for negotiation, especially for tailored programmes. "There is certainly price sensitivity. Some of the new providers, the new universities in particular, came into the market with very different price structures," says Mr Tanner. "It's a question of differentiating between the quality of providers, but within the broad bands of similar offerings there is some negotiation. There are one or two courses where demand is so high that price is non-negotiable. It's a bit like trying to get a discount on a new Mercedes Benz; some schools take a similar view with their leading programmes."

In general, fierce competition among a host of providers is good news for potential buyers. There is greater flexibility than ever before. However, there remains an elite body of schools which continue to charge premium prices. A glance at one particular course, Finance for non-financial managers, reveals a great variation in price. The daily rate ranges from $250 to $1,200, but there are add-ons such as accommodation and meals to consider.

Is the provider in touch?

Relevance is of paramount importance in executive programmes. The integration of theory and practice is a critical issue for every school, every company and every programme. Once again, this is reflected in the growth of tailored programmes.

In assessing providers, companies should look at the amount of project work involved on a programme and whether the provider makes use of action learning and teamwork.

The quality and relevance of research carried out by a school is also an indication of the priority it attaches to addressing real business concerns. Some idea of a school's research output can be gauged by its publications. Has it produced any well-known or influential books, articles or reports in a particular area? Is the research too esoteric or concentrated in a particular area or industry? (In the UK there are useful research ratings published by the Higher Education Council.)

The role of research is explained by Nigel Nicholson, research dean at London Business School: "We are dedicated to disseminating knowledge. We are a knowledge organisation and recognise that knowledge flows in a number of directions. We aim to synthesise three elements: research, teaching and active involvement in companies. What you do in class feeds into research. The active way we work with executives means that the classroom is a laboratory. The class is our raw material. We work with them. Case work on client companies means that we learn from them and vice versa. They are a constant source of material." It is worth asking a school about the role played by research in its work and how it balances research and teaching.

Does the provider have a good reputation?

There is no denying that, in the era of employability, a name everyone recognises can be useful on an executive's résumé. Big names, such as Harvard, Wharton and Stanford in the US, or INSEAD, London Business School and IMD in Europe, have a prestige which is important to many purchasers. Attendance on a course at Harvard, even if it was for three weeks over 20 years ago, is held up by executives as a sign of their worth. But this does not mean that a big-name school will always provide the right programme at the right price at the right time. Reputations can go down as well as up.

Although business schools generally offer a broad range of programmes, many have particular areas of expertise. London Business School, for instance, excels in finance and INSEAD has a world-famous Euro-Asia Centre.

Prospective customers are advised to talk to past participants or other clients of a particular school in order to gauge its current standing.

How good is the school's faculty?

In the world of the business-school faculty, market forces prevail. There is a merry-go-round of academics moving from school to school. In recent years the leading US schools have responded by recruiting faculty members with international credentials to attract a more cosmopolitan mix of participants on programmes. There is a constant scramble to recruit rising teaching stars from the leading PhD programmes.

As a result standards are high and becoming even higher. The lack of European business education was such that in 1970 only one member of INSEAD's faculty had a business doctorate—all now do. An interesting issue for potential purchasers is how the performance of faculty is rated. Is it related to teaching or research, or a combination of the two? It is worth considering the quality of both: a high rating in research does not necessarily mean a high rating in teaching.

How good are the facilities?

Campus visits are a useful means of assessment. The quality of accommodation, sports facilities and other amenities contributes to the learning experience. From an educational perspective, a well-stocked library and good computer facilities are important ingredients.

In recent years nearly all the major schools have invested heavily in improving their facilities. Cranfield School of Management in the UK recently spent £6m on a new state-of-the-art Management Development Centre. London Business School is involved in a four-year project costing about £20m which will be completed by 2000.

All the major business schools seem to be caught in a relentless cycle of fund-raising and building. In 1995, for example, INSEAD launched the INSEAD Campaign which aimed to raise FFr700m ($140m). In the world of one-upmanship, the school with the biggest executive development centre is king, for a while at least.

How international is the school?

The international mix of participants and faculty on programmes is of growing importance to companies competing in a global marketplace. The leading business schools are keen to stress their international credentials. Some are undoubtedly more international than others, and some are not as cosmopolitan as they would like people to believe.

In this respect European schools are well ahead of their North American and Asian competitors. Faculty and participants are routinely drawn from dozens of countries. For example, at INSEAD the 50 participants on its Advanced Management Programme commonly come from over 20 countries. However, INSEAD is no longer a glorious exception. Typically, among the 50 or so participants on Templeton College's Advanced Management Programme, there can be as many as 24 different nationalities. (Significantly, the largest single nationality on this programme is North American.) Other leading European schools, including London Business School, IMD and Spain's IESE, can make similar claims.

European schools believe their international appeal will tempt more North American managers on to their programmes in the future, and they may be right. However, although North American schools generally lag behind in terms of international faculty and participants, most are improving. And there are exceptions, most notably Thunderbird, which has long-established global credentials. Other schools are committed to becoming more international, but one of the main problems they must address is their teaching materials and benchmarks, which generally have an American bias.

How and where is the programme delivered?

Geographical location remains an important element in any decision. However, clients are putting increasing pressure on the leading North American and European schools to deliver programmes wherever in the world they are required. Schools are now frequently able to do this. Wharton, for example, offers a number of programmes outside the US. Since 1992 it has run an annual programme in Taipei, and it plans to run a series of programmes in Bangkok, Shanghai, Hong Kong, Jakarta, Kuala Lumpur, Manila, Japan and Israel.

More schools are pooling resources

Alternatively, schools can join together to expand their reach. For example, PRIME is a global development programme offered by six schools: Copenhagen Business School, ESADE in Barcelona, HEC in Paris, Rotterdam School of Management, SDA Bocconi in Milan and WU-Wien in Vienna. The five-week programme is spread over six months and is tailored to provide insights into the diversity of European cultures, with a week spent in five of the schools' home cities.

Another element is the market orientation of the company. A company with its sights set firmly on a particular market may perceive an important advantage to be gained from sending managers on programmes within that region. For example, companies with an interest in China may consider the Chinese University of Hong Kong; or if they have important business interests in eastern Europe, CMC Graduate School of Business near Prague in the Czech Republic may be an option.

In future, geography may be less of an issue as technology overcomes distances and reduces dependency on local providers.

How long is the programme?

For modern executives time is at a premium. "If we can do without someone for a week, we can probably do without them for good," noted one American chief executive. There is a clear trend now towards shorter programmes, driven by the unwillingness of companies to commit managers to programmes that will keep them away from their jobs for long periods.

At the top end of the market, for example, schools such as Kellogg and Michigan in the US, and INSEAD and London Business School in Europe offer four-week senior executive programmes in place of the longer Harvard Advanced Management Programme (AMP) model. Templeton College, Oxford, and Duke University's Fuqua School of Business both offer their own four-week versions of the AMP.

After 38 years MIT's Sloan School has cancelled its eight-week Programme for Senior Managers. Harvard itself, however, has so far bucked the trend, only trimming its AMP to nine weeks. Its resistance is based on a long-held belief that providing sufficient time for participants to reflect on issues away from the workplace is part of the intrinsic value of the Harvard experience. Other schools plump for something in the middle: Stanford's Executive Programme lasts six and a half weeks; and Wharton's AMP lasts five weeks.

Longer programmes cement relationships between students and members of faculty. London Business School questions whether there is a widespread need for shorter programmes. It reports consistent demand for its flagship, four-week open programmes, the Accelerated Development Programme and the Senior Executive Programme. Even so, London Business School demonstrates the growing flexibility on offer. One of its new programmes, Dynamics of strategy, runs as an evening programme with participants attending one class per week over two months.

Whether four weeks or ten weeks is the ideal duration for such programmes is debatable. Most will in any case be divided into a series of shorter modules, with executives returning to their jobs in between. The pressure from the market is for shorter programmes, although the purpose of the course is an important factor in determining duration. Programmes which aim to teach specific skills lend themselves more readily to short, sharp treatments.

Is the school in touch with technology?

A school's ability to understand and utilise technology is now of paramount importance, and for some companies it may determine their selection. Business schools are not generally a good source of IT-related executive programmes. They have left this market to specialists, although there is an IT element in an increasing number of programmes.

Many schools are also reluctant to abandon traditional teaching methods. For an industry which invented the phrase "leading edge", it is disappointing that a lot of management education falls into the "talk and chalk" category. The Annual UCLA Computer Usage Survey for 1997 included 252 business schools in 15 countries. It found that computer operating budgets, as a percentage of total operating budgets, had risen from 3% in 1985 to 3.3% in 1997. Such a miserly increase hardly suggests participation in a revolution.

Some schools are leading through technology

The Colegio de Dirección at Spain's Instituto de Empresa (IE) has set up a Department of Knowledge Technologies. Its aim is to foster understanding of the managerial challenges created by technology and to adapt the school's teaching content and methods to the latest technology. Such initiatives are becoming widespread as business schools somewhat belatedly enter the technological revolution.

Inevitably, there are a number of schools which have used technology to steal a march on the competition. Henley Management College in the UK, for example, has a well-established reputation for distance learning. Technology has long been embedded in its approach to executive programmes. According to Henley's principal, Ray Wild, technology is creating a new sort of business school. "Schools and their faculty must learn to reverse the traditional direction of their work," he says. "Instead of conveying information to recipients they will work in the opposite direction—back up the supply chain. They must design and provide learning opportunities for their markets, and provide directed access to relevant information, whatever its source, to support that learning. Academic work will certainly give rise to new information. But for most schools, for most of the time, information, ever increasing in quantity and perishability, will be outsourced, as they focus on their distinctive role of creating real-time learning opportunities and on-line support."

US schools such as Michigan and Duke University's Fuqua are now embracing technology with enthusiasm. Alan F White, senior associate dean at MIT's Sloan School of Management, says: "The new techniques and technologies of distance learning hold the potential to revolutionise executive education."

Whether or not this will turn into a revolution is open to debate. But consumers should be aware of a school's attitude to and use of technology. Beware of Luddites, and be suspicious of over-zealous converts who believe that technological wizardry is a substitute for substance. Consumers also need to be aware of schools which have an abundance of equipment but do not actually use it. The UCLA Computer Usage Survey found that 85% of business schools had access to distance-learning and teleconferencing equipment, but only 39% admitted to regularly using it.

What are the networking opportunities?

It is worth scrutinising providers' client lists when choosing programmes, to discover which corporate cultures managers are likely to be exposed to. One of the main benefits of sending managers on open programmes is the opportunity to work alongside managers from different organisations, sectors and nationalities. In many cases, contacts made on programmes endure beyond the duration of the programme and become an important addition to the participant's network.

How can the benefits be measured?

The most important question for any company is the return on investment. Unfortunately, there are no easy answers, but London Business School is one of a number of schools trying to address the issue by linking evaluation to learning sets, learning logs and other tools to make it "part of a virtuous cycle that endures after the programme has finished". Dena Michelli, the school's business development officer for executive programmes, explains: "In this way we try to pick up what participants get out of the experience. We repeat the process again six months after the programme to review what's actually happened. So the manager might say: 'This is what I did with my team based on X that I learned on the programme; this had the effect Y on the way we operate, which had the impact on the bottom line of Z.' In this way you can begin to get a sense of the return on the investment."

Consumers should check whether schools offer post-programme analysis. Any sort of follow-up is useful, but a systematic approach to understanding the impact of programmes is particularly beneficial for all concerned.

Chapter 6
Key issues in executive education

The growth areas

In recent years there have been important changes to the content of many programmes. This reflects the changing environment in which many companies and managers now operate, and their increasing focus on matching programmes to the strategy of the business.

In particular, there has been a rise in demand for:

- new and softer skills;
- global perspectives;
- personal development; and
- practical programmes.

New and softer skills

Widespread restructuring has led to demands for new skills and competencies, as well as for communication and interpersonal skills, traditionally regarded as soft skills. Many of the competencies identified by companies as crucial to the future of their business are less technical and more behaviour-oriented. The traditional command and control management style is being replaced with an approach geared towards creating a culture and environment in which employees can work more effectively.

Softer skills and behaviours include effective leadership, coaching, facilitating, mentoring and other interpersonal competencies. A 1997 report by the UK's Industrial Society found that leadership is now the main topic in management development programmes, closely followed by communication skills and appraisal interviews. Other popular topics were change management, coaching and mentoring skills.

These softer skills dominate lists of core competencies identified by major organisations. BP demands nine core competencies from its senior managers, including leadership and team-building skills. IBM UK has six competencies for senior executives: intellect, tenacity, vision, impact, skills in active management and skills in general management. Providers focusing on meeting these needs are well placed to gain business. Interestingly, business schools often have in-depth knowledge of the competency-based approach without actually putting it into practice themselves or organising their programmes along these lines.

Global perspectives

Global aspirations and expectations have created a need for a more international perspective on programmes. Companies want to create a cadre of managers who can manage across borders and who have an enlightened view of the global economy. This has sparked rapid growth in truly international programmes, the delivery and content of which span different continents.

One of Fuqua School of Business's courses, for example, is the Global Executive Program (GEP)*. The six-week programme is held at different locations around the world, including Europe, Asia and the Americas. It aims to provide participants, typically high-potential managers in their 40s, with an understanding of the business drivers in different regions. "We also travel to the companies and talk about the challenges," explains Wanda Wallace, managing director of executive programmes at Fuqua. "The sessions really start hanging together as participants build up the bigger picture of the factors driving business. So the programme is not aimed at someone who will be managing the Japanese operation, but at how Japan fits into the global economy." With continuing globalisation, programme delivery and content will become ever more international.

Personal development

A change in the psychological contact between employers and managers, recognition of the need for continuous professional development and awareness of the concept of employability has led to the current popularity of personal development programmes. These are geared towards the personal and career development of individuals. Typical of the genre is a programme called Emotional Intelligence: The Untapped Edge for Success. This covers self-motivation, persistence in the face of frustration, mood management, and the ability to empathise, think and hope. Traditional it is not.

Major programmes also now boast a more personal element. INSEAD's Advanced Management Programme, for example, features a health-management module led by a team of fitness experts. Sessions include physical and mental fitness training as well as counselling on stress management. This is becoming increasingly common.

Practical programmes

The practical usefulness of what people learn at business schools has always been questioned. Peter Drucker has observed: "Classrooms construct wonderful models of a

---

* The 1998 GEP has been postponed until 1999.

non-world." Henry Mintzberg, who works at McGill University and INSEAD, notes: "Business schools train people to sit in their offices and look for case studies."

Such criticism may be consigned to history, according to Jonathan Slack, chief executive of the UK Association of Business Schools. "Business schools have always had to struggle with balancing academic respectability with a problem solving approach companies want. They appear to be doing that by not being too theoretical and making it more relevant," he says.

Business schools are moving towards helping their customers make things happen. "Programmes cover topics such as major strategic change and the problems of major upheaval, and an enormous part of that is the human side," says Ian Tanner, director of the executive centre at Manchester Business School. "At a theoretical level you can look at how you bring about this sort of change, and the nature of leadership in organisations where the old hierarchy is dropping away. But what people are really interested in is: how do we actually do it? How do we find and develop the people to lead it? And how do we manage the people affected by it?"

Functional programmes

It is not all change, however. Although newer, more fashionable subjects attract attention, the traditional basics continue to generate substantial revenue. Specific functional skills remain the meat and drink of executive programmes. Demand for courses on how to read a balance sheet, the basics of marketing and operations management, for example, remains strong, as does demand for courses in sales techniques, negotiating skills and public speaking.

Functional specialism is also alive and well. For example, finance programmes are making a typically understated comeback. Among London Business School's most popular executive programmes is its Masters in Finance (MiF). Launched as recently as in 1993, the full-time MiF is already highly competitive with about ten applicants for every place. It is a specialist programme providing a thorough training in the principles and practice of finance. Interestingly, the MiF is deliberately positioned as a specialist programme for individuals who have already decided that they want their future career to be in an area requiring an in-depth knowledge of finance. It is not a top-up programme for the forgetful. According to Anthony Neuberger, director of the full-time MiF, the success of the programme should not come as a surprise: "The complexities of the financial markets and the sophistication required for financial management have generated a major educational need."

Outlining the origins of the course, Paul Marsh, director of the part-time version, explains: "Financial expertise, knowledge and training have become crucial for the success of companies and the careers of the individuals who work in them. No other management field has undergone such rapid changes, or experienced such exciting progress over the last decade. This was reflected in unprecedented demand for our long-established finance executive programmes, but some participants said they wanted to earn a formal qualification, and to study the field in even greater depth and breadth. The MiF grew out of this demand."

The demand for executive programmes suggests that managers are being pragmatic, seeking specialist knowledge as well as softer skills. In doing so they are being highly realistic. The most successful managers generally possess broad general management skills and expertise in a particular function.

Functions plus

Even traditional functional skills do not stand still. Functional programmes are now commonly supplemented by a range of new elements. Some of the more popular issues covered are:

- appraisal interviewing;
- benchmarking;
- managing information systems;
- managing the outsourcing decision;
- marketing on the Internet;
- project management;
- risk management.

Chapter 7
Regional trends

North America

The story of management thinking and of management education is predominantly an American one. The concept of the business school originated in the US and, during the last three decades, the world has sought to emulate its example.

The executive education market in North America is highly developed and sophisticated. The challenges and problems faced by business schools within this market are generally those mentioned earlier: increasing competition; rising expectations from consumers; and perpetually growing demands on resources. But many of these trends are particularly acute in this region. For example, in North America it is increasingly clear that business schools are divided into those competing internationally (a small elite group); those competing nationally (the majority); and those competing locally against a myriad of smaller training and consulting firms.

North American business schools are not, by European standards, highly international. The majority of faculty members are normally North American and the programme content is American-based. Most schools are moving towards greater internationalism, but it remains to be seen how far they are capable of going. As a result, some schools find themselves competing directly with foreign schools for the first time. As observed earlier, it is notable that the largest national grouping on some programmes in Europe is North American. Competition with European schools is probably not of great significance for elite North American schools. For the majority, however, it poses interesting and demanding questions.

A business school is not like McDonald's. It cannot replicate itself around the world through franchises (although this is an increasingly attractive alternative for MBA programmes). The schools likely to succeed in the future are those which establish partnerships and joint ventures with foreign business schools. This will enable them to deliver truly global programmes, broaden the global experience of their faculty and bring a global perspective to teaching and research.

An interesting alternative already being explored by some North American schools is to link up with major broadcasting companies to spread their message globally. This would meet the needs of developing markets, but would not add the much-needed global element to North American executive education.

Europe

European business schools were originally cast in the American mould. Over recent years, however, faith in the American management model appears to have slipped. (This is not the case in eastern Europe, where the emerging business schools are usually American-based, for example, the US Business School in Prague.)

Leading thinkers are increasingly to be found in European business schools. London Business School, for example, is home to Sumantra Ghoshal and Arie de Geus, as well as hosting visits from Gary Hamel. France's INSEAD is home to rising stars such as Chan Kim as well as long-established luminaries such as Yves Doz. "There is a European school of theory which is much less deterministic than American models. It is concerned with creating things dynamically and there is a critical mass of people who think along similar lines," says London Business School's Don Sull, an American and one of the new generation of Europe-based academics.

Europe is a packed and burgeoning market for executive development in all its manifestations. A report by the UK Association of Business Schools (ABS) suggests that UK business schools are among the country's top 50 exporters, attracting over £400m per year from other countries. Despite such statistics, Jonathan Slack, chief executive of the ABS, predicts: "There is unlikely to be much of an increase in the number of business schools in Europe. Some will seek to internationalise, while others will take a more regional role. Most will compete at a national level."

The international challengers are a small number of leading schools, including INSEAD, IMD, London Business School, Ashridge and Cranfield. Other European schools have demonstrated an ability to carve out effective niches. Henley Management College and Edinburgh Business School, for example, are leaders in the distance-learning market. With growing competition, the pressure is on many of the younger schools to justify their existence either through better targeting of their programmes or through imaginative alliances with other organisations.

Asia

The Asian executive education market is perhaps the most exciting in the world. Growth is enormous, and many parts of Asia are currently experiencing an unprecedented increase in the range and quality of programmes on offer. As Narayan Pant, deputy chairman of executive programmes at the National University of Singapore, notes: "The growth in the number of programmes in our region has been virtually exponential."

Asia is also developing its own strain of management thinking which is not brash in the American mould, but cerebral and low-key, spiritual as well as material, informed by the

West but gaining thoroughly Asian insights. When it started in 1968 the Asian Institute of Management in Manila, Philippines, the region's first Western-style business school, used only materials from Harvard. Now 60% of case studies for its MBA programme are written in-house or come from other Asian schools.

Asian thinkers are at the forefront of some of the most important areas of management research. Japan's Kenichi Ohmae has provided much of the impetus to studies of globalisation, and Ikujiro Nonaka has done a great deal to push knowledge management to the top of the managerial agenda. (Mr Nonaka holds the first professorship dedicated to the study of knowledge and its impact on business at the University of California's Haas School of Business as well as being professor of management at Japan's Hitosubashi University.) Their achievements are symptomatic of a broader change in perspective. Today's Asian management theorists often have a more truly global perspective than their Western counterparts.

There is a real sense that Asian business schools are a force for change. Their potential is often intriguing. What, for example, will be the input of the China Europe International Business School in Shanghai to Chinese thinking in the next decade? Equally interesting is the future role of Hong Kong. Kam-Hon Lee, dean of business administration at the Chinese University of Hong Kong, expresses confidence: "The 21st century is the Asia-Pacific century. Among Asia-Pacific countries, China is set to play an especially prominent role in that new order. Hong Kong will become of paramount importance in China. It serves, and will continue to serve, as the regional headquarters of business operations in the area and is universally regarded as the business gateway to China."

Although there are many unanswered questions, the quality of executive programmes offered in many Asian markets is far higher than before. Increasingly, they address senior management issues, such as strategic planning, rather than simply concentrating on functional issues. Many of the providers have products and programmes which stand up well against more established courses in North America and Europe, and their local knowledge and cultural awareness can represent substantial added value. In the Asian market, too, tailored programmes are growing in popularity.

Part 2

Directory of open programmes

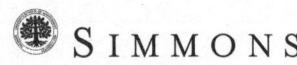

Introduction

Part 2 of *Which executive programme?* is a directory of open (or public) programmes selected from leading business schools throughout the world. The featured programmes meet a number of criteria. They have to have been offered for more than one year by schools with an established track record. Their content is aimed at middle and senior managers. All the programmes are three days or more in length and are delivered in English or a major European language.

Programmes are divided by subject matter as follows.

- Finance (page 41)

- General management 1: executive and advanced executive programmes (page 67)

- General management 2: other programmes (page 91)

- Human resources (page 147)

- International management (page 163)

- Leadership (page 171)

- Marketing (page 197)

- Personal development (page 221)

Each section is preceded by a brief introduction outlining the key issues in the subject area. Within the subject entries programmes are further divided geographically into: North America; the UK; Europe excluding UK; and the rest of the world.

For contact details as well as further information about the schools, including tailored (or customised) programmes, readers should refer to Part 3 of the report where the schools are listed alphabetically by region.

Finance programmes

Finance for non-financial managers is a traditional course which has been offered for many years. It remains the dominant programme in the area of finance and comes in a bewildering variety of options and formats. However, many business schools do not offer a wide range of financial programmes, and there are few programmes offering a genuinely international perspective on financial issues. INSEAD's Corporate Financial Strategy in Global Markets programme is one of the exceptions.

Financial training for senior managers and directors is generally offered only by the most prestigious schools. Northwestern University's Kellogg Graduate School of Management runs programmes on Cost Management Strategies and Corporate Financial Strategy; and Harvard Business School offers Finance for Senior Executives and Corporate Financial Engineering.

The market for financial programmes is likely to grow in the next few years. Senior managers will need training in concepts such as economic value added, which are becoming increasingly common, as well as the ability to understand and manage the financial implications of globalisation and events such as the advent of the single European currency.

Programmes are arranged alphabetically by provider in the following regions:

- North America (page 42)

- UK (page 57)

- Europe excluding UK (page 60)

- Rest of world (page 63)

North America

The Anderson School at UCLA—Executive Education Programs

▪ Finance for Non-Financial Executives

Location: The Anderson School at UCLA, Los Angeles, CA, US

Participants: Executives and managers who are not financial experts but must make or understand financial decisions

Frequency: Twice a year

Duration: 6 days

Cost: $4,950 incl accommodation, meals, books, materials

Aims: To help participants understand the financial management of their organisations and acquire the tools for financial decision-making

Main topics: Perspectives on balance sheets, income statements, cash-flow statements, annual reports; assessing accounting procedures and financial statements; valuation of companies; making capital budgeting and hedging decisions; corporate financing options; the role of the stock market; shareholder wealth

Notes: A basic knowledge of spreadsheets will help participants. A half-day optional quantitative spreadsheet workshop is held at the beginning of the programme. Computers and software are provided

Berkeley Center for Executive Development—Haas School of Business

▪ Financial Analysis for Non-Financial Managers

Location: Berkeley Centre for Executive Development, Berkeley, CA, US

Participants: Executives with little or no training in accounting and finance

Frequency: Twice a year

Duration: 3 days

Cost: $2,375 incl accommodation, meals, taxes

Aims: To help participants understand, interpret and communicate financial data

Main topics: Strategic significance of financial information; strategic profitability analysis; motivating and measuring financial performance; motivating and measuring managerial performance

Carlson School of Management—University of Minnesota

- ## Finance for Non-Financial Managers

Location: Carlson School, Minneapolis, MN; West Bank Campus, Minneapolis, MN, US

Participants: Executives and managers with little or no work experience in financial areas

Frequency: Twice a year

Duration: 4 days

Cost: $2,800 incl meals, materials

Aims: To provide participants with the tools to understand the financial functions of their organisations and contribute to the creation of shareholder value

Main topics: The finance view of the firm; introduction to financial statements; basic financial statement analysis; the time value of money; alternative rules for project selection; net present value analysis; economic value added; risk, return of the cost of capital; creating shareholder wealth

University of Chicago—Graduate School of Business

- ## Finance for Executives

Location: Gleacher Center, University of Chicago Graduate School of Business, Chicago, IL, US

Participants: Executives in areas such as marketing, sales, manufacturing, engineering; general managers who have been promoted through these routes

Frequency: Three times a year

Duration: 5 days

Cost: $3,850 incl some meals, materials

Aims: To meet the needs and concerns of managers who may not have formal training in the uses and interpretation of financial information

Main topics: Financial statement analysis and cash-flow forecasting; financing decisions; investment decisions and value creation

Columbia Business School

■ **Finance and Accounting for the Non-Financial Executive**

Location: Arden House, Harriman, NY, US; New York City, NY, US

Participants: Executives whose main expertise is outside accounting and financial management; marketing, sales and operations managers; corporate development officers

Frequency: 5 times a year (one of these programmes is run in New York City)

Duration: 1 week

Cost: $5,200 incl accommodation, meals, materials (Arden House); $4,500 excl accommodation, meals (New York City)

Aims: To provide participants with an understanding of the key concepts in finance and finance reporting

Main topics: Development of financial statements; financial statement integration and analysis; activity-based costing and management; performance measures; mergers and acquisitions; valuation; financial statement analysis; taxes and business strategy; risk and return; cost of capital; achieving financial excellence

Darden Executive Education—University of Virginia

■ **Financial Management for Non-Financial Managers**

Location: Darden School, Charlottesville, VA, US

Participants: General managers and managers in areas such as marketing, sales, manufacturing, engineering with non-financial backgrounds

Frequency: 3 times a year

Duration: 6 days

Cost: $4,950 incl accommodation, meals

Aims: To enable non-financial managers to interpret and utilise financial data in daily decisions and work more effectively with the financial managers of the organisation

Main topics: Financial reporting and analysis; introduction to basic accounting; published annual reports; financial ratios; current asset management; cost information and decision-making; operating budgets; capital budgeting; managing under changing prices; management control systems

Fisher College of Business—The Ohio State University

■ Academy for Financial Executives

Location: Fisher College of Business, Columbus, OH, US

Participants: Senior and middle managers

Frequency: Once a year

Duration: 1 week per year for 2 years

Cost: $4,400 (or $2,200 per session) incl accommodation, most meals, materials

Aims: To prepare participants to meet the challenges facing the financial services industry

Main topics: Emerging trends, issues and paradigms for the financial services industry; marketing financial products and services; profitability analysis and evaluation; managing and improving individual performance; business and economic environment; financial risk: analysis and evaluation; effective leadership; assessing a bank's financial viability; financial strategies for community banks; negotiation strategies; what makes an employee valuable; strategy formulation

■ The Essentials of Accounting and Finance for the Non-Financial Manager

Location: Fisher College of Business, Columbus, OH, US

Participants: Non-financial managers in areas such as marketing, sales, human resources, manufacturing, engineering

Frequency: 3 times a year

Duration: 3 days

Cost: $1,195 incl meals, materials

Aims: To enable participants to better understand financial statements and analysis

Harvard Business School

■ Corporate Financial Engineering: Advancing Business Strategies

Location: Harvard Business School, Boston, MA, US

Participants: Senior financial executives, individuals reporting to these officials

Frequency: Once a year

Duration: 4 days

Cost: $4,000 incl accommodation, most meals, materials and participation in the optional module

Aims: To examine the application of financial engineering in traditional treasury activities and risk management programmes, and in designing new business models and strategies

Main topics: Which risks a firm should manage; how financial engineers can make stock ownership more palatable to employees; how firms can substitute financial contracts for bricks and mortar; basics of financial engineering (optional)

■ Creating Value Through Corporate Restructuring

Location: Harvard Business School, Boston, MA, US

Participants: General managers, CEOs, CFOs

Frequency: Once a year

Duration: 3 days

Cost: $4,000 incl accommodation, most meals, materials

Aims: To teach participants to identify and respond to potential restructuring opportunities by focusing on financial strategies aimed at repositioning and revitalising companies

Main topics: How corporate spin-off creates value; when a firm should consider downsizing and how the level and timing of employee layoffs should be determined; financial strategies that create the most value when firms are highly leveraged

■ Finance for Senior Executives

Location: Harvard Business School, Boston, MA, US

Participants: Senior executives from non-financial backgrounds

Frequency: Once a year

Duration: 2 weeks

Cost: $9,500 incl accommodation, most meals, materials

Aims: To help participants gain a clear understanding of the flow and management of financial resources

Main topics: Setting corporate and divisional goals; forecasting performance; biases within financial systems and structures; incentives; profitability, value gaps and corporate control; managing cash flow; shareholder value

■ Strategic Finance for Small Business

Location: Harvard Business School, Boston, MA, US

Participants: Owners, presidents and CEOs of small, privately owned companies

Frequency: Once a year

Duration: 1 week

Cost: $6,000 incl accommodation, most meals, materials

Aims: To strengthen participants' understanding of financial strategy

Main topics: Determining and satisfying financial needs; dealing with the financial community and investors; evaluating buyout offers; managing cash flow and proactive financial planning

■ Valuation

Location: Harvard Business School, Boston, MA, US

Participants: Senior executives

Frequency: Once a year

Duration: 3 days

Cost: $4,000 incl accommodation, most meals, materials

Aims: To teach participants how to determine the optimal valuation tool for their organisations and use it for effective decision-making

Main topics: Choosing the valuation tools most appropriate for specific opportunities; implementing the proper valuation methodologies; making effective management decisions based on value

Richard Ivey School of Business—University of Western Ontario

■ Financial Analysis for Non-Financial Executives

Location: Spencer Hall, London, Ontario, Canada

Participants: Managers in non-financial roles, presidents, CEOs, vice-presidents, directors and managers in HR, marketing, operations, etc

Frequency: Twice a year

Duration: 5 days

Cost: C$5,250 incl accommodation, meals, materials

Aims: To help participants' improve their ability to understand and use financial information in making strategic and operational decisions

Main topics: External reporting; planning and control; problem-solving; measuring value added

Johnson Graduate School of Management—Cornell University

■ Finance and Accounting for Non-Financial Managers

Location: Cornell University, Ithaca, NY, US

Participants: Managers in operations, marketing, sales, HR, engineering, R&D and general management with non-financial backgrounds

Frequency: Twice a year

Duration: 1 week

Cost: $4,300 incl accommodation, meals, materials

Aims: To help participants use accounting information and financial analysis techniques in planning and evaluating manufacturing, marketing, capital spending and financing decisions

Main topics: The role of accounting information in planning, decision-making and performance evaluation; financial statement analysis; cash-flow analysis and net present value; capital budgeting and capital expenditure analysis; using cost data in management decision-making; integrated financial analysis for planning and performance evaluation

Jesse H Jones Graduate School of Management—Rice University

■ Finance and Accounting for Executives

Location: Rice University, Houston, TX, US

Participants: Executives and entrepreneurs whose experience has not included accounting and finance

Frequency: 6 times a year

Duration: 4 days

Cost: n/a

Aims: To clarify finance and accounting and make them understandable with practical, easy-to-implement ideas

Main topics: Assessment of financial reports; accounting systems and the accounting process; assessing the firm's performance, analysing cash flow and evaluating capital investment decisions; analysing budgeting concepts and procedures; developing a financial plan

J L Kellogg Graduate School of Management—Northwestern University

■ Corporate Financial Strategy

Location: James L Allen Center, Evanston, IL, US

Participants: Executives and general managers involved in capital budgeting, M&A analysis and financial decisions; executives in strategic and financial planning, treasury functions; commercial and investment bankers

Frequency: Twice a year

Duration: 5 days

Cost: $4,600 incl accommodation, meals, materials

Aims: To enhance the ability of participants to develop, evaluate and implement financial strategies

Main topics: Evaluation of investment programmes; financial reporting; resource allocation; financing strategies; the cost of capital; innovative financial instruments; investment and financing interactions; mergers and acquisitions; leveraged buy-outs; international investments

■ Cost Management Strategies

Location: James L Allen Center, Evanston, IL, US

Participants: Managers whose decisions have a direct impact on profitability

Frequency: Once a year

Duration: 4 days

Cost: $2,900 incl accommodation, meals, materials

Aims: To help managers understand the real costs and profit drivers of their businesses

Main topics: Strategic cost management; cost-management systems; activity-based costing; cost drivers and performance measures

■ Finance for Executives

Location: James L Allen Center, Evanston, IL, US

Participants: Executives who make or contribute to financial decisions, managers in marketing, operations, HR and engineering with non-financial backgrounds

Frequency: Twice a year

Duration: 5 days

Cost: $4,600 incl accommodation, meals, materials

Aims: To teach participants to apply modern financial concepts to a broad range of managerial decisions

Main topics: Interpreting financial reports; evaluating investments; financial decisions and value creation

- ## Merger Week: Creating Value Through Strategic Acquisitions and Alliances

Location: James L Allen Center, Evanston, IL, US

Participants: Senior executives with corporate development, planning and finance responsibilities

Frequency: 3 times a year

Duration: 5 days

Cost: $5,200 incl accommodation, meals and materials

Aims: To address the challenges involved in creating value and to provide participants with the skills to avoid the most frequent pitfalls

Main topics: Industry attractiveness and competitive analysis; financial analysis; value-based performance measures, negotiations, post-merger strategy and integration; strategic alliances

Kenan-Flagler Business School—University of North Carolina at Chapel Hill

- ## Financial Analysis for Non-Financial Managers

Location: University of North Carolina, Chapel Hill, NC, US

Participants: Non-financial managers

Frequency: 3 times a year

Duration: 3 days

Cost: $1,950

Aims: To enable managers to fully understand the financial position of their companies

Main topics: Financial statements and the accounting process; cash flows; interest, risk and decision-making; investment and capital budgeting decisions; financial statement analysis; financial performance measures

McGill Executive Institute—McGill University

■ Accounting and Finance for Non-Financial Executives

Location: McGill Executive Institute, Montreal, Canada; University of Toronto, Rotman School of Management, Toronto, Canada

Participants: Executives, managers and small-business owners with non-financial backgrounds

Frequency: 7 times a year

Duration: 4 days

Cost: C$1,595 incl lunches, materials

Aims: To provide participants with a solid understanding of business accounting and finance

Main topics: The financial reporting system; the financial information system; analysis for financial decisions; operations and corporate planning and control; strategic planning and control

University of Michigan Business School

■ Corporate Financial Management

Location: Executive Education Center, Ann Arbor, MI, US

Participants: Executives involved in investment and financial decisions, general managers

Frequency: Twice a year

Duration: 6 days

Cost: $5,200 incl accommodation, meals, materials

Aims: To heighten participants' understanding of important elements in the financial management process

Main topics: Role of strategy in finance; resource allocation and performance evaluation; economic value added; domestic and international capital markets; cost of capital; strategic issues in resource allocation; financing instruments; financial risk management; mergers and acquisitions

■ Financial Analysis, Planning and Control

Location: Executive Education Center, Ann Arbor, MI, US

Participants: Senior managers who need to use and understand financial data for decision-making

Frequency: Twice a year

Duration: 5 days

Cost: $4,875 incl accommodation, meals, materials

Aims: To explore the managerial uses of financial information within an organisation

Main topics: Financial performance measurement; transfer pricing; investment-centre performance measurement; budgeting and control of non-manufacturing expenses; planning and control of diversified companies; cost systems and product profitability; analysing alternative choices of action

■ Finance for the Non-Financial Manager

Location: Executive Education Center, Ann Arbor, MI, US

Participants: Non-financial managers in areas such as marketing, sales, manufacturing, engineering; general managers who have been promoted through these functions

Frequency: 4 times a year

Duration: 5 days

Cost: $5,200 incl accommodation, meals, materials

Aims: To help participants develop financial policy and better understand the impact of financial decisions on the firm's profitability

Main topics: Decision-making in business; financial statements; budgeting; financial analysis; asset management; liabilities management

Notes: This programme is also offered in Hong Kong; Taipei, Taiwan; Bangkok, Thailand

■ Finance for Strategic Decision Making: a Program for Non-Financial Managers

Location: Executive Education Center, Ann Arbor, MI, US

Participants: Non-financial managers who have already attended a basic finance programme

Frequency: Twice a year

Duration: 5 days

Cost: $5,200 incl accommodation, meals, materials

Aims: To familiarise non-financial managers with financial aspects of strategic decisions, and provide an understanding of financing decisions and how they enhance shareholder value

Main topics: Creating shareholder value through financial decisions valuation; capital structure and financing policy; corporate restructuring; performance evaluation; risk management

Owen Graduate School of Management—Vanderbilt University

■ Finance and Accounting for Non-Financial Managers

Location: Owen Graduate School of Management, TN, US

Participants: Managers with non-financial backgrounds

Frequency: Twice a year

Duration: 5 days

Cost: $1,995 incl accommodation, most meals, materials

Aims: To enable participants to update their knowledge of financial statements and other accounting data

The Mary Jean and Frank P Smeal College of Business Administration—Pennsylvania State University

■ **Financial Analysis for Strategic Management**

Location: Penn State University, PA, US

Participants: General, functional and staff managers who need a better understanding of the role of finance in their organisations

Frequency: Twice a year

Duration: 10 days

Cost: $6,700 incl accommodation, meals, materials

Aims: To help participants increase their financial acumen and confidence

Main topics: Corporate strategy; financial objectives; capital structure and the cost of capital; capital markets and valuation; mergers and acquisitions; evaluation of global business opportunities

Notes: This programme includes a computerised business simulation

University of South Carolina—Daniel Management Center

■ **Finance for the Non-Financial Manager**

Location: Daniel Management Center, Columbia, SC, US

Participants: Middle and upper-level managers from profit-making organisations with little or no background in finance

Frequency: 3 times a year

Duration: 3 days

Cost: $995

Aims: To enable participants to interact effectively with financial experts

Main topics: Strategic role of finance and financial management; understanding financial statements; analysis of company performance; valuation; relation between earnings and value; valuation principles applied to capital expenditure decisions; the impact of major corporate decisions; a framework for creating value

Stanford Graduate School of Business—Stanford University

■ **Financial Management Program**

Location: Graduate School of Business, Stanford, CA, US

Participants: Senior managers

Frequency: Once a year

Duration: 2 weeks

Cost: $10,500 incl accommodation, meals, books, study materials

Aims: To augment and expand participants' knowledge of corporate finance

Main topics: Valuation; capital structure; financial forecasting; dividend policy; risk management; fixed income securities; governance

Leonard N Stern School of Business—New York University

■ **Understanding the Basis and Consequences of Managerial Financial Decisions**

Location: Stern School of Business, New York City, NY, US

Participants: Non-financial managers in manufacturing, marketing, sales, purchasing, engineering, operations; strategic and business unit leaders; recently promoted general managers

Frequency: Once a year

Duration: 5 days

Cost: $3,900 incl some meals, materials

Aims: To allow participants without a financial background to integrate financial concepts in decisions that determine the success and profitability of their organisations

Main topics: Links to strategic business management; business performance measurement; fundamental accounting concepts; understanding financial statements and annual reports; cost analysis and business decisions; budgeting and forecasting; project evaluation; asset management; liabilities management

Thunderbird—American Graduate School of International Management

■ **Financial Issues in Global Competition**

Location: Thunderbird, Glendale, AZ, US

Participants: Non-financial and financial managers with international responsibilities

Frequency: Once a year

Duration: 1 week (Sunday pm-Friday noon)

Cost: $4,500 incl accommodation, meals

Aims: To increase participants' understanding of the global financial environment and to improve their skills in handling problems and issues in this area

Main topics: Global financial systems; financial forecasting and analysis; rate determination; foreign exchange needs and products; international investment analysis; performance measurement systems; organisational impacts

Wharton School—University of Pennsylvania—Aresty Institute of Executive Education

■ **Creating Value Through Financial Management**

Location: Wharton School, Philadelphia, PA, US

Participants: Senior managers who need to upgrade their financial skills

Frequency: Twice a year

Duration: 5 days

Cost: $5,950 incl accommodation, meals

Aims: To provide participants with a deeper understanding of how to build and track organisational value

Main topics: External equity and the cost of capital; capital budgeting; financial policy; company diversification policy; risk adjusted profit; control and review; mergers; multinational finance; the mix of debt

■ **Finance and Accounting for the Non-Financial Manager**

Location: Wharton School, Philadelphia, PA, US

Participants: Senior managers with non-financial backgrounds

Frequency: 6 times a year

Duration: 5 days

Cost: $6,250 incl accommodation, meals

Aims: To provide participants with the knowledge to make better financial decisions

Main topics: Accounting terminology and assumptions; valuation concepts; financial statements; distinguishing income from cash flow; the accounting process; the quality of earnings; financial decision-making; analysis of financial reports

University of Wisconsin-Madison—Graduate School of Business

■ **Finance and Accounting for Non-Financial Executives**

Location: Management Institute, University of Wisconsin-Madison, WI, US

Participants: Executives, directors and managers with non-financial backgrounds

Frequency: 5 times a year

Duration: 3 days

Cost: n/a

Aims: To teach participants how to use financial information and reports as an effective management tool

Main topics: Balance sheets and income statements; cash-flow analysis; return on investment; budgeting

UK

Ashridge Management College

▪ Advanced Finance for Managers

Location: Ashridge Management College, Berkhamsted, UK

Participants: Senior managers with knowledge of basic finance

Frequency: Twice a year

Duration: 5 days

Cost: £2,850 incl accommodation, meals

Aims: To help participants tackle more challenging financial decision-making

Main topics: Company appraisal through financial analysis; strategic cost management; investment appraisal; developing shareholder value; foreign exchange and treasury management; raising finance; acquisitions and divestments

▪ Finance for Managers

Location: Ashridge Management College, Berkhamsted, UK

Participants: Senior and middle managers

Frequency: 5 times a year

Duration: 5 days

Cost: £2,500 incl accommodation, meals

Aims: To help participants understand the financial aspects of their jobs to aid decision-making

Main topics: Measuring business performance; financial planning; financial analysis; management information and control; project evaluation; investment appraisal

Notes: Participation in this programme can lead towards the Ashridge Diploma in General Management

▪ Strategy and Finance

Location: Ashridge Management College, Berkhamsted, UK

Participants: Senior managers

Frequency: 3 times a year

Duration: 5 days

Cost: £3,000

Aims: To provide the practical tools for strategic and financial analysis at a senior level

Main topics: Evaluating the determinants of profitability; value companies; evaluating competitive advantage; organisational growth and acquisitions; competitor performance

Cranfield School of Management

■ Boardroom Finance for Strategic Decisions

Location: Cranfield School of Management, Cranfield, UK

Participants: Senior managers

Frequency: 4 times a year

Duration: 5 days

Cost: £2,950 incl accommodation

Aims: To help participants gain a better understanding of internal financial and external market information

Main topics: Understanding and interpreting financial information; planning and control; investment appraisal

London Business School

■ Financial Seminar for Senior Managers

Location: London Business School, London, UK

Participants: Senior managers from non-financial backgrounds who are experiencing an increasing need to make decisions using financial information

Frequency: Twice a year

Duration: 5 days

Cost: £3,900

Aims: To enable participants to carry out detailed financial analysis and evaluations

Main topics: Analysis and interpretation of financial statements; interpretation of management accounting information; project appraisal and valuation using net present value techniques

Manchester Business School

■ **Finance for Non-Financial Managers**

Location: Manchester Business School, Manchester, UK

Participants: Senior managers who need to improve their knowledge of finance and accounting

Frequency: Once a year

Duration: 1 week

Cost: £1,300 (residential); £975 (non-residential)

Aims: To provide managers with skills to evaluate the financial implications for strategic decisions taken at business and corporate levels

Main topics: Corporate reporting and analysis; corporate finance—project appraisal; management planning and control; corporate finance—financial markets

Templeton College

■ **The Oxford Senior Executive Finance Programme**

Location: Templeton College, Oxford, UK

Participants: Senior directors, newly promoted executives from specialist backgrounds, fast-track executives, corporate planners and strategists

Frequency: Twice a year

Duration: 6 days

Cost: £4,000 incl accommodation, meals

Aims: To provide participants with a broad competence in financial management and strategy

Main topics: Finance and accounting; assessing financial health; linking financial targets and business objectives; financing growth; performance measurement; valuation, capital budgeting and cost of capital; business unit and company values; financing decisions, financial structure and corporate finance; risk management; international finance

Notes: Emphasis is placed on the relationship between finance, strategy and operations, and on the global financial environment

Europe excl UK

ESADE—Escuela Superior de Administración y Dirección de Empresas

■ Finance for Non-Financial Managers: A General Approach

Location: ESADE, Barcelona, Spain; Madrid, Spain

Participants: General managers

Frequency: Once a year

Duration: 64 hours over 3 months (Barcelona: Wednesdays 9 am-6.45 pm; Madrid: Fridays 9 am-7 pm)

Cost: Pta420,000

Aims: To provide participants with a solid understanding of how financial management fits into the overall framework of their corporate vision

Main topics: Reading, interpreting and analysing financial reports; utilising financial information to support decision-making processes and overall corporate strategy

HEC Executive Development Center

■ CESA Finance

Location: HEC, Paris, France

Participants: Finance specialists, managers of medium-sized companies wishing to acquire financial expertise, managers who have not yet had responsibilities in finance

Frequency: Once a year

Duration: 20 days (4 5-day modules)

Cost: FFr47,000

Aims: To examine the concepts, theories and techniques of financial management

Main topics: Value analysis and risk management; creating strategic value and financial strategy; value integration in general management strategy

Notes: The programme language is French

■ Global Corporate Finance

Location: HEC, Paris, France

Participants: Finance analysts, controllers, treasurers, directors, consultants

Frequency: Once a year

Duration: 5 days

Cost: FFr22,000

Aims: To provide participants with an overview of current corporate financial issues in a changing global environment

Main topics: Financial markets; global developments in corporate finance; mergers and acquisitions in Europe

IMD—International Institute for Management Development

■ Strategic Finance

Location: IMD, Lausanne, Switzerland

Participants: Senior financial professionals, general managers with responsibility for the finance function

Frequency: Once a year

Duration: 6 days

Cost: Swfr8,000 incl some meals, materials

Aims: To examine the impact of an increasingly volatile environment on the role of the senior financial executive

Main topics: Assessing financial health; pan-European control; new venture analysis; mergers and acquisitions; economic values as a change driver; financial ethics (case history); leveraged buy-outs; financial restructuring

INSEAD—European Institute of Business Administration

■ Corporate Financial Strategy in Global Markets

Location: INSEAD, Fontainebleau, France

Participants: Finance directors, consultants, treasurers, controllers, financial analysts

Frequency: Once a year

Duration: 11 days

Cost: FFr46,000

Aims: To increase participants' awareness of global financial markets, the new instruments available and how to use them

Main topics: Value-based strategy and corporate financial policy (valuation methods; optimal finance strategies; managerial and strategic options; financial restructuring dynamics (corporate restructuring; leveraged and management buy-outs; share repurchase and shareholder communication)

■ Finance for Executives

Location: INSEAD, Fontainebleau, France

Participants: Managing directors, vice-presidents, general, functional and regional managers

Frequency: Twice a year

Duration: 10 days

Cost: FFr43,000 incl some meals, materials

Aims: To focus on the general principles of corporate finance and the link between finance and other functional areas of the corporation

Main topics: Financial accounting and analysis; analysis of investment decisions; corporate strategy, financing and valuation; corporate risk management

Maastricht School of Management

■ Financial Management

Location: Maastricht School of Management, Maastricht, Netherlands

Participants: Senior executives working in medium or large enterprises, consultants in the areas of general management, information systems and control

Frequency: Once a year

Duration: 14 weeks

Cost: G15,500 incl field-work expenses, materials

Aims: To enhance the ability of participants to make good investment and financing decisions

Main topics: Introduction to corporate accounting; cost accounting; management control and auditing; corporate investment decision-making; capital structure analysis and dividend policy; role and function of security markets; portfolio management; corporate risk management; management of financial derivatives

■ Financial Restructuring

Location: Maastricht School of Management, Maastricht, Netherlands

Participants: Finance, accounting and strategy executives

Frequency: Once a year

Duration: 2 1-week modules

Cost: n/a

Aims: To understand how restructuring decisions in the area of finance can enhance shareholder value

Main topics: Corporate strategy; valuation framework; buy-outs; mergers and acquisitions; optimising financial strategies

Rest of world

University of Cape Town—Graduate School of Business

■ Essentials of Managerial Finance

Location: Graduate School of Business, Cape Town, South Africa

Participants: Senior and middle managers from non-financial backgrounds

Frequency: Once a year

Duration: 6 days

Cost: R7,210 incl accommodation

Aims: To provide a practical understanding of financial decisions and their applications

Main topics: Financial reporting; cost management; financial analysis; working capital management; financial planning; cost of capital; capital investment appraisal; management of risk and return; factors that influence the valuation of a business; recent developments in taxation

Monash Mt Eliza Business School

■ Strategic Finance for Executives

Location: Mt Eliza, Australia

Participants: Senior and middle managers from all industries and disciplines

Frequency: Twice a year

Duration: 5 days

Cost: A$5,450

Aims: To give participants the frameworks and practical tools to ensure that functional strategies are integrated with financial strategies to maximise the value of their decisions

Main topics: Managing risks and cash flows; capital investment; creating strategic value; activity-based costing; monitoring strategic actions

National University of Singapore—Graduate School of Business

■ Accounting and Finance Programme

Location: National University of Singapore

Participants: Non-financial and non-accounting managers

Frequency: Twice a year

Duration: 1 week

Cost: S$2,200

Aims: To provide participants with a working knowledge of the principles of accounting and finance

Main topics: Interpreting financial statements; working capital requirements and the cash-flow cycle; cash flow analysis; ratio analysis; capital budgeting; budgeting for cost control; performance measurement; choosing accounting policies; creative accounting techniques; off-balance-sheet financing techniques; firm valuation

■ Financial Management Programme

Location: National University of Singapore

Participants: Senior executives; general, senior and finance managers; functional department managers

Frequency: Once a year

Duration: 2 weeks

Cost: S$3,600

Aims: To enable participants to gain a good grasp of the fundamentals of financial management

Main topics: Economic value added; overview of foreign exchange markets; assessing and hedging foreign exchange risks; financial analysis of the firm; valuation of the firm; assessing and hedging corporate risks; predicting corporate failure; making corporate investments; strategic management of working capital; corporate mergers and acquisitions; determining optimal corporate borrowing; innovative financial instruments; assessing and hedging interest rate risks

Wits Business School—University of the Witwatersrand

■ Effective Financial Management

Location: Wits Business School, Johannesburg, South Africa

Participants: Managing directors, finance directors, chief accountants, corporate treasurers, commercial and business development managers, planners

Frequency: Once a year

Duration: 3 days

Cost: R4,950 incl materials, meals

Aims: To examine modern developments in corporate finance and their practical application; to focus on an integrated approach to financial analysis, planning, risk management, valuation

Main topics: Risk, return and the cost of capital; valuation; capital market instruments; measuring and creating value; derivatives; economic environment of risk

■ Finance for Non-Financial Managers

Location: Wits Business School, Johannesburg, South Africa

Participants: Marketing, technical or personnel executives; professionals such as lawyers, architects and quantity surveyors who need a knowledge of financial terminology and analysis

Frequency: Twice a year

Duration: 5 days

Cost: R7,350 incl materials, refreshments

Aims: To develop understanding of the financial decision framework and the skills needed to use financial reports

Main topics: Accounting concepts; assessing the financial health of a firm; planning future financial performance; sources of finance; evaluating investments

General management 1: executive and advanced executive programmes

The inherent vagueness of the term general management has proved no barrier to the development of a profusion of programmes under its generic umbrella. At their heart is one of the founding fathers of business school education: the four-week executive programme. This examination of general management, which can be likened to a quick trip through the contents of an MBA programme, has stood the test of time. There is no sign of its popularity diminishing; indeed, the trend is towards executive programmes aimed at specific audiences. One step up the scale are advanced or senior executive programmes, which are executive programmes with added intellectual substance and prestige.

Programmes are arranged alphabetically by provider in the following regions:

- North America (page 68)

- UK (page 81)

- Europe excluding UK (page 84)

- Rest of world (page 86)

North America

Amos Tuck School of Business

■ Tuck Executive Program

Location: Amos Tuck School, Hanover, NH, US

Participants: General managers, country managers and experienced functional managers who set strategy

Frequency: Once a year

Duration: 4 weeks

Cost: $20,000 incl accommodation, meals, materials

Aims: To address the challenges of globalisation, strategic innovation, industry redefinition and new competitive strategies

Main topics: Developing a general manager's perspective; managing the challenges of globalisation; creating the future; transferring what you learn

The Anderson School at UCLA—Executive Education Programs

■ Advanced Executive Program

Location: The Anderson School at UCLA, Los Angeles, CA, US

Participants: Senior executives responsible for initiating and implementing international business strategies

Frequency: Once a year

Duration: 2 weeks

Cost: $14,000 incl accommodation, meals, books, materials

Aims: To explore the latest strategies for maximising global competitive advantage

Main topics: Knowledge and application of organisational requirements; development and practice of analytical problem-solving skills; testing concepts through group discussion and questioning; interpreting new trading blocs and new trade agreements; identifying opportunities with emerging firms in transition markets; tapping into emerging economies such as China, South Korea, Mexico

■ The Executive Program

Location: The Anderson School at UCLA, Los Angeles, CA, US

Participants: General and senior managers

Frequency: Twice a year

Duration: 13 or 26 weeks

Cost: $11,500 incl meals, books, materials

Aims: To enhance the professional development competencies of executives and managers in a comprehensive general management programme

Main topics: Organisation and management; managerial economics; managerial problem-solving and creativity; managerial accounting and finance; business strategy; human resource management; marketing management; operations and technical management; information technology and systems; global strategy

Notes: The programme can be taken either as 2 13-week semesters with classes held once a week or as an accelerated programme of 1 13-week semester with classes held twice a week

Berkeley Center for Executive Development—Haas School of Business

■ Berkeley Executive Program

Location: Berkeley Center for Executive Development, Berkeley, CA, US

Participants: Senior and high-potential executives who already possess significant general management and/or functional responsibilities substantially affected by global competition and change

Frequency: Twice a year

Duration: 4 weeks

Cost: $18,500 incl meals, taxes

Aims: To renew intellectual capital and empower the executive to act as change agent for achieving organisational effectiveness

Main topics: Understanding the forces shaping contemporary business realities and strategic choices; creating strategies that support corporate priorities; understanding global competitive environments; co-ordinating the use of key corporate resources, processes, capabilities and people; developing and orchestrating people skills and strategies; organisational behaviour in different countries

Notes: This programme emphasises a multidisciplinary approach and features scenario-based planning

■ Berkeley Advanced Management Program

Location: Berkeley Center for Executive Development, Berkeley, CA, US

Participants: Senior and middle managers destined for expanded leadership roles who need to strengthen general management, strategic decision-making and implementation skills

Frequency: Twice a year

Duration: 3 weeks

Cost: $13,875 incl accommodation, meals, other social activities, taxes

Aims: To help transform executives from specialist to multi-competency managers

Main topics: Macroeconomics and financial markets; the human aspect of the managerial challenge; implementing corporate policy choices; the market-focused organisation; configuring the organisation; values, ethics and the legal environment; negotiation as a strategic tool; finance as a performance measurement and control tool

Carlson School of Management—University of Minnesota

■ Minnesota Executive Program

Location: Various conference centres in Minnesota, US

Participants: Senior executives, general managers, managers who are about to enter either of these categories

Frequency: Once a year

Duration: 4 weeks (4 1-week modules spread over 3 months)

Cost: $12,900 incl materials

Aims: To integrate the functional areas of management into a strategic framework

Main topics: General strategy; marketing; finance; operations management; information systems; economic systems; human resources

Notes: This programme includes an optional module on finance for non-financial managers

Carnegie Mellon University—Graduate School of Industrial Administration

■ Program for Executives

Location: Carnegie Mellon University, Pittsburgh, PA, US

Participants: Senior managers with 15-25 years' work experience

Frequency: Twice a year

Duration: 4 weeks

Cost: $16,800 incl accommodation, most meals, taxes

Aims: To broaden perspectives and strengthen skills in general management

Main topics: The global environment; corporate strategy; strategic marketing; management accounting; operations management; financial management; leadership in a complex organisation

Notes: This programme includes a business simulation and there is an optional media skills workshop

Columbia Business School

■ The Columbia Senior Executive Program

Location: Arden House, Harriman, NY, US

Participants: Senior general managers, directors, presidents, country managers; senior executives expected to take up such posts within 2 years

Frequency: 3 times a year

Duration: 4 weeks

Cost: $20,000 incl accommodation, meals, materials

Aims: To help participants identify, develop and acquire new concepts and approaches to leading and managing in the changing global marketplace

Main topics: Global business environment; achieving functional excellence; leading and managing change; individual development and action planning

Notes: Content and participants are notably international, being drawn from 40 countries. Participants prepare case studies of real business issues in their organisations, which are discussed with faculty and other participants

Darden Executive Education—University of Virginia

■ The Executive Program

Location: Darden School, Charlottesville, VA, US

Participants: Managers and executives with around 12 years' experience who have or are about to have significant general management responsibilities

Frequency: Once a year

Duration: 6 weeks

Cost: $29,900 incl accommodation, most meals

Aims: To explore the challenges and opportunities facing organisations as they move into the 21st century

Main topics: Managing through teams; managing the change process; leadership; service excellence; managing the total enterprise; managing for collaborative relationships; managing a sustainable system; managing in a global context; managing in the 21st century; creating value in a global economy

Fisher College of Business—The Ohio State University

■ Executive Development Program

Location: Fisher College of Business, Columbus, OH, US

Participants: Senior and middle managers

Frequency: Once a year

Duration: 4 1-week sessions

Cost: $13,000 ($3,250 per session) incl accommodation, most meals, materials, taxes

Aims: To help participants expand and broaden their leadership and management skills in order to manage more effectively across functions

Main topics: Leadership development; strategic thinking; managing change; effective marketing; human resource management; quality management; financial management

Notes: This is one of the oldest programmes of its kind in the US; it has prepared more than 3,200 managers

Fuqua School of Business—Duke University

■ Advanced Management Program

Location: Fuqua School of Business, Durham, NC, US

Participants: Senior managers making the shift from implementing strategy to formulating it

Frequency: Twice a year

Duration: 4 weeks (2 2-week modules)

Cost: $19,000 incl accommodation, meals, materials

Aims: To prepare executives for the responsibilities of senior general management

Main topics: Successful strategic concepts for domestic and international environments; leadership and corporate culture; decision-making as a strategic tool; growth by acquisition; internal growth strategies; corporate restructuring and strategic alliances in a changing world

Goizueta Business School—Emory University

■ Executive Development Consortium

Location: Goizueta Business School, Atlanta, GA, US

Participants: Senior managers

Frequency: Twice a year

Duration: 3 weeks (3 1-week modules over 5 months)

Cost: $11,300 incl meals, materials

Aims: To extend the knowledge and skills base of senior executives by targeting emerging management practices and establishing or reinforcing the network of ties among a select set of firms

Main topics: Corporate strategy and the senior executive; corporate transformation and the global context; leadership and organisational dynamics

Harvard Business School

■ Advanced Management Program: The International Senior Managers' Program

Location: Harvard Business School, Boston, MA, US

Participants: Senior executives with 15 or more years' experience

Frequency: Twice a year

Duration: 9 weeks

Cost: $40,500 incl accommodation, most meals, materials

Aims: To explore the latest management thinking and provide participants with the insights, tools and management techniques to lead and change their organisations

Main topics: Innovative policy and implementation ideas; the political, economic, social, cultural and ethical aspects of domestic and international corporate performance; corporate renewal; global competition

University of Illinois at Urbana-Champaign— Executive Development Center

■ Executive Development Program

Location: University of Illinois, Urbana, IL, US

Participants: Managers with potential for increased responsibility who have moved or will be moving from functional to general management

Frequency: Once a year

Duration: 3 weeks

Cost: $12,600 incl accommodation, most meals

Aims: To enhance executive growth through the development and application of new knowledge

Main topics: Personal awareness; interpersonal effectiveness; organisational complexity; environmental scanning; organisational effectiveness; leadership; intellectual capital; agility; globalisation; functional areas

Richard Ivey School of Business—University of Western Ontario

■ Western Executive Program

Location: Spencer Hall, London, Ontario, Canada

Participants: Executives with 10-25 years' experience in general management or with senior responsibility

Frequency: Twice a year

Duration: 4 weeks

Cost: C$19,500 incl accommodation, meals, materials

Aims: To sharpen participants' strategic, general management and leadership skills

Main topics: Core aspects of business including marketing, managerial accounting, finance and human resource management; strategic planning; leadership; management of change

Notes: As well as enhancing their leadership skills, participants will develop a global network of high-performing executives in a wide range of industries

Johnson Graduate School of Management—Cornell University

■ Executive Development Program

Location: Cornell University, Ithaca, NY, US

Participants: Senior managers who hold or are about to assume general management responsibilities

Frequency: Once a year

Duration: 4 weeks

Cost: $15,500 incl accommodation, meals, materials

Aims: To enable participants to enhance strategic vision, develop a general management perspective, advance managerial skills, build cross-functional competencies and acquire effective techniques for managing change

Main topics: Improving individual and organisational productivity; enhancing leadership and decision-making skills; managing in the global environment; strategy development and implementation

Joseph M Katz Graduate School of Business— University of Pittsburgh

■ Management Program for Executives

Location: Katz Graduate School of Business, PA, US

Participants: Vice-presidents; general, regional, divisional, marketing managers with 8-10 years' managerial experience

Frequency: Once a year

Duration: 4 weeks

Cost: $15,000 incl accommodation, some meals, materials

Aims: To enable managers to rethink the ways in which they manage and think globally

Main topics: Strategic leadership; human resource management and organisational behaviour; global business; managing transformation; marketing management; financial management

Notes: MPE is one of the oldest executive development programmes in the US. Special features include an interactive management simulation, a global business panel, self-assessment and counselling

J L Kellogg Graduate School of Management— Northwestern University

■ Advanced Executive Program

Location: James L Allen Center, Evanston, IL, US

Participants: Senior managers who have or will soon have general management or cross-functional responsibilities

Frequency: Twice a year

Duration: 4 weeks

Cost: $18,500 incl accommodation, meals, materials

Aims: To help participants develop the knowledge and skills necessary to formulate clear, comprehensive strategies for their organisations, as well as to translate new strategies into co-ordinated multifunctional actions

Main topics: The role of the general manager; leadership; developing market-driven strategies; management of organisational change and innovation

■ Executive Development Program

Location: James L Allen Center, Evanston, IL, US

Participants: Managers with 10 or more years' experience considered to have senior management potential

Frequency: 3 times a year

Duration: 3 weeks

Cost: $13,800 incl accommodation, meals, materials

Aims: To give participants a broad perspective on the function and environment of management and a fuller understanding of the concepts and analytical tools required for higher-level responsibilities

Main topics: Functional areas of management; macroeconomic theory and policy; international finance; negotiation; competitive analysis; new leadership challenges

Kenan-Flagler Business School—University of North Carolina at Chapel Hill

■ Advanced Management Program

Location: University of North Carolina, Chapel Hill, NC, US

Participants: Experienced managers in need of a general management orientation

Frequency: Twice a year

Duration: 4 weeks (1 week per month over 4 months) or 3 consecutive weeks

Cost: $16,900 incl accommodation, meals, materials

Aims: To acquire cutting-edge concepts and techniques for more creative problem-solving and decision-making

Main topics: The business environment of the 21st century; managing the global environment; strategy formulation and development; strategy implementation and general management perspective; leadership strategy

Notes: This programme is now in its 46th year

McGill Executive Institute—McGill University

■ Advanced Management Course

Location: McGill Executive Institute, Montreal, Canada

Participants: Experienced managers

Frequency: Once a year

Duration: 12 Monday evenings, 2 weekends (1 is the closing session)

Cost: C$2,900 incl some meals, materials

Aims: To integrate the topics covered in the Executive Development Course and develop skills in strategic management

Main topics: Managerial accounting and control; human resource management; business strategy; marketing; international business; business game

■ Executive Development Course

Location: McGill Executive Institute, Montreal, Canada

Participants: People with some managerial experience or who hold professional or specialist positions

Frequency: Once a year

Duration: 12 Monday evenings, 2 weekends (1 is the closing session)

Cost: C$2,900 incl some meals, materials

Aims: To examine critical issues in key functional areas and introduce participants to essential management skills

Main topics: Finance; marketing; business strategy and policy; managerial negotiations; human resource management; managing information technology

Notes: A computer-based, market simulation business game is used to integrate, apply and test the concepts developed during the course. Participants who successfully complete the course receive a certificate from the McGill Executive Institute

University of Michigan Business School

■ The Executive Program

Location: Executive Education Center, Ann Arbor, MI, US

Participants: Senior executives with strategic responsibilities

Frequency: 3 times

Duration: 4 weeks

Cost: $22,500 incl accommodation, meals, materials

Aims: To expand participants' perspectives on issues, policy and the external environment

Main topics: Corporate strategy; financial analysis; economics; strategic marketing, planning and management; human resource management; information and decision technology

MIT Sloan School of Management—Massachusetts Institute of Technology

■ Greater Boston Executive Program

Location: Sloan School of Management, Cambridge, MA, US

Participants: High-potential middle managers

Frequency: Once a year

Duration: 15 1-day sessions over 4 months

Cost: $4,500 incl meals, materials

Aims: To introduce relevant ways of thinking about and dealing with the management of human, technical and economic resources

Main topics: Finance, managerial accounting and strategy; economic analysis and policy; marketing; operations management and organisation; organisation studies; readings in power and responsibility

The Mary Jean and Frank P Smeal College of Business Administration—Pennsylvania State University

■ Executive Management Program

Location: Penn State University, PA, US

Participants: Senior and upper-middle managers

Frequency: Twice a year

Duration: 4 weeks

Cost: $16,500 incl accommodation, meals, materials

Aims: To explore the policy-level perspective required of today's business leaders

Main topics: Strategic management; operational effectiveness; multidimensional thinking; network building

Notes: This programme includes a 360-degree feedback instrument, Internet session and computerised business simulation

■ Program for Executive Development

Location: Penn State University, PA, US

Participants: Executives who are successful in one or two functional areas and are considered to have general management potential

Frequency: Once a year

Duration: 3 weeks

Cost: $12,500 incl accommodation, meals, materials

Aims: To provide a broad-based general management educational experience

Main topics: Strategic management; management processes; functional management; multidimensional thinking

Notes: This programme includes a 360-degree feedback instrument, Internet session and computerised business simulation

Stanford Graduate School of Business—Stanford University

■ Stanford Executive Program

Location: Graduate School of Business, Stanford, CA, US

Participants: Senior executives of major corporations with 15 or more years' significant management experience

Frequency: Once a year

Duration: $6\frac{1}{2}$ weeks

Cost: $30,700 incl accommodation, meals, books, study materials

Aims: To help participants develop conceptual frameworks for effective management; strengthen strategic knowledge; enhance professional capabilities for organisational leadership; and build an international network of business associates

Main topics: Business, government and the changing environment; strategic leadership; management control and financial reporting; advanced countries in the world economy; microeconomies with names; marketing management; winning through innovation; financial management; business process design; competitive advantage through people; strategic management in the globalising economy

Wharton School—University of Pennsylvania—Aresty Institute of Executive Education

■ Advanced Management Program

Location: Wharton School, Philadelphia, PA, US

Participants: Senior line or functional executives

Frequency: 3 times a year

Duration: 5 weeks

Cost: $32,500 incl accommodation, meals

Aims: To examine the challenges and consequences of global competition from the perspective of the senior executive

Main topics: Global competition; critical thinking; group behaviour and leadership

University of Bradford Management Centre

■ Senior Executive Programme

Location: Bradford Management Centre, Bradford, UK; Paris, France

Participants: Senior managers

Frequency: Once a year

Duration: 16 days

Cost: £7,950 incl accommodation

Aims: To enable managers to have a direct impact on the future direction of the organisation

Main topics: Managing people in times of change; marketing management; employment law; financial management; strategic management and business policy (incl International aspects of strategy with EAP, Paris)

Cranfield School of Management

■ Advanced Development Programme

Location: Cranfield School of Management, Cranfield, UK

Participants: Managers about to take on general management responsibilities

Frequency: Twice a year

Duration: 3 1-week modules

Cost: £8,750

Aims: To prepare participants for longer-term senior general management roles

Main topics: Managing strategically; managing change; managing performance

Durham University Business School

■ The Durham Senior Management Programme

Location: Durham University Business School, Durham, UK

Participants: Senior managers

Frequency: Twice a year

Duration: 1 week

Cost: n/a

Aims: To give senior managers a cross-functional perspective of their business

Main topics: Business context; best practice and knowledge; project management; personal development

Henley Management College

■ Senior Management Programme

Location: Henley Management College, Henley-on-Thames, UK

Participants: Business unit, general and divisional managers; managing directors, directors

Frequency: 4 times a year

Duration: 4 weeks (4 consecutive or 2 2-week modules)

Cost: £10,950 incl accommodation, meals

Aims: To provide participants with the confidence to lead their organisations through complex and changing circumstances by providing them with the managerial knowledge and skills essential for success

Main topics: Personal managerial skills; business knowledge; awareness; business management including international change, managing strategic change, scenarios and strategy formulation

Notes: Participants work with 7-8 others in syndicates throughout this programme and a variety of teaching methods are used

London Business School

■ Senior Executive Programme

Location: London Business School, London, UK

Participants: Senior managers

Frequency: Twice a year

Duration: 4 weeks

Cost: £14,500 incl accommodation, meals, taxes

Aims: To help managers become more effective leaders through focusing on the essential strategic leadership skills needed to plan, direct and control the organisation of today and the future

Main topics: Strategic leadership skills; creating the future; innovating and creating value; leading people and change; achieving radical performance improvement; managing in the global economy; topics in international business; learning from leaders

Notes: "This is an elite programme, with elite participants," says LBS; each programme has on average 40 participants

Manchester Business School

■ Advanced Management Development Programme

Location: Manchester Business School, Manchester, UK

Participants: Executives who hold or are about to hold positions which require broad strategic competencies

Frequency: Twice a year

Duration: 2 weeks

Cost: £8,250 incl accommodation and meals

Aims: To deepen and widen participants' understanding of the changing international business environment and the dynamics influencing general management in a national and international context

Main topics: Industry and competitive analysis; management of customer-driven marketing; managerial competencies for the future; management accounting and finance; the geopolitical environment; the world economic picture; corporate strategy; multicultural challenges in business; implementation of strategy; human talent management

Notes: Participants are selected to ensure a broad and diverse range of experience and are encouraged to indicate specific aspects of each topic they would particularly like to discuss

Templeton College

■ The Oxford Advanced Management Programme

Location: Templeton College, Oxford, UK

Participants: Managing directors, chief executives, general managers, divisional directors, presidents

Frequency: 3 times a year

Duration: 4 weeks

Cost: £14,000 incl books, accommodation, meals, excursions

Aims: To give participants an overview of the business enterprise and its operations, especially how to respond to change in a global environment, and to provide a personal growth opportunity for high achievers

Main topics: Operations and service management; information management; marketing strategy; negotiation; financial management; financial policy; leadership; organisation and change; business policy; briefings; simulation

Notes: This is one of the longest-running executive development programmes in Europe. Its approach combines the Harvard case study and the specialist Oxford tutorial. Notable are the Oxford Briefings, where leading Oxford thinkers explore current issues

Europe excl UK

ESADE—Escuela Superior de Administración y Dirección de Empresas

■ Senior Management Programme

Location: ESADE, Barcelona, Spain

Participants: General managers

Frequency: Once a year

Duration: 310 hours over 8 months (Mondays 9 am-6.45 pm, Tuesdays 9 am-1.45 pm plus 4 intensive course modules)

Cost: Pta2.15m

Aims: To update the personal and professional skills of senior managers responsible for designing a global vision for their companies' future

Main topics: Introduction to finance for managers; complexity comprehension: finance management, information systems, business strategy, strategic marketing; personnel and managerial development; human resources management

Notes: This programme includes a business game, and a business plan is prepared for each participant's company

IMD—International Institute for Management Development

■ Program for Executive Development

Location: IMD, Lausanne, Switzerland

Participants: High-potential senior and middle managers

Frequency: Twice a year

Duration: 10 weeks (2 5-week modules)

Cost: Swfr40,000 incl some meals, materials

Aims: To provide participants with a learning environment for the exploration of contemporary management issues

Main topics: Module 1: Leading the business (foundations of teamwork and management; managing contradictions; creativity, innovation and change; cross-functional integration); Module 2: Leading the multibusiness enterprise (leading within the business unit; creating value from the centre; international business strategy; the CEO's agenda)

Notes: The programme can be taken as 2 consecutive 5-week modules or as 2 separate 5-week modules with a break in between; it can be extended to earn an executive MBA

INSEAD—European Institute of Business Administration

■ Advanced Management Programme

Location: INSEAD, Fontainebleau, France

Participants: General managers, senior functional managers

Frequency: 3 times a year

Duration: 4 weeks

Cost: FFr110,000 incl some meals, materials

Aims: To strengthen managerial competencies to deal with greater competition and to make managers more sensitive to the need for constant reassessment

Main topics: Management accounting and performance measurement; operations management; marketing; organisational behaviour; global assessment: economics and politics; business policy; financial management

Notes: INSEAD also offers a general management programme in French

Nijenrode University—The Netherlands Business School

■ Advanced Management Programme

Location: Netherlands Business School, Nijenrode, Netherlands

Participants: Experienced managing directors and entrepreneurs

Frequency: Once a year

Duration: 6 workshops

Cost: G35,000

Aims: To enable participants to reflect on their roles as leaders, managers and strategists

Main topics: Macroeconomic trends; financing and strategy; organisational structures and corporate culture; ethical dilemmas; strategy and marketing; leadership

Rest of world

University of Cape Town—Graduate School of Business

■ Executive Management Programme

Location: Graduate School of Business, Cape Town, South Africa

Participants: Senior executives with at least 12 years' managerial experience who have demonstrated significant achievement and potential for further development

Frequency: Once a year

Duration: 20 days

Cost: R28,800

Aims: To explore the challenges and opportunities facing organisations as they move into the 21st century

Curtin Business School

■ Executive Development Programme

Location: QV1 Campus, Graduate School of Business, Perth, Australia

Participants: Senior public-sector managers

Frequency: Once a year

Duration: 12 days (residential), 17 days (non-residential); each mode offered every other year

Cost: A$5,000

Aims: To develop the range and flexibility of participants' managerial competencies and increase their understanding of the environmental factors affecting public-sector management

Main topics: Strategic planning; government policy and practice; project management; communication and conflict management; dealing with the media; managing change; team-building; customer focus in the public sector; activity-based management; public service ethos; industrial relations; contract management and leadership

Notes: A leadership management development profile is produced for each participant

Macquarie Graduate School of Management— Macquarie University

■ Advanced Management Programme

Location: Macquarie Graduate School, Sydney, Australia

Participants: Senior managers who hold or are about to hold general management or senior functional posts

Frequency: Once a year

Duration: 3 weeks

Cost: A$15,500 incl accommodation, meals

Aims: To enable participants to develop a better understanding of key business issues and acquire a set of tools and frameworks to analyse an organisation's operational strengths and weaknesses

Main topics: Creating sustainable advantage through competitive strategies; developing managerial effectiveness; strategic marketing; financial analysis for strategic management; human resource management; the global enterprise; ethical issues in management; team-building; negotiation skills; crisis and media management; operations and IT; project management; managing change

Notes: This programme, now in its 24th year, uses a business simulation and there is an outdoor team-building exercise

Melbourne Business School—University of Melbourne

■ Executive Development Programme

Location: Melbourne Business School, Melbourne, Australia

Participants: High-potential managers

Frequency: Twice a year

Duration: 4 weeks

Cost: A$16,000 incl accommodation, meals, materials

Aims: To expose managers to the latest management theory and practice; to broaden participants' management perspective beyond their own functional speciality and help them become effective leaders

Main topics: Business value of information technology; managing financial resources; strategies for success; concepts of strategic management; operations and services; managing people in the learning organisation; marketing; winning negotiations; business, government and economic decisions; insights into the role of the chief executive

Monash Mt Eliza Business School

■ Advanced Management Programme (Consulting Project)

Location: Mt Eliza, Australia

Participants: Executive directors, managing directors, general managers, chief executives

Frequency: Twice a year

Duration: 27 days

Cost: A$19,550

Aims: To provide managers with the insights, tools and latest strategic thinking to drive their organisations into a position of market supremacy

Main topics: The core strategy module provides a framework for competitive strategy development. Submodules include: cultivating strategic leadership; managing strategic change; managing strategic resources; developing the global manager

Notes: This programme is now in its 41st year. Participants are awarded the Graduate Certificate in Management

■ Advanced Management Programme (Work-based Project)

Location: Mt Eliza, Australia

Participants: Executive directors, managing directors, general managers, chief executives

Frequency: Once a year

Duration: 13 days plus 6 days

Cost: A$14,900

Aims: To provide managers with the insights, tools and latest strategic thinking to drive their organisations into a position of market supremacy

Main topics: The core strategy module provides a framework for competitive strategy development. Submodules include: cultivating strategic leadership; managing strategic change; managing strategic resources; developing the global manager

Notes: This programme is now in its 41st year. Participants are awarded the Graduate Certificate in Management

Wits Business School—University of the Witwatersrand

■ Executive Development Programme

Location: Wits Business School, Johannesburg, South Africa; National University of Singapore

Participants: Managers with functional expertise who are about to assume general management responsibilities

Frequency: Once a year

Duration: 4 weeks

Cost: R34,000 incl materials, meals, visit to Singapore

Aims: To increase participants' knowledge of the functional areas of an enterprise, broaden their outlook and improve their skills in dealing with people

Main topics: The sociopolitical environment; global strategy; economic environment and international business; managing the employment relationship; managing and controlling financial resources; creating the marketing edge; achieving world-class operations management; organisational transformation and development; gaining and sustaining competitive advantage; developing and leading the entrepreneurial organisation

Notes: In 1998 participants visit Singapore for some modules. Global business strategy, marketing and the field trips are undertaken during a 9-day period which includes a visit to Malaysia

General management 2: other programmes

With functional specialism becoming less fashionable, in management theory at least, general management programmes covering a broad range of subjects are prospering. These include programmes which seek to convert specialists into generalists and those aimed at high-potential managers. The latter are particularly important as companies seek to retain and develop their best people. Within this category we have included programmes covering a number of other popular topics, including competition, change management (still a favoured subject), strategy in all its manifestations (new angles are continually being explored), as well as operations, technology and manufacturing.

Programmes are arranged alphabetically by provider in the following regions:

- North America (page 92)

- UK (page 117)

- Europe excluding UK (page 126)

- Rest of world (page 136)

North America

Amos Tuck School of Business

■ Managing in Hypercompetitive Industries

Location: Amos Tuck School, Hanover, NH, US

Participants: Senior managers

Frequency: Twice a year

Duration: 3 days

Cost: $4,200 incl accommodation, meals, materials

Aims: To present a powerful, dynamic approach to mapping strategy

Main topics: The value of strategic market disruption in shifting the rules of competition; achieving strategic dominance by building temporary advantages; shifting the rules of competition to gain the advantage of speed and surprise; why traditional strategic models fail in hypercompetitive environments; managing the dynamics of strategic manoeuvring in 4 arenas of competition (price quality, know-how and timing, strongholds and deep pockets)

■ Strategic Revolution: Transforming Industries and Organizations

Location: Amos Tuck School, Hanover, NH, US

Participants: General and business development managers

Frequency: Once a year

Duration: 5 days

Cost: $5,200 incl accommodation, meals, materials

Aims: To examine the strategy revolution that is occurring in leading-edge organisations today

Main topics: Making the shift from re-engineering to value creation and growth; identifying existing core competencies and those needed to build for the future; exploring opportunities for creating new industries; identifying the leadership capability required for innovation and growth; moving from traditional strategic planning to transformational thinking

■ Update 2000: A Senior Management Forum

Location: Amos Tuck School, Hanover, NH, US

Participants: Senior executives

Frequency: Once a year

Duration: 5 days

Cost: $5,400 incl accommodation, meals, materials

Aims: To understand the innovations that will move leading-edge organisations into the new century

Main topics: Transforming industries and organisations; the rise of strategic cost management; mergers and acquisitions strategies; hypercompetition; Internet business models; the new marketing concept; corporate communication; real options; decision-making

Arthur D Little School of Management

■ Managing Organisational Change

Location: Cambridge, Massachusetts

Participants: Senior managers, strategic planners, chief information officers

Frequency: Once a year

Duration: 5 days

Cost: $5,000 incl accommodation

Aims: To help participants build competence in the use of an integrated model to respond to changes more quickly and efficiently

Main topics: Strategic flexibility and change readiness; hidden leverage; operational alignment; change cycle acceleration

Babson College—School of Executive Education

■ Forging and Managing Strategic Alliances

Location: Babson College, Wellesley, MA, US

Participants: General managers, senior functional managers, alliance managers

Frequency: Twice a year

Duration: 3 days

Cost: $3,200 incl accommodation, meals, materials, taxes

Aims: To examine best practices in successfully forging, structuring and managing multiple alliances around the world

Main topics: Linking strategic plans to alliances; evolution of alliances; global alliances and implications; organisational challenges; the role of the alliance manager; the role of management; managing multiple alliances; best practices and research

Berkeley Center for Executive Development—Haas School of Business

■ Implementing Strategy: The Four Factors of Strategic Implementation

Location: Berkeley Centre for Executive Development, Berkeley, CA, US

Participants: Business unit managers, business owners, general managers with responsibility for strategy implementation; other managers who wish to increase their contribution to overall str'ategy implementation

Frequency: Once a year

Duration: 3 days

Cost: $1,900 incl accommodation, meals, taxes

Aims: To help participants understand more clearly and gain control over the fundamental forces determining the successful implementation of their strategies and objectives

Main topics: The four factors of strategy implementation; designing effective organisational structures; managing organisational knowledge and learning; performance measurement and incentive compensation systems; leadership and management of corporate culture

Notes: This programme uses Toshi Shibano's framework, the Four Factors of Strategic Implementation

Carlson School of Management—University of Minnesota

■ Minnesota Management Academy

Location: Carlson School, Minneapolis, MN; West Bank Campus, Minneapolis, MN, US

Participants: Managers, supervisors and team members from services, manufacturing, government and non-profit organisations

Frequency: Twice a year

Duration: 1 week

Cost: $2,300 incl accommodation, meals, materials

Aims: To give participants an opportunity to assess their management skills and learn through group processes

Main topics: Essentials of management; management for quality and continuous improvement; high performance from individuals and teams; interpersonal and organisational communication; leadership and change

■ **Minnesota Management Institute**

Location: Various conference centres in Minnesota, US

Participants: Individuals in significant operational positions who are responsible for translating strategy into action

Frequency: Once a year

Duration: 3 weeks (3 1-week modules over 4 months)

Cost: $7,800 incl materials

Aims: To give successful executives an opportunity to acquire and develop new skills in functional areas; to reflect and broaden their management perspectives; and to exchange information with managers from other organisations

Main topics: Strategy; finance; marketing; operations; communications; risk/project management; international economies; information systems; human resources; organisational behaviour/self insights

Notes: This programme includes outdoor learning and live cases

Carnegie Mellon University—Graduate School of Industrial Administration

■ **Global Information Management**

Location: Carnegie Mellon University, Pittsburgh, PA; New York, NY, US

Participants: Executives, managers and professionals responsible for using information technology to achieve productivity and performance goals

Frequency: Twice a year

Duration: 1 week

Cost: $2,350 incl most meals

Aims: To help participants exploit business information for competitive advantage

Main topics: Strategic use of information resources; IT inside the organisation; IT across the value chain; exploiting the untapped value of business information

- ## Management in Technology Organizations

Location: Carnegie Mellon University, Pittsburgh, PA, US

Participants: Senior and middle managers in technical organisations and departments, non-technical managers new to the technology environment, technologists about to assume management responsibilities

Frequency: Twice a year

Duration: 1 week

Cost: $2,950 incl most meals

Aims: To familiarise participants with best practices in technology management and to enhance their leadership and interpersonal skills

Main topics: Managing engineering, design and development; market-focused innovation management; developing high-performance work groups; nurturing and utilising intellectual assets; cost and value analysis in the product development process; gathering international competitive intelligence; optimising the engineering/manufacturing interface

Notes: This programme is a collaboration between Carnegie Mellon and Pittsburgh universities

University of Chicago—Graduate School of Business

- ## Executive Program in Corporate Strategy

Location: Gleacher Center, University of Chicago Graduate School of Business, Chicago, IL, US

Participants: Vice-presidents, general managers, strategic planners, consultants, corporate and business planners, functional directors

Frequency: 3 times a year

Duration: 5 days

Cost: $3,850 incl some meals, materials

Aims: To focus on the formulation and implementation of a company's strategy in today's complex and competitive environments

Main topics: Industry analysis and positioning; competitive advantage, sustainability and entry; corporate-level strategy; strategy implementation; competitive dynamics and game theory; strategic scenario analysis; new venture strategy: the role of the general manager; technology strategy; strategic thinking

Columbia Business School

■ Business Strategy

Location: Arden House, Harriman, NY, US

Participants: General managers of divisions, business units or product groups; vice-presidents or directors of departments responsible for strategic planning; corporate planners; line managers responsible for strategy implementation

Frequency: Twice a year

Duration: 2 weeks

Cost: $12,500 incl accommodation, meals, materials

Aims: To teach participants how to approach business strategy as an ongoing process and a way of thinking

Main topics: Dynamic framework for strategy formulation; global issues in strategy formulation; financial implications of strategy; managing global joint ventures; levers of executive leadership; strategy implementation: the role of symbols and themes; implementing global strategies; managing strategic innovation and change; strategic alliances and core competencies

Notes: Week 1 is spent studying the analysis and creativity involved in formulating effective strategies. Week 2 is dedicated to strategy implementation, including application to specific strategic problems faced by participants' own companies

■ Leading Organizational Change and Renewal

Location: Arden House, Harriman, NY, US

Participants: General managers, managers of new products or services, strategic planning executives

Frequency: Once a year

Duration: 1 week (Sunday pm-Friday pm)

Cost: $5,200 incl accommodation, meals, materials

Aims: To build the organisation architecture, sound strategy, teamwork and communication required to succeed now and prepare for the future

Main topics: Strategic innovation; technical change and innovation; organisational culture and innovation; business strategy, technology strategy and organisations; competitors, customers and strategic innovation; executive leadership and managing change; management of large system change

Notes: Companies are encouraged to send teams of 4-6 people who will work on specific issues in separate sessions with faculty. The team will return with a joint action plan for lasting change

■ The Learning Organization: Driving Superior Performance

Location: Arden House, Harriman, NY, US

Participants: Senior executives with general management responsibilities, senior human resource executives, business unit heads

Frequency: Twice a year

Duration: 4 days

Cost: $3,200 incl accommodation, meals, materials

Aims: To teach participants how to translate theory into a set of practical measures for creating and sustaining learning organisations that deliver superior results

Main topics: Strategies and systems for creating the learning organisation; knowledge management in the learning organisation; leadership in the learning organisation; building the vision for the learning organisation

Edwin L Cox School of Business—Southern Methodist University

■ Management of Managers: Leadership, Change and Renewal

Location: Cox School of Business, Dallas, TX, US

Participants: Senior and upper-middle executives

Frequency: Twice a year

Duration: 1 week

Cost: $4,450

Aims: To enable participants to become more effective and to derive more personal satisfaction from their corporate positions

Main topics: Managing world-class organisations; the context of leadership; leadership and decision styles; decision-making and creativity; designing learning organisations; perceptions of behaviour: the Profilor 360-degree feedback instrument; managerial relationships; movitating and influencing others; managing your career; renewal and wellness action planning

Notes: This programme features a global management simulation; outdoor team-building; an international negotiation simulation; and executive wellness

Darden Executive Education—University of Virginia

■ Creating Successful Alliances and Partnerships

Location: Darden School, Charlottesville, VA, US

Participants: Senior and middle managers; alliance managers and teams

Frequency: Twice a year

Duration: 6 days

Cost: $4,950

Aims: To help participants understand the critical aspects of strategic alliances

Main topics: Forms of alliances; partner selection; evolution of alliances; role of the alliance manager; managerial competencies for alliance success; managing a network of alliances; evaluating success

■ Creating and Sustaining the High-Performing Organization

Location: Darden School, Charlottesville, VA, US

Participants: Leaders and managers at all levels

Frequency: Twice a year

Duration: 6 days

Cost: $4,950

Aims: To challenge participants to think and act in ways that will contribute to high performance

Main topics: Frameworks and concepts supporting the high-performance organisation; designing and implementing a performance improvement process; providers and receivers of high performance

Notes: This programme was called Creating the High Performance Workplace and has been offered since 1985

■ Developing Managerial Excellence: A Program for High-Potential Managers

Location: Darden School, Charlottesville, VA, US

Participants: Bright, experienced, assertive, enthusiastic managers who are moving at a rapid pace to positions of increasing responsibility

Frequency: Twice a year

Duration: 3 weeks

Cost: $14,500 incl accommodation, most meals

Aims: To develop high-potential managers, broaden their perspectives, and improve their individual and organisational accomplishments

Main topics: Developing integrated functional area plans and allocating corporate assets; building and managing teams effectively; exerting influence in the absence of direct authority; managing a new role

Notes: This programme was known as the Young Manager's Program and has been running since 1985

■ Managing Critical Resources

Location: Darden School, Charlottesville, VA, US

Participants: Recently appointed general managers, individuals with general management potential and 10 years' functional experience

Frequency: 4 times a year

Duration: 2 weeks

Cost: $9,900 incl accommodation, most meals

Aims: To provide cross-functional insights into the creation and use of human, financial, operational and marketing resources

Main topics: Understanding financial statements; consumer analysis and marketing segmentation; the role of the operations manager; product line development and policy; materials management issues; pricing policy; cost analysis; creating service excellence in operations; managing interpersonal conflict; high-performance work systems; branding and channel management; organisational structure and systems; management of quality

Notes: This programme has been offered since 1968

■ Managing Individual and Organizational Change

Location: Darden School, Charlottesville, VA, US

Participants: Managers concerned with change

Frequency: Twice a year

Duration: 4 days

Cost: $3,700

Aims: To help participants understand change and manage it more effectively

Main topics: Psychological and social aspects of change; self-management; strategies for effectively managing change; principles and values in the change process; alignment factors

■ Manufacturing Management Program: Developing World-Class Capability

Location: Darden School, Charlottesville, VA, US

Participants: Managers responsible for planning and executing manufacturing operations at plant, division or corporate level; staff professionals and line managers intending to follow a career in the manufacturing function

Frequency: Twice a year

Duration: 2 weeks

Cost: $9,900 incl accommodation, most meals

Aims: To increase participants' effectiveness in creating and managing a world-class manufacturing operation

Main topics: Manufacturing planning and control systems and competitive strategy; managing the supply chain; global sourcing decisions; implementing a manufacturing strategy; the engineering-manufacturing interface; workforce planning and safety capacity; global manufacturing competition; successful manufacturing management

■ Strategic Management for Line Managers

Location: Darden School, Charlottesville, VA, US

Participants: Executives who have taken on strategic responsibilities, plan to do so or face an impending strategic challenge

Frequency: Once a year

Duration: 5 days

Cost: $4,950 incl accommodation, meals

Aims: To give line managers a strategic perspective

Main topics: Industry and competitor analysis; business strategy; competitive advantage; strategy formulation and competitive dynamics; strategic leadership; strategic intent; strategic change; corporate culture as a source of competitive advantage

Fuqua School of Business—Duke University

■ Program for Manager Development

Location: Fuqua School of Business, Durham, NC, US

Participants: New general managers and those about to assume general management responsibilities

Frequency: 3 times a year

Duration: 2 weeks (split and consecutive sessions are available)

Cost: $8,400 incl accommodation, meals, materials, taxes

Aims: To prepare high-potential managers for future leadership in their organisations

Main topics: Delivering customer value; building leadership performance; strategic thinking and competitive analysis; creating competitive advantage through people; creating shareholder value

Notes: The programme includes a 3-day business simulation integrating team-building with management skills and decision analysis, and an outdoor leadership programme

Harvard Business School

■ Competition and Strategy

Location: Harvard Business School, Boston, MA, US

Participants: Senior executives

Frequency: Once a year

Duration: 1 week

Cost: $8,500 incl accommodation, most meals, materials

Aims: To devise new business strategies using cutting-edge concepts in competitive strategy development and implementation

Main topics: Formulating new competitive strategies; state-of-the-art thinking in competition and strategy; action learning in the participant's organisation

■ Creating Corporate Advantage: Strategy in the Multi-business Firm

Location: Harvard Business School, Boston, MA, US

Participants: Chief executives, business unit managers

Frequency: Once a year

Duration: 3 days

Cost: $5,000 incl accommodation, most meals, materials

Aims: To examine how success depends on combining a firm's assets, skills and capabilities with its ability to leverage resources across traditional business boundaries

Main topics: Vision; corporate advantage; scope and portfolio choice; co-ordination and control

■ The General Manager Program

Location: Harvard Business School, Boston, MA, US

Participants: Country managers, business unit managers, general managers from multibillion-dollar companies

Frequency: Once a year

Duration: 2 3-week sessions separated by on-site organisational analysis

Cost: $29,500 incl accommodation, most meals, materials

Aims: To prepare participants for recently acquired or expanded general management roles

Main topics: Resource allocation; new product and process development; country management; market entry; industry exit; corporate renewal

Notes: There is a sliding scale of discounts for more than 2 participants from the same company

■ Making Corporate Boards More Effective

Location: Harvard Business School, Boston, MA, US

Participants: Chief executives, board directors

Frequency: Twice a year

Duration: 3 days

Cost: $5,000 incl accommodation, most meals, materials

Aims: To explore critical issues facing board members

Main topics: Board composition; director selection; CEO evaluation and compensation; the board's role in strategic planning and positive change

---

■ Program for Management Development

Location: Harvard Business School, Boston, MA, US

Participants: Managers who have just taken up or who are about to take up general management posts

Frequency: Once a year

Duration: 10 weeks

Cost: $40,500 incl accommodation, most meals, materials

Aims: To help participants understand functions beyond their specialism and prepare them for their roles as general managers

Main topics: New ways to approach and solve general management challenges; effective methods for enhancing strategic thinking and diversifying thought processes; understanding the role of technology in participants' businesses

Richard Ivey School of Business—University of Western Ontario

■ Operations Management Program

Location: Spencer Hall, London, Ontario, Canada

Participants: Operations and production managers in the services and primary and secondary manufacturing sectors

Frequency: Twice a year

Duration: 2 weeks

Cost: C$9,350 incl accommodation, meals, materials

Aims: To improve the total performance of line and staff managers involved in the production of goods and the offering of services

Main topics: Developing skills and practices to expand current operation abilities; interpersonal skills; the role of operations in overall corporate strategy; diagnosing and analysing operations problems; developing winning strategies and successful implementation plans

Johnson Graduate School of Management—Cornell University

■ Executive Program for Midsized Companies

Location: Cornell University, Ithaca, NY, US

Participants: Senior executives from public or private companies with revenue of $5m-500m and strategic business units of larger companies

Frequency: Once a year

Duration: 1 week

Cost: $4,300 incl accommodation, meals, materials

Aims: To focus on the unique challenges facing medium-sized companies

Main topics: Leadership and the future; creating and sharing vision; interpersonal relationships in executive teams; corporate culture; competitive strategy; scenario planning; analysing the competition; marketing-driven strategies; customer-driven focus; customer feedback; strategic decision-making; managing uncertainty; strategic capital structure decisions; capital expenditure and strategies; evaluating investment alternatives; forecasting rates of return for new products and services; valuation of corporations

Notes: It is suggested that teams of executives attend this programme to maximise its effectiveness

■ **Manufacturing Executive Program**

Location: Cornell University, Ithaca, NY, US

Participants: Senior managers in manufacturing

Frequency: Once a year

Duration: 1 week

Cost: $4,300 incl accommodation, meals, materials

Aims: To help participants effectively position their companies for global competition

Main topics: Manufacturing strategy; re-engineering and TQM; managerial styles; measuring productivity and quality; activity-based and life-cycle costing; real-time control of manufacturing; high-performance teams; managing change; managing technology and innovation; time-based competition; the future of manufacturing

■ **Strategic Decision Making and Critical Thinking**

Location: Cornell University, Ithaca, NY, US

Participants: Senior managers

Frequency: Twice a year

Duration: 1 week

Cost: $4,300 incl accommodation, meals, materials

Aims: To help participants learn how to enhance the effectiveness of their own personal style and improve the dynamics of the groups they manage and interact with

Main topics: Critical factors that influence decision outcomes; key phases of decision-making; thinking frames and styles; strategic thinking; creating multiple scenarios; gathering intelligence; environmental scanning; managing conflict within groups and teams; maximising impact; barriers to implementation

Jesse H Jones Graduate School of Management—Rice University

■ **Rice Program for Managers**

Location: Rice University, Houston, TX, US

Participants: Professionals from diverse industries newly appointed to managerial roles

Frequency: Once a year

Duration: 12 days over 3 months (Thursday, Friday, Saturday, every other week for 7 weeks)

Cost: n/a

Aims: To introduce a broad range of management functions to enable participants to improve performance

Main topics: Finance and accounting; strategy and marketing; leadership and organisation

J L Kellogg Graduate School of Management— Northwestern University

■ Changing Strategic Direction

Location: James L Allen Center, Evanston, IL, US

Participants: General managers, heads of major functions, directors of strategic planning, senior M&A specialists

Frequency: Once a year

Duration: 1 week

Cost: $ 4,600

Aims: To help participants develop a comprehensive vision for their organisations

Main topics: Characteristics of a sound strategy; global competitive environment; sources of competitive advantage; strategic role of core competencies; building a strategic platform; defining and influencing corporate culture; organisational learning; barriers to strategic change; using IT for strategic advantage

■ Creating and Managing Strategic Alliances

Location: James L Allen Center, Evanston, IL, US

Participants: Managers involved in the creation and/or implementation of strategy alliances

Frequency: Twice a year

Duration: 4 days

Cost: $2,950 incl accommodation, meals, materials

Aims: To help managers understand the latest advances in creating and managing different types of strategic alliances

Main topics: Strategic alliance structures and key success factors; negotiating alliances; joint ventures; licensing arrangements; designing alliances; strategic and operational considerations

Kenan-Flagler Business School—University of North Carolina at Chapel Hill

■ Program for Manager Development

Location: University of North Carolina, Chapel Hill, NC, US

Participants: High-potential managers

Frequency: Twice a year

Duration: 2 weeks

Cost: $8,500

Aims: To prepare managers for the leadership challenges of the 21st century

Main topics: The emergent environment; the leadership challenge; negotiation strategies; the strategic mindset; creating a market-driven orientation; managing a culturally diverse workplace; the global village; managing change and conflict; operations management; financial analysis; shareholder value; strategic financial management

Krannert Executive Education Programs—Purdue University

■ Engineering/Management Program

Location: Purdue University, West Lafayette, IN, US

Participants: Senior and middle managers, engineers

Frequency: Once a year

Duration: 1 week

Cost: $2,295 incl accommodation, meals, transport

Aims: To offer participants the opportunity to update or enhance their technical skills and managerial abilities

Main topics: Participants can select up to 4 courses from a master list of 16, arranged in 4 course "series", including: engineering and technical courses; functional management courses; communication courses; human and intellectual resources courses

McGill Executive Institute—McGill University

■ The Effective Manager

Location: McGill Executive Institute, Montreal, Canada; University of Toronto, Rotman School of Management, Toronto, Canada

Participants: Managers, professionals, entrepreneurs

Frequency: 4 times a year

Duration: 3 days

Cost: C$1,395 incl lunches, materials

Aims: To help participants master the demands made on their lives at individual, interpersonal and organisational levels

Main topics: The paradox of change; focusing on results; getting organised; tracking your progress; focusing on your career; networking; problem-solving; meeting for results; managing conflict; stress demystified

■ Essential Management Skills

Location: McGill Executive Institute, Montreal, Canada; University of Toronto, Rotman School of Management, Toronto, Canada

Participants: Experienced managers wishing to renew their knowledge and skills; potential and newly appointed managers and supervisors

Frequency: 6 times a year

Duration: 5 days

Cost: C$1,795 incl lunches, materials

Aims: To improve the performance of managers and their teams

Main topics: Decision-making; managing and supervising; time management

■ Project Management Process

Location: McGill Executive Institute, Montreal, Canada; University of Toronto, Rotman School of Management, Toronto, Canada

Participants: Managers involved in project management

Frequency: 5 times a year

Duration: 3 days

Cost: C$1,395

Aims: To help participants develop effective techniques for contemporary project management

Main topics: Scope control; time control; procurement; cost control and budgeting; role of the microcomputer; integrating scope, time and cost; project organisation

■ Strategy for Managers

Location: McGill Executive Institute, Montreal, Canada; University of Toronto, Rotman School of Management, Toronto, Canada

Participants: Managers who need to strengthen their abilities to think strategically; line managers whose experience has been primarily in one function; professionals whose position requires a broader perspective

Frequency: Twice a year

Duration: 3 days

Cost: C$1,595 incl lunches, materials

Aims: To give participants a strategic perspective on their businesses

Main topics: Industry analysis; corporate strengths, weaknesses, opportunities and threats; understanding industry trends and directions; understanding deliberate and emergent strategies; internal alignment of strategy, structure, systems, etc; systems design; managing culture; strategy implementation

University of Michigan Business School

■ Linking Customer Satisfaction, Quality and Financial Performance

Location: Executive Education Center, Ann Arbor, MI, US

Participants: Functional managers, executives with broad responsibilities

Frequency: Twice a year

Duration: 5 days

Cost: $4,900 incl accommodation, meals, materials

Aims: To provide participants with a broad exposure to current practice and cutting-edge concepts and methods in customer satisfaction

Main topics: Concept of customer asset management; customer satisfaction and financial performance: the state of the art, the role of quality; setting up a quality, satisfaction and profit measurement system

■ Managing Critical Issues

Location: Executive Education Center, Ann Arbor, MI, US

Participants: General managers, team leaders

Frequency: Once a year

Duration: 2 weeks

Cost: $10,000 incl accommodation, meals, materials

Aims: To focus on the critical issues facing organisations in the current competitive business environment

Main topics: Identifying business challenges in the 21st century; globalisation; quality and continuous improvement; positioning the firm for growth; context and environment of innovation; identifying strategies for effective change

■ Management Development Program

Location: Executive Education Center, Ann Arbor, MI, US

Participants: Managers moving into positions where multifunctional perspectives are required; experienced managers wishing to update their skills; small-business senior executives

Frequency: Once a year

Duration: 2 weeks

Cost: $9,800 incl accommodation, meals, materials

Aims: To give a holistic view of the elements of achieving success in an increasingly global and competitive business environment

Main topics: Strategic management; marketing and customer orientation; finance; measurement, reporting and analysis; leadership and change

■ Management II: Mid-Management Development Program

Location: Executive Education Center, Ann Arbor, MI, US

Participants: Middle managers with 3-8 years' management experience

Frequency: 8 times a year

Duration: 5 days

Cost: $5,100 incl accommodation, meals, materials

Aims: To develop participants' skills in dealing with people

Main topics: Leadership and management styles; associate empowerment; interpersonal communication; creative thinking and problem-solving; delegating for results; setting the motivational climate

Notes: This programme is also offered in Hong Kong

■ Management of Managers

Location: Executive Education Center, Ann Arbor, MI, US

Participants: Senior and middle managers with more than 8 years' management experience

Frequency: 9 times a year

Duration: 5 days

Cost: $5,200 incl accommodation, meals, materials

Aims: To provide a conceptual framework to enable participants to identify and formulate a personalised action plan

Main topics: Organisational leadership roles; developing effective managerial competencies; managing and empowering individuals and teams (clan); managing and winning in a competitive environment (market); managing organisational process and design (hierarchy); managing innovation and transformation "adhocracy"; action planning and synthesis

Notes: This programme is also offered in Hong Kong

■ **Strategy: Formulation and Implementation**

Location: Executive Education Center, Ann Arbor, MI, US

Participants: Senior managers, vice-presidents, general managers, functional directors

Frequency: Twice a year

Duration: 6 days

Cost: $5,200 incl accommodation, meals, materials

Aims: To provide participants with knowledge of successful techniques for long-range organisational planning and strategy formulation and implementation

Main topics: Competitive strategy; customer satisfaction; planning process; emerging organisation forms; organisational processes

Owen Graduate School of Management—Vanderbilt University

■ **Effective Management Techniques**

Location: Owen Graduate School of Management, TN, US

Participants: Senior managers

Frequency: Twice a year

Duration: 3 days

Cost: $1,395 incl most meals, materials

Aims: To teach practical methods and systematic procedures as aids in managing others

MIT Sloan School of Management—Massachusetts Institute of Technology

■ **Corporate Strategy**

Location: Sloan School of Management, Cambridge, MA, US

Participants: Senior line managers, staff planners

Frequency: Once a year

Duration: 1 week

Cost: $4,850 incl accommodation, meals, materials

Aims: To help participants gain a deeper understanding of modern corporate strategy and strategic management

Main topics: Corporate culture and organisational structure; global strategic management; financial theory and financial strategy; managing the strategy-technology interface

■ Management of Change in Complex Organizations

Location: Sloan School of Management, Cambridge, MA, US

Participants: Senior managers

Frequency: Once a year

Duration: 1 week

Cost: $4,650 incl accommodation, meals, materials

Aims: To provide a research-based perspective on emerging managerial problems and consider ways these problems can and should be addressed

Main topics: Developments in organisational theory and the shape of contemporary organisations

Simmons Graduate School of Management

■ Managing for Results

Location: Simmons Graduate School of Management, Boston, MA, US

Participants: Women at all levels

Frequency: Twice a year

Duration: 1 week

Cost: $3,000 incl accommodation, meals, materials

Aims: To provide participants with improved communication skills, innovative strategies for expanding power and influence, and enhanced leadership skills

Main topics: Leadership strategies and communication strategies

Notes: Each participant's skills are individually assessed and her workplace environment analysed

■ Program for Developing Managers

Location: Simmons Graduate School of Management, Boston, MA, US

Participants: Women who are high-potential middle managers, new senior managers, technical specialists

Frequency: Twice a year

Duration: 4 weeks

Cost: $10,000 incl accommodation, meals, materials

Aims: To give participants a broader understanding of the quantitative and strategic areas of business and help build more focused leadership skills

Main topics: Functional courses (accounting, finance, etc) and behavioural aspects of management

Notes: As with other Simmons programmes, case studies on women managers are used

The Mary Jean and Frank P Smeal College of Business Administration—Pennsylvania State University

■ Developing Managerial Effectiveness

Location: Penn State University, PA, US

Participants: Middle managers

Frequency: 3 times a year

Duration: 1 week

Cost: $4,200 incl accommodation, meals, materials

Aims: To expand participants' strategic and financial perspectives and hone their managerial skills

Main topics: Role of the manager; strategic management; financial planning and control; managerial leadership

Notes: This programme features use of a 360-degree feedback instrument and a computerised business simulation

University of South Carolina—Daniel Management Center

■ Developing Profit Center Managers

Location: Daniel Management Center, Columbia, SC, US

Participants: Divisional and plant managers; staff, department and functional heads; assistant vice-presidents of larger firms

Frequency: 3 times a year

Duration: 4½ days

Cost: $1,995

Aims: To give managers an opportunity to act as senior executives and make decisions from a much broader perspective

Main topics: Strategic thinking and decision-making; viewing the enterprise across functions, divisions and culture; integrating production, marketing and financial decisions; using teamwork and internal networks

Notes: This programme uses a computer-driven business simulation

- ## Management Development Program for Engineers and Technical Professionals

  Location: Daniel Management Center, Columbia, SC, US

  Participants: Newly appointed managers making the transition from engineering or technology to management; project engineers, department managers or others in supervisory roles

  Frequency: 3 times a year

  Duration: $4\frac{1}{2}$ days

  Cost: $1,595

  Aims: To broaden the perspectives and enhance the management skills of technical people

  Main topics: From projects to people; leadership styles; planning and controlling; performance management; communication and influencing skills; delegation and empowerment; strategic management; team leadership

Stanford Graduate School of Business—Stanford University

- ## Executive Program for Growing Companies

  Location: Graduate School of Business, Stanford, CA, US

  Participants: Senior managers of small companies

  Frequency: Twice a year

  Duration: 2 weeks

  Cost: $10,500 incl accommodation, meals, books, study materials

  Aims: To challenge assumptions, test ideas and formulate frameworks for action

- ## Executive Program in Strategy and Organization

  Location: Graduate School of Business, Stanford, CA, US

  Participants: Managers who have assumed, or are about to take on, the strategic direction of their organisations

  Frequency: Once a year

  Duration: 2 weeks

  Cost: $10,500 incl accommodation, meals, books, other materials

  Aims: To offer an integrated view of the problems of strategic management, the internal culture and organisation of a firm, and the non-market forces that affect its long-term success

  Main topics: Strategic management; internal culture and organisational non-market forces

- **Strategic Uses of Information Technology**

  Location: Graduate School of Business, Stanford, CA, US

  Participants: Senior managers responsible for the strategic direction of their companies

  Frequency: Once a year

  Duration: 1 week

  Cost: $5,700 incl accommodation, meals, books, study materials

  Aims: To help participants integrate technology, operating procedures and people into a cohesive strategy for the future

Wharton School—University of Pennsylvania—Aresty Institute of Executive Education

- **Critical Thinking: Real-World, Real-Time Decisions**

  Location: Wharton School, Philadelphia, PA, US

  Participants: Senior and middle managers

  Frequency: Twice a year

  Duration: 3 days

  Cost: $3,750 incl accommodation, meals

  Aims: To present a variety of strategies for framing problems and when to apply them

  Main topics: Framing the problem; gauging uncertainty; consequences of risk; decision-making under pressure; interactive decision-making; modelling, forecasting and data-mining

- **Executive Development Program: The Transition from Functional to General Management**

  Location: Wharton School, Philadelphia, PA, US

  Participants: Functional specialists moving to general management positions that integrate several functions, products, regions or operations

  Frequency: 4 times a year

  Duration: 2 weeks

  Cost: $14,250 incl accommodation, meals

  Aims: To address the challenges of leading cross-functional teams

  Main topics: Examining critical issues in finance, marketing, operations, technology, strategy and globalisation; exploring the skills needed to build teams, foster creativity and manage conflict and change

  Notes: This programme uses a business simulation; at least 40% of participants come from outside the US

■ Implementing Strategy

Location: Wharton School, Philadelphia, PA, US

Participants: Senior managers

Frequency: Twice a year

Duration: 5 days

Cost: $5,950 incl accommodation, meals

Aims: To show the relationship between strategy formulation and implementation and help participants anticipate the requirements for success

Main topics: Strategy implementation model; strategy and organisational structure; integrating short- and long-term operating objectives; managing human resources; developing effective incentives and controls; managing strategic change

■ Strategic Thinking and Management for Competitive Advantage

Location: Wharton School, Philadelphia, PA, US

Participants: Senior managers

Frequency: Twice a year

Duration: 5 days

Cost: $5,950 incl accommodation, meals

Aims: To teach participants strategies to build their organisations' competitive advantage

Main topics: Strategic planning; firm capabilities and competitive advantage; strategic alliances; management of technology and innovation; economic, technical, social and political forces affecting international firms

■ Winning in the Next Millennium: Strategies for Driving Change

Location: Wharton School, Philadelphia, PA, US

Participants: Senior managers

Frequency: Twice a year

Duration: 3 days

Cost: $3,750 incl accommodation, meals

Aims: To provide participants with new perspectives on and different approaches to their businesses

Main topics: Competitive dynamics; globalisation; the changing nature of work; managing without commitment; preparing for the age of electronic commerce

Notes: Organisations are encouraged to put teams of executives through this programme

UK

Ashridge Management College

■ Directors' Strategy Programme

Location: Ashridge Management College, Berkhamsted, UK

Participants: Directors or senior executives with strategic responsibility

Frequency: Twice a year

Duration: 5 days

Cost: £3,200 incl accommodation, meals

Aims: To enable participants to lead and influence the strategy development process more effectively

Main topics: Leading the strategic process; environmental, industry and competitor analysis; strategy formulation; strategic relationships; implementing strategic change

■ General Management Programme

Location: Ashridge Management College, Berkhamsted, UK

Participants: Managers moving from functional to more general management posts

Frequency: 5 times a year

Duration: Modular (2 12-day sessions) or 4 weeks (plus 2-day follow-up)

Cost: £11,075 incl accommodation, meals, follow-up workshop (£10,250 without workshop)

Aims: To develop participants' ability to take a general management perspective both in running operational processes and in managing change

Main topics: Major business disciplines; integrative management exercises and simulations; identifying individual learning priorities and creating development plans for the future

Notes: Participation in this programme can lead to the Ashridge Diploma in General Management

■ Influencing Strategies and Skills

Location: Ashridge Management College, Berkhamsted, UK

Participants: Managers whose success depends on influencing and persuading others without using formal authority

Frequency: 6 times a year

Duration: 5 days

Cost: £2,700 incl accommodation, meals

Aims: To sharpen participants' ability to influence and persuade others

Main topics: Goal-oriented influencing; key success factors; influencing skills; presenting a persuasive case

Notes: Participation in this programme can lead to the Ashridge Diploma in General Management

■ Innovative Business Development

Location: Ashridge Management College, Berkhamsted, UK

Participants: Senior managers

Frequency: Twice a year

Duration: 5 days

Cost: £2,700 incl accommodation, meals

Aims: To focus on practical ways to grow business, from idea generation to implementation

Main topics: Innovation context; creativity; benchmarking; innovative partnerships; managing a pilot and new venture planning; implementation

■ Managing Corporate Community Involvement (CCI)

Location: Ashridge Management College, Berkhamsted, UK

Participants: Senior managers

Frequency: Twice a year

Duration: 3 days

Cost: £1,550 incl accommodation, meals

Aims: To enable participants to develop strategies for the benefit of the community and their organisations

Main topics: Strategic development of CCI; making a business case for CCI; designing a secondment programme; developing partnerships; maximising the returns on CCI

■ Project Management in Action

Location: Ashridge Management College, Berkhamsted, UK

Participants: Project team leaders, members of teams

Frequency: Twice a year

Duration: 3 days

Cost: £1,850 incl accommodation, meals

Aims: To provide hands-on experience of managing a project from inception to completion

Main topics: Managing the project plan; managing clients' expectations; managing team priorities; project scope and budget

Notes: Considerable time is spent on application of the frameworks to participants' own issues

■ Strategic Decisions

Location: Ashridge Management College, Berkhamsted, UK

Participants: Senior executives involved in strategic decisions

Frequency: Twice a year

Duration: 5 days

Cost: £3,200 incl accommodation, meals

Aims: To provide senior executives with tools and frameworks to improve the quality of their strategic decision-making through awareness of analytical and process issues

Main topics: Strategic appraisal; decision-making styles; decision process tools; roles in the decision process; financial appraisal

■ Strategic Management Programme

Location: Ashridge Management College, Berkhamsted, UK

Participants: Managers responsible for leading business units or teams

Frequency: 4 times a year

Duration: 3 weeks or 2 modules of 7 and 6 days each (plus 2-day follow-up)

Cost: £9,500 incl accommodation, meals, 1-day follow-up workshop

Aims: To help leaders of teams or business units develop and implement more effective strategies

Main topics: Strategic and competitive analysis; strategic choices and processes; finance and strategy; corporate culture and strategy; leadership styles and skills; managing change; vision; making strategy work; measuring business performance; recognising personal strengths and weakness as a force for change

Notes: A programme tutor visits participants 3 months after completion of the programme. Participation in this programme can lead to the Ashridge Diploma in General Management

■ Strategy and Organisation

Location: Ashridge Management College, Berkhamsted, UK

Participants: Senior managers

Frequency: Twice a year

Duration: 5 days

Cost: £3,200 incl accommodation, meals

Aims: To examine the link between strategy, key organisational components and business success

Main topics: The dynamics of organisations; developing strategic options; structuring the organisation; leadership; re-engineering; culture; changing the organisation

Notes: Diagnostic questionnaires help clarify organisational approaches and key issues. An individual, detailed action plan is produced

Cranfield School of Management

■ Breakthrough Strategic Thinking

Location: Cranfield School of Management, Cranfield, UK

Participants: Middle managers about to take on higher-level responsibilities

Frequency: Twice a year

Duration: 2 days (plus 1-day review workshop)

Cost: £1,550

Aims: To enable managers to build personal competitive advantage through strategic skills

Main topics: Strategic analysis; strategic decision tools; strategic choice and implementation; strategic project management

■ Business Growth and Development

Location: Cranfield School of Management, Cranfield, UK

Participants: Owner-managing directors

Frequency: Once a year

Duration: Modular over 6 weekends

Cost: £5,500

Aims: To enable managers in smaller businesses to manage their growth and development more effectively

Main topics: Competitive strategy; financial controls; managing change; motivation; team-building; leadership; raising finance; recruitment

■ Developing Managerial Competence

Location: Cranfield School of Management, Cranfield, UK

Participants: Managers in the early stages of their careers who have the potential to succeed

Frequency: 3 times a year

Duration: 12 days

Cost: £5,600 incl accommodation, meals and a 24-hour follow-up event

Aims: To provide a managerial frame of reference for those new or fairly new to management, building on potential for promotion or significantly increased responsibility

Main topics: Competitive strategy; marketing; finance and management accounting; the managerial role; human resource development; managing information; leadership and teamwork; operations management; business simulation; personal development

Notes: This programme offers a 24-hour optional report-back facility

■ General Management for Specialists

Location: Cranfield School of Management, Cranfield, UK

Participants: Senior general managers with specialist responsibilities

Frequency: 4 times a year

Duration: 12 days

Cost: £7,400 incl accommodation, meals

Aims: To improve managerial effectiveness by exploring the range of different management disciplines

Main topics: Strategy management; leadership and teamwork; financial management; marketing management; operations management; information systems

■ Implementing Business Process Change

Location: Cranfield School of Management, Cranfield, UK

Participants: Managers who need to review, design or implement business processes

Frequency: Twice a year

Duration: 5 days (plus 2 days)

Cost: £3,100 incl accommodation

Aims: To further participants' understanding and implementation of changes to business processes

Main topics: Determining objectives and processes; communication issues; developing an IT strategy; managing the impact of change on people

■ Logistics Management Programme

Location: Cranfield School of Management, Cranfield, UK

Participants: Managers responsible for logistics, materials, distribution or customer services, and those who need an understanding of supply chain decisions

Frequency: Twice a year

Duration: 5 days

Cost: £2,250 incl accommodation

Aims: To teach participants more about the logistics process

Main topics: Customer service management; logistics cost analysis; logistics planning; information systems; managing a logistics network

■ Managing European Supply Chains

Location: Cranfield School of Management, Cranfield, UK

Participants: Managers responsible for logistics in strategy or planning

Frequency: Once a year

Duration: 3 days

Cost: £1,600 incl accommodation

Aims: To cover the key aspects of logistics

Main topics: Strategy building; manufacturing logistics; managing the European logistics function; cultural perspectives; integrating IT systems; service strategies

■ Senior Manager's Programme

Location: Cranfield School of Management, Cranfield, UK

Participants: Managers holding or about to hold strategy-making positions

Frequency: 3 times a year

Duration: 12 days

Cost: £7,900 incl accommodation, meals and a 24-hour follow-up event

Aims: To enable participants to make a more effective contribution to the direction and performance of their organisations by focusing on strategic leadership

Main topics: Organisational strategy and implementation; strategic human resources; business economics; finance strategy; leadership; marketing strategy; information systems; operations management; international environment; change strategies

Notes: There is an optional report-back 6 months after the programme

■ World Class Manufacturing

Location: Cranfield School of Management, Cranfield, UK

Participants: Manufacturing directors and managers

Frequency: Twice a year

Duration: 5 days

Cost: £2,600 incl accommodation

Aims: To enable managers in manufacturing companies to generate and implement manufacturing strategies

Main topics: Manufacturing strategy; comparative performance measurement; time productivity; involving the workforce

Henley Management College

■ Bridging Customer and Shareholder Value

Location: Henley Management College, Henley-on-Thames, UK

Participants: All types of executive

Frequency: Twice a year

Duration: 3 days

Cost: £1,450

Aims: To build strategies that tie together customer and shareholder value

Main topics: The market value process and how to create value in product securities markets; building a first cut strategy

■ Business Transformation Programme

Location: Henley Management College, Henley-on-Thames, UK

Participants: Directors and senior managers

Frequency: Twice a year

Duration: 1 week

Cost: £2,950 incl accommodation, meals

Aims: To help develop the organisation's ability to build and leverage core competencies, to stay ahead through innovation and to pursue "heroic goals despite resource constraints"

Main topics: New dimensions in strategic thinking; business transformation; changing the market, not just the organisation; managing radical change; developing an innovative and responsive organisation

■ Developing Managerial Effectiveness

Location: Henley Management College, Henley-on-Thames, UK

Participants: General and departmental managers

Frequency: 4 times a year

Duration: $5\frac{1}{2}$ days

Cost: £2,475 incl accommodation, meals

Aims: To learn, understand and practise the interpersonal skills necessary for effective management

Main topics: Leadership; communication; motivation; use of authority

■ Putting Strategy into Action

Location: Henley Management College, Henley-on-Thames, UK

Participants: Strategic planners, senior and middle managers

Frequency: Twice a year

Duration: $5\frac{1}{2}$ days

Cost: £2,475

Aims: To enable participants to carry out their strategic responsibilities in a professional and effective manner

Main topics: Leadership of strategic issues; implementation of strategy; use of appropriate tools and techniques

London Business School

■ Accelerated Development Programme

Location: London Business School, London, UK

Participants: Middle managers

Frequency: 3 times a year

Duration: 4 weeks (4 consecutive or 2 2-week modules)

Cost: £12,950 incl accommodation, meals, taxes

Aims: To develop the managers of today into the leaders of tomorrow by accelerating development in technical, people and strategic skills

Main topics: Technical skills (finance and accounting, marketing, operations, information management); people skills (personal and interpersonal skills); strategic skills (understanding the international business environment, articulating a broader vision, offering a sense of direction)

Notes: Includes a 6-month follow-up questionnaire and an outdoor weekend

■ Systems Thinking and Strategic Modelling

Location: London Business School, London, UK

Participants: General and senior functional managers, planners and strategy advisers

Frequency: Twice a year

Duration: 5 days

Cost: £4,100

Aims: To focus on skills for systems thinking and informed use of modelling and simulation in the context of practical business problems

Main topics: The application of strategic modelling to growth management; human resources policy; technology transitions; competitive strategy and manufacturing policy

Notes: Participants also work in small teams on strategic topics of their own choice

Manchester Business School

■ Quality Master Class in Service Quality

Location: Manchester Business School, Manchester, UK

Participants: Senior and middle managers who wish to help their organisations in the drive towards business excellence

Frequency: Once a year

Duration: 5 days

Cost: £1,800 incl accommodation and meals

Aims: To provide a participative forum in which participants can acquire a greater knowledge of advanced ideas and concepts

Main topics: Quality self-assessment; quality techniques; benchmarking; culture change; teamwork; quality costs; re-engineering; customer satisfaction measurement

Notes: The programme is relevant to managers from the manufacturing and services sectors

CMC Graduate School of Business

■ Strategic Management

Location: CMC Graduate School of Business, Prague, Czech Republic

Participants: Directors and senior executives of international industrial and trade corporations

Frequency: Once a year

Duration: 5 days

Cost: n/a

Aims: To examine the most recent trends and approaches in corporate strategy

Main topics: The transition from competition to supercompetition in international markets; international competitiveness; the organisational transformation of large corporations; new HR strategies

ESADE—Escuela Superior de Administración y Dirección de Empresas

■ Management Control

Location: ESADE, Barcelona, Spain; Madrid, Spain

Participants: Senior managers

Frequency: Twice a year

Duration: Barcelona: 102 hours over 5 months (Thursdays 9 am-6.45 pm); Madrid: 72 hours over 3 months (Tuesdays 9.30 am-7 pm)

Cost: Pta635,000 (Barcelona); Pta390,000 (Madrid)

Aims: To explore ways of ensuring that managers can successfully adapt and change

Main topics: Design of organisational structures through effective definition of responsibility business centres; training on budgeting systems, measuring and interpreting results

■ Owner/Managers Programme: Development Strategy

Location: ESADE, Barcelona, Spain

Participants: Owners and managers of companies

Frequency: Once a year

Duration: 180 hours over 13 weeks (Fridays 9 am-6.45 pm, Saturdays 9 am-1.45 pm)

Cost: Pta690,000

Aims: To provide participants with the tools necessary to design successful development strategies

Main topics: Training in different management areas; preparation of a development plan for each participant's business; presentation and discussion of development plans

ESSEC Executive Programs

■ General Management Program

Location: ESSEC IMD, Paris

Participants: Senior managers

Frequency: Once a year

Duration: 9 months (Fridays and Saturdays)

Cost: n/a

Aims: To help participants develop their skills and become motors of change in their businesses

Notes: The programme language is French

Groupe CPA

■ General Management Programme

Location: CPA centres in France: Jouy-en-Josas, Lille, Lyon, Nice, Paris, Toulouse; and Madrid, Spain

Participants: Experienced senior managers

Frequency: n/a

Duration: 12 weeks (full-time, modular or weekly options)

Cost: FFr136,500

Aims: To deal with the problems encountered by senior managers

Main topics: Management fundamentals; managing complexity; strategic planning and action; managing change

Notes: The programme emphasises an integrated concept of management and is organised into 3 phases of increasing complexity. Participants are expected to reach solutions in line with the organisation's overall interests rather than those of a particular activity

HEC Executive Development Center

■ CESA Company Control and Management

Location: HEC, Paris, France

Participants: Middle and senior managers

Frequency: Once a year

Duration: 15 days (3 5-day modules)

Cost: FFr42,000

Aims: To train participants to control successfully the performance levels of their companies

Main topics: Practical approaches to new controlling methods; controlling efficient performance measurement; financial information and corporate management; information systems and new organisational modes

Note: The programme language is French

■ CESA Strategic Management

Location: HEC, Paris, France

Participants: General managers

Frequency: Once a year

Duration: 15 days (3 5-day modules)

Cost: FFr55,000

Aims: To help participants develop a systematic and dynamic vision of their companies

Main topics: Current trends in global competition; managing corporate transformation; developing corporate identity

Notes: The programme language is French

■ Strategies for Competitive Success: Formulation and Implementation

Location: HEC, Paris, France

Participants: Experienced European managers involved in strategic decision-making in their organisations

Frequency: Once a year

Duration: 5 days

Cost: FFr22,000 incl lunch

Aims: To provide a perspective of strategic management via European and American approaches

Main topics: Analysing the competitive environment; creating sustainable competitive advantage; creating customer value; growing and expanding versus re-engineering and downsizing; forming strategic alliances; designing effective structures and systems; managing performance; competing globally; promoting strategic change

IESE—International Graduate School of Management—University of Navarra

■ Achieving Breakthrough Service

Location: IESE, Barcelona, Spain

Participants: General, marketing, HR and operations managers with decision-making roles

Frequency: Once a year

Duration: 6 days (Sunday pm-Friday pm)

Cost: $9,000 incl accommodation, meals, taxes

Aims: To help participants develop strategies and implement plans to achieve superior service

Main topics: Service strategy; customer loyalty; customer satisfaction; human resources; information technology; re-engineering; managing change

Notes: This is a joint-venture programme with Harvard Business School. The course is also run in Bariloche, Argentina, in association with Instituto de Altos Estudios Empresariales

■ Global Programme for Management Development

Location: IESE, Barcelona, Spain

Participants: Experienced executives and managers involved in formulating company strategy

Frequency: Once a year

Duration: 12 days (Sunday pm-Friday pm)

Cost: $14,000 incl accommodation, meals, taxes

Aims: To enable participants to develop competitive strategies in global markets

Main topics: Strategy; customer focus; value orientation; human resources; international interdependencies; operations and technology

Notes: This is a joint-venture programme with the University of Michigan which is also run in Shanghai, China, with the China Europe International Business School

■ Global Programme for Management Development—China

Location: Shanghai, China

Participants: Global managers who have operations in China or are considering establishing them and wish to increase their knowledge of global issues

Frequency: Once a year

Duration: 12 days (Sunday pm-Friday pm)

Cost: $14,000 incl accommodation, meals, taxes

Aims: To enable participants to develop competitive strategies in global markets with a special focus on China

Main topics: Strategy; customer focus; value orientation; human resources; international interdependencies; operations and technology. China-specific topics: the economy; state-owned enterprises, selecting partners; negotiating joint ventures; legal issues; human resources; capital markets

Notes: This is a joint-venture programme with the University of Michigan. It presents a condensed version of the GPMD Europe outline and provides participants with specific knowledge of how to do business in and with China

---

■ Management in the Information Age: Aligning Information Technology and Business Strategy

Location: IESE, Barcelona, Spain

Participants: Senior executives from a range of industries wishing to enhance their organisations' strategic direction

Frequency: Once a year

Duration: 1 week

Cost: $7,000 incl accommodation, meals, taxes

Aims: To explore and analyse the impact of information technology on today's organisations and how it can be leveraged to make more effective business decisions

Main topics: Delivering goods and services in new ways; maximising customer service and loyalty; creating an environment conducive to individual and organisational learning; adapting to change; moving to a new process management approach; understanding electronic markets

---

■ Strategic Management of Technology-based Companies

Location: IESE, Barcelona, Spain

Participants: General and functional managers intending to move into general management in technology-intensive industries

Frequency: Once a year

Duration: 12 days (Sunday pm-Friday pm)

Cost: $13,000 incl accommodation, meals, taxes

Aims: To analyse the key processes and address the strategic challenges and opportunities of technology-intensive businesses

Main topics: Strategic leadership; negotiation; transformation; new product development; market orientation; restructuring and revitalising; supply chain; manufacturing and development; high-technology intrapreneurship; technology management for internal ventures

IMD—International Institute for Management Development

■ Differentiation Through Service

Location: IMD, Lausanne, Switzerland

Participants: Managers responsible for service operations in both service and manufacturing industries

Frequency: Once a year

Duration: 2 weeks

Cost: Swfr12,000

Aims: To improve a company's competitiveness by leveraging services to create value-added for the customer

Main topics: Seeing the company through the customers' eyes; creating differences through customer service; managing customer expectations to avoid disappointments; the profitable art of recovering from mistakes; creating outstanding customer loyalty programmes; reorienting the organisation to customers and service; linking HR management and quality to service; sustaining the service effort through technology

■ Managing Corporate Resources

Location: IMD, Lausanne, Switzerland

Participants: Senior managers

Frequency: Twice a year

Duration: 4 weeks

Cost: Swfr24,000 incl some meals, materials

Aims: To develop participants' capability to integrate business functions and manage change in the context of implementing a well-defined business unit strategy and increase their effectiveness as members of a general management team

Main topics: Industry and competition analysis; shaping business policies; mobilising the business unit; the role of the general manager

■ Managing the Innovation Process: from Idea and Technology to Market

Location: IMD, Lausanne, Switzerland

Participants: Senior managers

Frequency: Once a year

Duration: 6 days

Cost: Swfr9,000 incl some meals, materials

Aims: To provide participants with a holistic framework, management concepts and insights from best practice to help them implement innovation

Main topics: There are two intertwined themes, the "what" and the "how" of innovation. The "what" stream deals with 3 types of activities: generate; validate and choose; implement. The "how" stream deals with: process management mechanisms; innovation-specific skills; innovation climate and culture

Notes: Teams of executives are encouraged to participate in this programme

---

■ Managing Manufacturing: Transforming the Manufacturing Enterprise

Location: IMD, Lausanne, Switzerland

Participants: Senior executives from manufacturing companies

Frequency: Once a year

Duration: 2 weeks

Cost: Swfr12,000 incl some meals, materials

Aims: To help participants continuously "transform" their companies' manufacturing operations

Main topics: Transformation; lean manufacturing; supply/demand chain management; the people dimension

---

■ Orchestrating Winning Performance

Location: IMD, Lausanne, Switzerland

Participants: Senior and middle managers

Frequency: Once a year

Duration: 6 days incl 1 weekend

Cost: Swfr10,000 for first participant from a company, Swfr7,000 for each subsequent participant from same company incl some meals, materials

Aims: To give an overview of the latest research at IMD and exposure to the latest business thinking across relevant management issues

Main topics: Participants design their own courses by choosing from a varied menu of available options

Notes: Teams can use the services of a faculty facilitator throughout the programme for an additional fee of Swfr2,000 per person

INSEAD—European Institute of Business Administration

■ Achieving Outstanding Performance

Location: INSEAD, Fontainebleau, France

Participants: Directors, vice-presidents, general managers

Frequency: Twice a year

Duration: 3 days

Cost: FFr36,000 incl some meals, materials

Aims: To better understand how to create and sustain outstanding performance

Main topics: Processes (including IT and process redesign); activities (including key performance indicators); people (including re-engineering managerial behaviour)

■ Competitive Strategy

Location: INSEAD, Fontainebleau, France

Participants: Directors, vice-presidents, general managers

Frequency: Once a year

Duration: 3 days

Cost: FFr28,000 incl some meals, materials

Aims: To enable participants to articulate an effective strategy for their organisations

Main topics: Creating and capturing customer value; establishing market dominance; managing the supply chain

■ The Strategic Management of Services

Location: INSEAD, Fontainebleau, France

Participants: Managing directors; business unit, HR, marketing and planning managers

Frequency: Once a year

Duration: 2 weeks

Cost: FFr61,000 incl some meals, materials

Aims: To help participants enhance their skills in leading service businesses

Main topics: Service delivery as a strategic weapon (marketing; operations and quality; people and organisations); implementation issues (distribution; strategic cost management; IT; re-engineering; strategic alliances)

Notes: This programme offers a health and fitness programme and includes the Markstrat Services Simulation

Maastricht School of Management

■ Managerial Control and Management Information Systems

Location: Maastricht School of Management, Maastricht, Netherlands

Participants: Senior executives, consultants in the area of management control and management information systems

Frequency: Once a year

Duration: 14 weeks

Cost: G10,000 incl field-work expenses, materials

Aims: To review the deficiencies of traditional control systems, the possible failings of existing systems and the latest developments in management control and performance

Main topics: Management control systems (analysis of strengths and weaknesses; illustrations of current systems; new paradigms); management information systems (computer software and hardware; information analysis; information strategy and planning; information strategy and control; inter-organisational systems)

■ Project Management

Location: Maastricht School of Management, Maastricht, Netherlands

Participants: Executives and managers of semi-government organisations, project analysts and loan officers of commercial and development banks

Frequency: Once a year

Duration: 14 weeks

Cost: G15,500 incl field-work expenses, materials

Aims: To provide a deeper understanding of the strategic, economic, organisational and management aspects of project management

Main topics: Innovation and the creation of projects; market analysis and research; technical analysis; economic analysis; planning the project; project organisation; computer-aided feasibility studies; project finance; environmental impact analysis; project management and implementation

Nijenrode University—The Netherlands Business School

■ Senior Management Forum (Semafor)

Location: Netherlands Business School, Nijenrode, Netherlands

Participants: Senior and middle managers

Frequency: Twice a year

Duration: 4 1-week modules and a ½-week module over 6 months

Cost: G23,500

Aims: To enable participants to take time out to reconsider their management skills

Main topics: European integration; philosophy and fine arts; corporate ethics; doing business in Brussels

---

Theseus Institute

■ Programme for Energising People

Location: Theseus Institute, Sophia Antipolis, France

Participants: Managers, project leaders

Frequency: Once a year

Duration: 1 week

Cost: Ecu5,400

Aims: To help instil in participants the skills and confidence to address uprooting, disorienting changes and create highly successful groups (dynamic action groups)

Main topics: Organisational behaviour; leadership and followership; team-building; personal development; communications and negotiation skills

Rest of world

Australian Graduate School of Management—University of New South Wales

■ Accelerated Development Programme

Location: Australian Graduate School of Management, Sydney, Australia

Participants: Managers with high potential

Frequency: Once a year

Duration: Module 1: 13 days; module 2: 6 days

Cost: A$13,950 incl accommodation, meals, materials

Aims: To provide young executives with the skills and knowledge to move from functional or unit management to general management

Main topics: Managing teams; finance and accounting; marketing; corporate strategy; organisational development; personal competencies; leadership; team membership; data gathering, synthesis and analysis; problem diagnosis; self-development

Notes: During the 5 months between modules participants are required to complete self-directed assignments. The programme involves significant pre-programme assessment and preparation including a workplace feedback survey of the participants' colleagues

■ Development Programme for Managers

Location: Australian Graduate School of Management, Sydney, Australia

Participants: Senior functional or general managers

Frequency: Once a year

Duration: 28 days

Cost: A$19,850 incl accommodation, meals, materials

Aims: To enable managers to improve their personal performance and the results of their organisations

Main topics: Corporate strategy; financial management and accounting; managing people and teams; marketing; negotiations; process improvement; strategic human resource management

Notes: Participants who also complete an optional assessment may receive credit for subjects in the AGSM's Executive MBA programme

■ General Manager Programme

Location: Australian Graduate School of Management, Sydney, Australia

Participants: Senior executives at divisional and corporate levels

Frequency: Once a year

Duration: 6 days

Cost: A$7,350 incl accommodation, meals, materials

Aims: To co-ordinate the disparate skills of the managerial function into a coherent strategy

Main topics: Integrating corporate strategy, marketing, operations and leadership; balancing short-term profit and long-term growth; generating, developing and differentiating between opportunities; examining the role of successful business leaders; finding and developing innovators

■ Organisational Change

Location: Australian Graduate School of Management, Sydney, Australia

Participants: Senior line and staff managers involved in implementing significant change programmes

Frequency: Once a year

Duration: 3 days

Cost: A$3,450 incl accommodation, meals, materials

Aims: To enable managers to achieve major change in their organisations

Main topics: Implications of business strategies for designing organisational change programmes; assessing the scale and nature of change needed; designing the change process; taking charge of change; skills required of an agent for change; designing human resource management systems to support change

University of Cape Town—Graduate School of Business

■ Accelerated Development Programme

Location: Graduate School of Business, Cape Town, South Africa

Participants: Employees with limited prior educational opportunities who are demonstrating their potential within the workplace

Frequency: Twice a year

Duration: 13 days

Cost: R7,116 incl accommodation

Aims: To help employees whose effectiveness and productivity could be significantly enhanced by increased understanding of the context in which they are operating

Main topics: History and purpose of business; basic principles of business; the functional areas of business; oral and written communication skills; writing a business plan

Notes: Between the residential modules participants undertake projects focusing on their business, supervised by the GSB and their line manager

■ Programme for Management Development

Location: Graduate School of Business, Cape Town, South Africa

Participants: Middle managers who have been or are about to be promoted to general management, or who are about to take on more responsibility in a specialist field

Frequency: Twice a year

Duration: 20 days

Cost: R24,000

Aims: To facilitate the transition from function-specific to general management

Notes: Established in 1967; in 1997 over 1,000 delegates attended the programme

Indian Institute of Management

■ Management Education Programme

Location: IIM, Vastrapur, Ahmedabad, India

Participants: Functional managers who have moved or are about to move into general management

Frequency: Once a year

Duration: 4½ months

Cost: Rs180,000 ($10,000 for participants from outside India) incl accommodation, materials

Aims: To provide management education for managers in the private and public sectors (and young owner managers) who are about to take on broader general management responsibilities

Main topics: Computer-based information systems; cost accounting and management control systems; decision analysis; economics; financial accounting and analysis; financial management; human resource management; international business; logistics management; managerial communication; marketing management; organisational behaviour; production and operations management; strategic management; managerial role and identity

■ Programme for Management Development

This is a 3-tier programme catering for the needs of middle, senior and top management

1. Middle Management Programme

Location: IIM, Vastrapur, Ahmedabad, India

Participants: Middle managers in functional departments

Frequency: Once a year

Duration: 4 weeks

Cost: Rs55,000 ($2,000 for participants from outside India) incl accommodation, materials

Aims: To enhance the managerial skills of middle managers to enable them to take on more responsibilities

Main topics: Economic environment and policy; marketing management; financial and cost accounting; financial management; investment analysis; quantitative aids for decision-making; computer-based management information systems; manufacturing management; organisational behaviour; management of personnel and industrial relations; management control systems; managerial communication; strategic management

2. Senior Management Programme

Location: IIM, Vastrapur, Ahmedabad, India

Participants: Senior executives who head functional departments and report to top management

Frequency: Once a year

Duration: 3 weeks

Cost: Rs50,000 ($1,750 for participants from outside India) incl accommodation, materials

Aims: To examine managerial issues and to develop fresh insights into the process of formulating plans, evaluating performance, and exercising control and co-ordination in functional areas in the context of overall organisational goals and objectives

Main topics: Business policy; computers and information management; economic environment; ethics in management; financial management; human resources management; management accounting and control; managerial communication; marketing management; operations management; organisational behaviour; stress management

3. Top Management Programme

Location: IIM, Vastrapur, Ahmedabad, India

Participants: Executives from the top management team who are actively involved in policy-making and managing whole or major parts of organisations with independent, multifunctional responsibilities

Frequency: Once a year

Duration: 1 week

Cost: Rs45,000 ($1,500 for participants from outside India) incl accommodation, materials

Aims: To review the current strategies of corporations and discuss issues concerning links between the business environment and corporate strategy in the context of the far-reaching changes that have taken place in business management in India and abroad

Main topics: The corporation and its environment: the interlinkages; the changed economic, sociopolitical, competitive and technological environment; organisational excellence; competitive strategy and competitive advantage; the generation and evaluation of strategic options; functional strategies in the context of corporate strategy; strategy, structure, systems and processes

■ Small and Medium Enterprises Programme

Location: IIM, Vastrapur, Ahmedabad, India

Participants: Entrepreneurs and owner managers; executives and officers of development agencies, banks and other financial institutions

Frequency: Once a year

Duration: 2 weeks

Cost: Rs35,000 ($1,500 for participants from outside India) incl accommodation, materials

Aims: To provide the concepts and skills necessary to manage and develop existing businesses; to provide research and consulting experience on the special managerial problems of small and medium-sized businesses

Main topics: Managerial accounting and control; financial management; operations management; marketing management; human resource management; economic environment and policy; strategic management; computer applications

■ Strategies for Competitive Advantage

Location: IIM, Vastrapur, Ahmedabad, India

Participants: Senior managers who are or are likely to be associated with formulating and implementing divisional or corporate strategies in a competitive environment

Frequency: Once a year

Duration: 6 days

Cost: Rs21,000 ($780 for participants from outside India) incl accommodation, materials

Aims: To provide the concepts, tools and techniques for identifying and analysing sources of competitive advantage

Main topics: Concept of competitive strategy; nature of competitive advantage; changing competitive environment in India; structure of competitive forces; anchors for formulating strategies for competitive advantage (cost, differentiation, focus, time, IT); strategies for globalisation and international competitiveness; issues in implementation

Macquarie Graduate School of Management— Macquarie University

■ Creative Business Development Programme

Location: Macquarie Graduate School, Sydney, Australia

Participants: Senior directors and executives, business development managers, business analysts

Frequency: Once a year

Duration: 3 days

Cost: A$2,950

Aims: To help managers with strategic responsibility develop their ability to formulate and implement innovative and achievable business development strategies

Main topics: Strategic analysis and focus; developing creative and innovative solutions; strategic implementation

■ Foundations of Management

Location: Macquarie Graduate School, Sydney, Australia

Participants: Functional managers wishing to enhance their careers

Frequency: Twice a year

Duration: 7 days

Cost: A$5,950

Aims: To help executives realise their full management potential

Main topics: Strategic management; marketing management; financial management; managing people; organisational behaviour; personal effectiveness; leadership; negotiation skills and conflict resolution

■ Strategic Management Programme

Location: Macquarie Graduate School, Sydney, Australia; Coolum, Queensland, Australia

Participants: Senior managers, strategic planning executives

Frequency: 4 times a year

Duration: 5 days

Cost: A$3,950 incl accommodation, meals

Aims: To provide an integrated approach to strategic thinking; a comprehensive perspective of the people, organisational and financial influences on strategic management; an understanding of industry analysis and competitive strategy; an insight into the strategies of Australian companies

Main topics: Understanding industry profitability; strategic responses to industry conditions; industry competitiveness and retaliation; creating shareholder wealth; corporate capability platforms; growth and diversification; strategic thinking and strategic intent; strategy formulation and implementation

Monash Mt Eliza Business School

■ Implementing Strategic Change

Location: Mt Eliza, Australia

Participants: Senior and middle managers from all functions and industries

Frequency: Twice a year

Duration: 5 days

Cost: A$5,450

Aims: To develop the knowledge and skills to formulate and implement strategy, and increase personal effectiveness in a change management role

Notes: The interactive workshop methodology allows participants to apply the skills, techniques and processes learned by discussing each other's strategic issues

■ Management Development Programme (Consulting Project)

Location: Mt Eliza, Australia

Participants: Senior and middle managers

Frequency: Twice a year

Duration: 27 days

Cost: A$15,500 incl accommodation, meals, materials, taxes

Aims: To develop managers beyond their specialities to prepare them for general management responsibilities

Main topics: The core theme is the management environment, with modules on internal environment and change; functional operations and management; external environment and strategy; leadership and managerial style

■ Management Development Programme (Work-Based Project)

Location: Mt Eliza, Australia

Participants: Senior and middle managers

Frequency: Once a year

Duration: 13 days plus 6 days

Cost: A$12, 900 incl accommodation, meals, materials, taxes

Aims: To develop managers beyond their specialities to prepare them for general management

Main topics: The programme begins with a 2-week module focusing on the theme of the management environment. The key competencies developed are leadership and change; external environment and strategy; corporate resource management; and managerial style. Participants apply the programme over the next 3 months then reassemble for a second 1-week module to present their projects

■ Managing in the Middle: Improving Workplace Performance

Location: Mt Eliza, Australia

Participants: Middle managers

Frequency: Twice a year

Duration: 5 days

Cost: A$4,250

Aims: To enable participants to understand the mechanics of how business operates to optimise staff performance

Main topics: Change management; team and people management; project and process management; negotiation; best practice and performance management

■ Senior Manager's Programme

Location: Mt Eliza, Australia

Participants: General and senior functional managers

Frequency: Twice a year

Duration: 6 days

Cost: A$4,950

Aims: To develop business and organisational performance by effectively integrating the functional and operational activities of the enterprise

Main topics: Managing and leading people; change management; negotiation; project management; performance management and measurement; best practice and performance improvement

National University of Singapore—Graduate School of Business

■ General Management Programme

Location: National University of Singapore

Participants: General and functional managers, managing directors

Frequency: Twice a year

Duration: 2 weeks

Cost: S$4,100

Aims: To help participants broaden their managerial perspective and improve their analytical and decision-making skills

Main topics: Understanding the context (scenarios for the future of Asian markets, globalisation); strategic thinking; marketing in Asia; strategic human resource management; strategic financial management; operations management

■ Operations Management Programme

Location: National University of Singapore

Participants: General, middle and operations managers

Frequency: Once a year

Duration: 2 weeks

Cost: S$3,600

Aims: To help participants understand the issues and problems encountered in the design, planning and control of productive systems

Main topics: Operations strategy and design; choice and management of technology; demand forecasting; aggregate planning; inventory planning and control; material requirements planning; operations scheduling; Japanese production systems; quality management; human aspects of operations; financial aspects of operations; theory of constraints; logistics and distribution; service operations management

■ Stanford-NUS Executive Programme

Location: National University of Singapore; Shanghai, China

Participants: General managers

Frequency: Twice a year

Duration: 3 weeks

Cost: US$9,200

Aims: To help participants broaden their managerial perspective and improve analytical and behavioural skills

Main topics: Management of financial resources; operations, information systems and management analysis; economic environment; marketing and business strategy; management of human resources; strategic management

■ Strategic Management Programme

Location: National University of Singapore

Participants: Senior and upper-middle managers

Frequency: Once a year

Duration: 2 weeks

Cost: S$4,000

Aims: To expose participants to the strategic challenges faced by organisations

Main topics: The content of strategy; strategy implementation; broad strategic trends and issues; Asian approaches to strategy; networks, alliances and acquisitions; business re-engineering; technology strategy; regionalisation

Wits Business School—University of the Witwatersrand

■ The Art of General Management

Location: Wits Business School, Johannesburg, South Africa

Participants: Managing directors, general managers, key members of the general management team

Frequency: Once a year

Duration: 3 days

Cost: R4,950 incl materials, meals

Aims: To help participants develop the skills and techniques required to become effective general managers

Main topics: Challenges facing general management; developing vision and direction; strategic positioning; general management and leadership; designing an effective organisation; from strategy to action—methods of effective implementation

Human resource programmes

Human resource (HR) management is a discipline whose time appears to have come. In the past, HR management, or personnel management as it was known, did not feature strongly among business school programmes. The skills of personnel professionals were mostly developed by professional bodies or training companies. Now, with growing recognition of the need to manage human resources imaginatively, efficiently and profitably, HR management is of paramount importance.

Business schools have responded as if they always knew that people mattered. Shrewdly, they have targeted the development of strategic skills as their principal opportunity. The HR programmes they offer focus on adding strategic skills to the armoury of HR specialists or on teaching HR skills to experienced managers with backgrounds in other disciplines.

Programmes are arranged alphabetically by provider in the following regions:

- North America (page 148)

- UK (page 153)

- Europe excluding UK (page 156)

- Rest of world (page 159)

North America

The Anderson School at UCLA—Executive Education Programs

- ## Advanced Program in Human Resource Management

  Location: The Anderson School at UCLA, Los Angeles, CA, US

  Participants: Senior HR executives, professionals and specialists from all industries, sectors and countries

  Frequency: Once a year

  Duration: 5 days

  Cost: $4,950 incl accommodation, meals, books, materials

  Aims: To enhance the contribution of HR management to organisational effectiveness and bottom-line business performance

  Main topics: Strategic planning frameworks; HR strategies; leadership and communication; building effective teams; performance management and rewards; effective organisational change; global and cross-cultural HR management; HR practices and business performance; CEO expectations of the HR function

Carlson School of Management—University of Minnesota

- ## Human Resource Executive Program

  Location: Oak Ridge Conference Center, Chaska, MN, US

  Participants: HR executives who lead major functions in their organisations

  Frequency: Once a year

  Duration: 5 days

  Cost: $2,600 incl materials

  Aims: To help participants further develop into effective strategic business leaders

  Main topics: Business strategy; HR competencies; personal effectiveness

Darden Executive Education—University of Virginia

■ Human Resource Forum: Key Strategic Human Resource Issues for the Next Century

Location: Darden School, Charlottesville, VA, US

Participants: HR professionals and senior professionals

Frequency: Once a year

Duration: 6 days

Cost: $4,950 incl accommodation, meals

Aims: To analyse business strategies and explore the development of HR strategies

Main topics: Business strategy; developing an HR strategy; role of the HR manager; managing diversity; the future of HR; leveraging organisational learning

Harvard Business School

■ Strategic Human Resource Management

Location: Harvard Business School, Boston, MA, US

Participants: Chief executives, HR managers, line managers

Frequency: Once a year

Duration: 1 week

Cost: $6,000 incl accommodation, most meals, materials

Aims: To explore the strategic role of the HR function

Main topics: Examining the impact of structures, systems, cultures and leadership on organisational effectiveness

University of Michigan Business School

■ Advanced Human Resource Executive Program

Location: Executive Education Center, Ann Arbor, MI, US

Participants: Senior HR executives, general managers

Frequency: Once a year

Duration: 2 1-week modules

Cost: $10,750 incl accommodation, meals, materials

Aims: To enhance the knowledge and competence of senior HR executives

Main topics: Participating and contributing to the management team (globalisation, business strategy, system change); preparing a leadership agenda for the HR function (leadership, organisation of the function, executive succession, board relations, shared mindset or culture, HR policies)

■ Human Resource Executive Program

Location: Executive Education Center, Ann Arbor, MI, US

Participants: Middle and senior HR managers

Frequency: Twice a year

Duration: 2 weeks

Cost: $10,400 incl accommodation, meals, materials

Aims: To enable participants to assess current HR management practices

Main topics: Strategic planning; strategic HR management; HR planning; international HR management; implementing change; performance appraisal systems; reward systems; training and development; labour relations; current issues

Notes: A 1-week version of this programme is also offered in Hong Kong

■ Global Employee Relations Strategy

Location: Executive Education Center, Ann Arbor, MI, US

Participants: Experienced company or union professionals with responsibility for organisational strategies affecting the employment relationship

Frequency: Once a year

Duration: 5 days

Cost: $5,200 incl accommodation, meals, materials

Aims: To broaden the understanding of industrial relations strategy in the context of global competition

Main topics: Global competition and strategic business implications; global labour markets and industrial relations systems; multinational company decision-making; formulating workplace strategies; achieving and sustaining competitive advantage

Rotman School of Management—University of Toronto

■ Advanced Program in Human Resource Management

Location: Rotman School of Management, Toronto, Canada

Participants: Senior executives, HR executives

Frequency: 3 times a year

Duration: 4 weeks over 9 months (1 1-week module every 2 months)

Cost: C$7,750 incl most meals, materials

Aims: To provide participants with the tools, knowledge and techniques to move from an administrative to a strategic perspective in human resources management

Main topics: Business economic strategy; financial accounting; business strategy; HR strategy; strategic cost management; compensation strategy; strategic planning for HR; HR strategic evaluation; managing the legal environment; organisations and change; managing diversity; employee relations strategy; understanding the legal environment; managing change; HR strategy; managing employee relations

Notes: This programme is a joint venture between the University of Toronto and the Human Resources Professionals Association of Ontario. Participants receive a Joseph L Rotman School of Management Certificate in Human Resources on completion

The Mary Jean and Frank P Smeal College of Business Administration—Pennsylvania State University

■ Human Resource Management Program

Location: Penn State University, PA, US

Participants: Vice-presidents, directors, HR managers, personnel, employee relations

Frequency: Once a year

Duration: 10 days

Cost: $7,200 incl accommodation, meals, materials

Aims: To improve the strategic leadership abilities of executives responsible for or influential in the management of human resources

Main topics: Organisational drivers of HR strategy; leadership in strategic HR management; financial planning and control; global business environment; creating HR systems for competitive advantage; achieving competitive effectiveness; strategic HR management

Stanford Graduate School of Business—Stanford University

■ **Human Resource Executive Program**

Location: Graduate School of Business, Stanford, CA, US

Participants: Senior HR managers, functional managers with HR responsibility

Frequency: Once a year

Duration: 1 week

Cost: $5,700 incl accommodation, meals, books, study materials

Aims: To examine how human resources can be directly linked to business strategy and provide a broad exposure to the latest thinking and practice in HR management

Wharton School—University of Pennsylvania—Aresty Institute of Executive Education

■ **Managing People: Power through Influence**

Location: Wharton School, Philadelphia, PA, US

Participants: Senior managers

Frequency: Twice a year

Duration: 3 days

Cost: $3,750 incl accommodation, meals

Aims: To examine perspectives and best practice in motivation and incentives

Main topics: Understanding organisations; human influence on organisations; politics of organisations; managing organisational conflict; organisational change; organisational paradoxes; managing people through multiple perspectives

UK

Ashridge Management College

■ Strategic Human Resource Management

Location: Ashridge Management College, Berkhamsted, UK

Participants: Senior HR professionals, senior line managers

Frequency: 3 times a year

Duration: 5 days

Cost: £2,950 incl accommodation, meals

Aims: To help optimise the human-resource contribution to strategy formulation and implement corporate strategy through HR management

Main topics: Strategic HR management, strategic concepts and tools; aligning HR with strategy; developing an HR strategy and plan; making implementation happen; the future of the HR function

Notes: This programme is offered in partnership with the Association for Management , Education and Development (AMED)

Cranfield School of Management

■ Managing People Effectively

Location: Cranfield School of Management, Cranfield, UK

Participants: Specialists and professionals seeking further management guidance

Frequency: 3 times a year

Duration: 5 days plus 3-day follow-up

Cost: £3,950 incl accommodation

Aims: To enable managers to balance technical expertise with people management skills

Main topics: Motivation; communication; teamwork; leadership; management style; stress management

Henley Management College

■ Developing Cultural Fluency

Location: Henley Management College, Henley-on-Thames, UK

Participants: HR professionals, managers of international and transnational operations

Frequency: Twice a year

Duration: 4 days

Cost: £1,800

Aims: To help participants understand how people's performance in transcultural work environments can be improved through programmes of training and development

Main topics: Cultural analysis techniques; cross-cultural managerial competencies; team-working skills

Notes: The programme introduces innovative training approaches designed to help people meet the challenges of working in a global marketplace

London Business School

■ HR Strategy in Transforming Organisations

Location: London Business School, London, UK

Participants: Senior HR managers and general managers

Frequency: Once a year

Duration: 5 days

Cost: £3,750 incl accommodation, meals

Aims: To strengthen personal competencies so that participants can help their organisations create sustainable competitive advantage through people processes

Main Topics: Analysis of participants' own organisations using a per programme diagnostic questionnaire; linking business strategy to human resources; managing meaning and change; the world in 2005; megatrends

Notes: The programme director will draw upon the findings of the Leading Edge Consortium, an extensive and detailed study of people management in the 1990s

Roffey Park Management Institute

■ The Strategic Human Resources Programme

Location: Roffey Park, Horsham, UK

Participants: HR specialists, managers, senior managers

Frequency: Twice a year

Duration: 3 days plus 3 2-day modules

Cost: £3,950 incl meals, accommodation

Aims: To deepen participants' understanding of strategic HR issues and enhance their skills to carry out HR strategies effectively

Main topics: Understanding the role of strategic HR; enhancing strategic HR skills; establishing a network of HR professionals; linking HR and business strategies

Notes: This programme is based on learning by doing, with live group sessions

CMC Graduate School of Business

- ## Work Organisation and Work Conditions

  Location: CMC Graduate School of Business, Prague, Czech Republic

  Participants: Line managers, HR managers

  Frequency: Once a year

  Duration: 3 days

  Cost: n/a

  Aims: To teach participants approaches and methods that enable them to use the organisation's human resources efficiently

  Main topics: The importance of human resources; designing work tasks; work time organisation and time management; development of the workplace and work environment; health and safety at work

HEC Executive Development Center

- ## CESA Human Resources

  Location: HEC, Paris, France

  Participants: Managers, present or future heads of HR departments

  Frequency: Once a year

  Duration: 15 days (3 5-day modules)

  Cost: FFr42,000

  Aims: To provide participants with practical tools to improve organisational performance

  Main topics: Current challenges of the HR function; functional tools and management systems; managing change and innovation within the organisation; managing cultural diversity

  Notes: The programme language is French, and there is a personalised corporate project

IMD—International Institute for Management Development

■ Mobilizing People

Location: IMD, Lausanne, Switzerland

Participants: Senior and middle managers

Frequency: Twice a year

Duration: 2 weeks

Cost: Swfr14,000 incl some meals, materials

Aims: To improve managers' ability to influence others and mobilise available human talent to meet objectives

Main topics: Developing individual energy; leading successful teams; mobilising the organisation

INSEAD—European Institute of Business Administration

■ Management of People

Location: INSEAD, Fontainebleau, France

Participants: General managers, HR vice-presidents and directors, management development managers, finance and administration directors

Frequency: Once a year

Duration: 1 week

Cost: FFr36,000

Aims: To examine the relationship between competitive business strategy and HR management and consider the key questions for high-performing organisations

Main topics: Business strategy and HR management; competitive HR strategy; leading change and organisational renewal; competitive advantage through HR management; managing cultural diversity; leadership

EM Lyon

■ **Cross-cultural Management: A Human Resource Perspective**

Location: Paris or Lyon, France

Participants: Senior or middle managers; current or future expatriates; managers hosting or working with expatriates; HR specialists

Frequency: Once a year in English; twice in French

Duration: 3 days

Cost: FFr9,000

Aims: To increase understanding of how the basic components of national culture have a direct impact on HR practices in multinational organisations

Main topics: HR and culture; mergers and acquisitions; expatriation

Notes: This programme uses multimedia case studies as well as videos and interactive discussions

Maastricht School of Management

■ **Building Human Resources Competence**

Location: Maastricht School of Management, Maastricht, Netherlands

Participants: Senior managers, HR directors

Frequency: Once a year

Duration: 2 1-week modules

Cost: n/a

Aims: To review the implications of business strategy in the management of human resources

Main topics: Changes in the business environment; strategy and the management of human assets; team-building, empowerment and the learning organisation; leadership and culture; transformation strategy

Rest of world

Australian Graduate School of Management—University of New South Wales

■ Managing the New Workplace Relations

Location: Australian Graduate School of Management, Sydney, Australia

Participants: Senior and middle managers, in particular employee relations and HR managers

Frequency: Once a year

Duration: 3 days

Cost: A$3,325 incl accommodation, meals, materials

Aims: To help participants recognise and think strategically about workplace relations issues

Main topics: Exploring the range of workplace relations choices available in Australia; reviewing the operation of the Workplace Relations Act; examining enterprise bargaining outcomes; developing professional skills in enterprise bargaining, advocacy and grievance handling; reviewing industrial relations practices in the Asia-Pacific region

■ Strategic Human Resource Management

Location: Australian Graduate School of Management, Sydney, Australia

Participants: HR specialists; general and line managers

Frequency: Twice a year

Duration: 6 days

Cost: A$6,985 incl accommodation, meals, materials

Aims: To enable participants to develop and apply a practical and strategic approach to the management of their workforce, and to identify and achieve competitive advantage from their people

Main topics: HR management issues for organisations; using analytical tools to identify the needs of organisations

Notes: A competency survey provides feedback for participants which can be used as a basis for their own development

University of Cape Town—Graduate School of Business

■ People Management for Line Managers

Location: Graduate School of Business, Cape Town, South Africa

Participants: Functional line managers with people management responsibilities

Frequency: Once a year

Duration: 6 days

Cost: R7,210 incl accommodation

Aims: To develop an understanding of the people management challenges specific to South African organisations

Main topics: The employment process; the control process; interaction

---

■ Strategic Human Resource Management

Location: Graduate School of Business, Cape Town, South Africa

Participants: Senior HR and industrial relations practitioners

Frequency: Once a year

Duration: 6 days

Cost: R7,210 incl accommodation

Aims: To redefine the HR contribution in terms of adding value to an organisation

Main topics: HR management and strategic fit; flexible work practices; implementing HR strategies; HR development; HR and service excellence; HR practices and organisational development; socio-political environment of business; industrial relations; trends in compensation management; incentive design process and pay for performance; leadership and culture

National University of Singapore—Graduate School of Business Administration

■ Human Resource Management Programme

Location: National University of Singapore

Participants: Directors and managers with responsibility for human resources

Frequency: Once a year

Duration: 2 weeks

Cost: S$4,000

Aims: To improve managerial competence in the design and implementation of HR systems

Main topics: Strategic HR management; HR planning; staff acquisition and retention; training and development; career planning and management; position analysis and performance management; compensation design and administration; management of regional executives; managing change in organisations; corporate culture; learning organisations; working effectively as a team; organisational restructuring

Wits Business School—University of the Witwatersrand

■ Strategic Human Resource Management

Location: Wits Business School, Johannesburg, South Africa

Participants: Senior and middle managers responsible for the implementation and management of HR strategies or processes

Frequency: Once a year

Duration: 5 days

Cost: R7,350 incl materials, meals

Aims: To equip managers with the knowledge and insights necessary to align HR strategy and processes with the imperatives for business success

Main topics: The evolving world of work and its impact on individuals; creating high-performance, globally competitive organisations; strategy and interactive planning in circumstances of uncertainty; building corporate and human competencies; new institutions and legislation and their implications; accommodating stakeholders in corporate governance and business decision-making; diversity management; managing in South African society; leading in the new world of work; performance management and productivity

International management programmes

Business schools are involved in an accelerating battle to improve their global credentials. They work hard to promote their global networks and their international faculty and participants. Some have a more truly global perspective than others, and it is generally accepted that North American schools lag behind their European counterparts, although there are a number of exceptions.

The international lead does undoubtedly come from Europe, in particular some of the region's leading schools, such as IMD, INSEAD and London Business School. INSEAD's six-week International Executive Programme represents a benchmark for the international programmes which many business schools profess to be seeking to create.

Programmes are arranged alphabetically by provider in the following regions:

- North America (page 164)
- Europe excluding UK (page 166)
- Rest of world (page 170)

North America

University of Michigan Business School

■ Global Program for Management Development

Location: Bangalore, India; Shanghai, China; Barcelona, Spain

Participants: Senior executives involved in decisions affecting global competition and strategy, joint ventures and strategic alliances

Frequency: Once a year in each country

Duration: 2 weeks

Cost: $12,000 (India) or $14,000 (China, Spain) incl accommodation, meals

Main topics: New thinking on business strategy; customer focus; value orientation; human resources and organisational capabilities; managing international interdependencies; operations and technology; the global economy

■ Managing International Alliances

Location: Executive Education Center, Ann Arbor, MI, US

Participants: Managers responsible for the formulation and implementation of global competitive strategies

Frequency: Twice a year

Duration: 3 days

Cost: $2,900 incl accommodation, meals, materials

Aims: To provide participants with an analytical framework for engaging in joint ventures, selecting joint-venture partners and designing management and control structures for joint ventures

Main topics: Strategic alliance as a management process; partner selection and negotiations; implementation of alliance strategies; alliances in non-traditional markets; critical tasks in alliance management; management processes in alliance firms

■ Managing International Operations in Global Markets

Location: Executive Education Center, Ann Arbor, MI, US

Participants: Managers and specialists entering foreign markets, developing strategies for global operations, operating in foreign locations; newly appointed country managers

Frequency: Twice a year

Duration: 5 days

Cost: $5,200 incl accommodation, meals, materials

Aims: To provide participants with an understanding of the complex global competitive environment

Main topics: Entry strategies and tactics; effective approaches to international markets; cultural dimensions of international business; managing international operations in regional markets; financing strategies for multinational operations; economics of foreign direct investment; foreign exchange and risk management; using international capital markets; strategies for global competition

Thunderbird—American Graduate School of International Management

■ Globalization: Merging Strategy with Action

Location: Thunderbird, Glendale, AZ, US

Participants: Upper-level managers (business unit, division or subsidiary heads) with international responsibilities

Frequency: Twice a year

Duration: 1 week (Sunday pm-Friday noon)

Cost: $4,500 incl accommodation, meals, materials

Aims: To improve global management skills; to enhance the ability to handle the issues of global competition; to relate personal and organisational goals to a broad strategic global setting

Main topics: Strategy in global industries; strategy implementation; international joint ventures and alliances; cross-cultural communication; international operations management

Europe excl UK

SDA Bocconi, Italy; ESADE, Spain; HEC Management Center, France; Rotterdam School of Management, Netherlands

▪ Programme for International Managers in Europe (PRIME)

Location: Vienna, Austria; Copenhagen, Denmark; Paris, France; Milan, Italy; Rotterdam, Netherlands; Barcelona, Spain

Participants: Executives with international responsibilities or potential

Frequency: Once a year

Duration: 5 weeks

Cost: Ecu12,000 incl taxes; Ecu4,000 for accommodation

Aims: To develop international awareness and the international managerial skills of participants

Main topics: Environment and visions; strategic decision-making; leadership; key business skills; organisation and performance

Notes: PRIME is a joint venture comprising Copenhagen Business School, Denmark; ESADE Business School, Spain; HEC Management Center, France; Rottterdam School of Management, Netherlands; SDA Bocconi, Italy; and WU-Wien, Austria. The programme involves sponsoring companies with the aim of achieving the benefits of both open and tailored programmes

ESADE—Escuela Superior de Administración y Dirección de Empresas

▪ Internationalising Small Businesses: Defining and Applying Strategy

Location: ESADE, Barcelona, Spain

Participants: Senior managers and entrepreneurs

Frequency: Once a year

Duration: 144 hours over 5 months (Fridays 9 am-6.45 pm)

Cost: Pta585,000

Aims: To examine and analyse the management styles and strategies of fast-growing, medium-sized companies

Main topics: Analysis of key issues for business competitiveness; diagnosis of participants' businesses' competitiveness; preparation of internationalisation plans for participants' businesses

Groupe CPA

■ European Management Programme

Location: Paris, France

Participants: Senior managers seeking a better understanding of the European environment

Frequency: Once a year

Duration: 1 week

Cost: n/a

Aims: To enhance awareness of competitive trends and EU policy; to provide a new perspective on European and world trends; to increase awareness of cultural diversity and provide new techniques for managing multicultural teams

Main topics: Strategic management; cross-cultural management; international alliances; cultural conflict and organisational change

Notes: The programme is offered by a consortium of 6 European schools: Groupe CPA, EADA (Spain), ISTUD (Italy), USW (Germany), CSC (Czech Republic) and POHTP (Finland)

IMD—International Institute for Management Development

■ Accelerating International Growth

Location: IMD, Lausanne, Switzerland

Participants: Managers responsible for their company's international expansion at the corporate level

Frequency: Once a year

Duration: 5 days

Cost: Swfr8,000

Aims: Explores various ways of handling the challenges faced by executives who have responsibility for establishing and developing the international activities of their companies

Main topics: Global strategy; global mindset; global human resources; alliances; learning from international growth

Notes: This strategy programme emphasises the soft aspects of global expansion that are less frequently covered in other programmes, but are most relevant for front-line managers with international responsibilities

INSEAD—European Institute of Business Administration

■ International Executive Programme

Location: INSEAD, Fontainebleau, France

Participants: Vice-presidents, managing directors, regional and senior functional managers, senior engineers

Frequency: Twice a year

Duration: 6 weeks

Cost: FFr135,000 incl some meals, materials

Aims: To provide a complete management development experience, including knowledge and skills on which to build in future years

Main topics: Organisational behaviour; human resource management; financial management; economic and political analysis; marketing management; accounting and control; quality and operations management; information technology; strategic management

Notes: The programme uses a general management simulation exercise, SIGMA, which is designed for executives who need a comprehensive and global view of their businesses

■ International Manufacturing Programme

Location: INSEAD, Fontainebleau, France

Participants: Manufacturing and technical directors; production, plant and quality managers

Frequency: Once a year

Duration: 2 weeks

Cost: FFr45,000 incl some meals, materials

Aims: To analyse the changing rules in manufacturing and production management and their implications for managers

Main topics: Global trends in manufacturing; managing global factory networks; managing global supply chains; managing quality; managing Internet products and process technologies; performance measures and activity-based costing; work design and international industrial relations; Asia and the "Pacific Century"; green manufacturing; developing core manufacturing competence

■ Managerial Skills for International Business

Location: INSEAD, Fontainebleau, France

Participants: Division managers, marketing directors, HR vice-presidents, regional managers, international project leaders

Frequency: Once a year

Duration: 2 weeks

Cost: FFr51,000 incl some meals, materials

Aims: To enhance cross-cultural management skills, understand international team working and tackle global organisation management

Main topics: Personal adaptability; cross-cultural skills; building the transnational network

---

■ Managing Multinational Enterprise: the Renewal Challenge

Location: INSEAD, Fontainebleau, France

Participants: Chief executives, general managers, group functional directors, executive vice-presidents, managing directors

Frequency: Once a year

Duration: 8 days

Cost: FFr52,000 incl some meals, materials

Aims: To provide participants with an opportunity and a structure to discuss and learn from best practice

Main topics: Strategic renewal; organisation renewal; the changing context for international business

---

Maastricht School of Management

■ Advanced Strategy in Global Enterprises

Location: Maastricht School of Management, Maastricht, Netherlands

Participants: Senior managers with planning responsibilities and at least 7 years' business experience

Frequency: Once a year

Duration: 2 1-week modules

Cost: n/a

Aims: To address major strategic challenges in global and domestic competition

Main topics: Global competition: winners and losers; managing industry foresight; developing capabilities for global advantage; building customer value; building alliances and network organisations; managing alliances and acquisitions; building and managing global companies; strategies for global alliances; managing corporate transformation

Rest of world

Wits Business School—University of the Witwatersrand

- ## Global Business Strategy

Location: Wits Business School, Johannesburg, South Africa

Participants: Senior managers

Frequency: Once a year

Duration: 5 days

Cost: R7,350 incl materials, meals

Aims: To provide participants with an understanding of the challenges facing South African companies in the global business environment and help them develop insights into how to overcome these challenges effectively

Main topics: Market entry; standardisation versus adaptation; international finance; human resources; international operations; global competitive advantage

Leadership programmes

A surprising number of leadership programmes are being offered at present. In an age of empowerment and teamworking, the quest to acquire leadership skills remains. After being neglected for many years, the study, research and teaching of leadership has grown rapidly with no let-up in the number of permutations and new angles on the subject.

Leadership programmes fall into a number of categories. First are the programmes aimed at high-potential managers. Their aim is to uncover and ignite any latent leadership potential. Second are those programmes targeted at senior leaders and those aimed at senior managers with a strong strategic orientation.

Third are programmes covering the mechanics of leadership, the skills which leaders need to acquire. A rapidly expanding area is that of leading teams. Group and team leadership is fashionable at present, as is the topic of leading change. Lastly, there are a small number of programmes that aim to develop leadership skills within particular groups, such as women managers or African-American managers.

Programmes are arranged alphabetically by provider in the following regions:

North America

The Anderson School at UCLA—Executive Education Programs

■ African-American Leadership Institute

Location: The Anderson School at UCLA, Los Angeles, CA, US

Participants: African-American executives and managers

Frequency: Twice a year

Duration: 4 days

Cost: $4,250 incl accommodation, meals, books, materials

Aims: To acquire the critical knowledge and skills to succeed as an African-American executive in today's business and social environment and to address leadership issues from a personal, interpersonal and organisational perspective

Main topics: Leadership; mentoring and personal development; successful career-building; team leadership and the group process; entrepreneurship; diversity and affirmative action; conversations about power

■ Leadership and Team Effectiveness Program

Location: The Anderson School at UCLA, Los Angeles, CA, US

Participants: Executives and managers with significant responsibility and professional experience

Frequency: Once a year

Duration: 6 days

Cost: $4,500 incl accommodation, meals, books, materials

Aims: To provide participants with the tools to address stressful demands and allow them to size up situations quickly and act effectively

Main topics: Learning when to be participative, when to be autocratic, and when to integrate and employ both approaches simultaneously; utilising teams and making them effective; using innovative techniques to analyse your leadership style

Babson College—School of Executive Education

■ Leadership and Influence

Location: Babson College, Wellesley, MA, US

Participants: Senior and middle managers

Frequency: Twice a year

Duration: 5 days

Cost: $4,300 incl accommodation, meals

Aims: To explore vision, teamwork and other leadership competencies

Main topics: Vision and communication; power and alliances; team development; coaching

Notes: This programme requires a pre-programme questionnaire on the leadership style of participants. It uses case studies, role simulations, peer reviews, video analysis and outdoor team-building

Carlson School of Management—University of Minnesota

■ Advanced Leadership Program

Location: Carlson School, Minneapolis, MN, US; West Bank Campus, Minneapolis, MN, US

Participants: Senior managers

Frequency: Once a year

Duration: 3 days

Cost: $2,000 incl materials

Aims: To enable participants to assume their executive leadership responsibilities and expand their long-term influence throughout their business environment and community

Main topics: Leadership trends, leadership choices, authenticity; paradoxes of leadership, rethinking competition, new paradigms; creative use of power; large-scale organisational transformation: how to accomplish fast and effective change without losing organisational identity; leadership and improvisation

University of Chicago—Graduate School of Business

■ **Enhancing Leadership Performance: the Leader as Teacher**

Location: Gleacher Center, University of Chicago Graduate School of Business, Chicago, IL, US

Participants: Vice-presidents, general managers, division and department heads, chief finance officers, chief operating officers

Frequency: 4 times a year

Duration: 5 days

Cost: $3,950 incl some meals, materials

Aims: To expand participants' conception of the leader's role and equip them to provide creative leadership in their organisations

Main topics: Exploring the teaching component in leadership; what's happening on your "watch"?; the metaphor of theatre as it relates to the individual as leader-teacher; strengthening performance skills as a leader-teacher; examining power in the role of the leader-teacher; injecting creativity into the role of the leader-teacher .

Columbia Business School

■ **Leading and Managing People**

Location: Arden House, Harriman, NY, US

Participants: Senior managers and heads of large corporations

Frequency: 5 times a year

Duration: 1 week (Sunday pm-Friday pm)

Cost: $5,600 incl accommodation, meals, materials

Aims: To equip managers for today's constantly changing business climate

Main topics: Managerial decision-making; feedback and recognition as management tools; team leadership; redeveloping the mature professional; managing change: exploring underlying assumptions; dimensions of culture and leader/manager behaviour; group dynamics; organisational culture and integrating feedback; leadership styles and teamwork

Notes: The tools used in the programme include the Burke-Litwin model of organisation performance and change and the Myers-Brigg type indicator of individual information processing and communication style

Darden Executive Education—University of Virginia

■ Creating the Future: the Challenge of Transformational Leadership

Location: Darden School, Charlottesville, VA, US

Participants: Senior executives

Frequency: Twice a year

Duration: 5 days

Cost: $4,950

Aims: To challenge executives to think in new ways about the future of their businesses and provide fresh perspectives on leadership strategies

Main topics: The challenge to executive leadership; the power of paradigms; creating a powerful new vision; mobilising commitment to the vision; translating vision into action; institutionalising the vision; leadership in action

■ Leadership for Extraordinary Performance

Location: Darden School, Charlottesville, VA, US

Participants: Senior managers

Frequency: 3 times a year

Duration: 5 days

Cost: $4,950 incl accommodation, meals

Aims: To nurture participants' clarity of vision and personal leadership

Main topics: Leadership practices and assumptions; high performance; performance breakthroughs; garnering commitment; coaching; feedback; mastering technology for results management

■ Power and Leadership

Location: Darden School, Charlottesville, VA, US

Participants: Managers who want to improve their leadership skills

Frequency: Twice a year

Duration: 5 days

Cost: $4,600 incl accommodation, meals

Aims: To enable managers to become more effective leaders

Main topics: General leadership framework; six steps to more effective leadership; language of leadership; values and style; ethical issues; goal setting; perspectives on leadership style

Fisher College of Business—The Ohio State University

■ Leadership Development for Women Managers

Location: Fisher College of Business, Columbus, OH, US

Participants: Women who want to improve their capacity to lead others

Frequency: Once a year

Duration: 3 days

Cost: $1,195

Aims: To develop and enhance the leadership potential of women managers

Main topics: The practices of exemplary leaders; legal issues for empowerment; lessons from experience; leadership, personality and teamwork; negotiations and conflict resolution

Notes: This programme includes outdoor leadership exercises

Goizueta Business School—Emory University

■ Developing Leaders in High-Potential Managers

Location: Goizueta Business School, Atlanta, GA, US

Participants: Senior and middle managers

Frequency: Once a year

Duration: 2 weeks (2 1-week modules)

Cost: $6,195 incl meals, materials

Aims: To help participants strengthen their analytical and managerial skills

Main topics: Topical perspectives on global management; concepts of business strategy; marketing concepts and market segmentation; relationship marketing; evaluating financial performance; quality; managerial accounting; corporate financial decision-making; learning through diagnosis in contemporary organisations; leading and implementing change; managing in the new team environment; organisational culture

Harvard Business School

■ **Owner/President Management Program**

Location: Harvard Business School, Boston, MA, US

Participants: Owners and chief executives of large companies

Frequency: Once a year

Duration: 3 weeks per year for 3 consecutive years

Cost: $14,250 incl accommodation, most meals, materials

Aims: To teach participants how to become more effective chief executives

Main topics: Managing growth to avoid outrunning cash flow; anticipating and dealing with changes in a volatile business environment; understanding the advantages of smaller companies when dealing with larger and more established firms; improving participants' ability to manage the transition in their role and style as the company grows

Johnson Graduate School of Management—Cornell University

■ **Strategic Leadership in an Uncertain World**

Location: Cornell University, Ithaca, NY, US

Participants: Senior managers

Frequency: Twice a year

Duration: 1 week

Cost: $4,500 incl meals, materials

Aims: To help participants assess their leadership skills, master the process of scenario planning and corporate strategy, and maximise their ability to lead change in their organisations

Main topics: Uncertainty and the call to action; 360-degree feedback; scenario planning; group decision-making; corporate strategy; leading organisational change

Notes: This programme includes a strategic computer simulation

Jesse H Jones Graduate School of Management—Rice University

■ Leadership Skill Development

Location: Rice University, Houston, TX, US

Participants: Individuals who are now or expect to be in leadership positions in their organisations

Frequency: Twice a year

Duration: 5 days over 2 months

Cost: n/a

Aims: To gain insights into the behaviour of others and acquire the skills necessary to become more effective leaders and improve performance

Main topics: Effective leadership; conveying expectations; effective delegation; leadership styles; developing leadership skills; innovation as a function of leadership

J L Kellogg Graduate School of Management—Northwestern University

■ Reinventing Leadership

Location: James L Allen Center, Evanston, IL, US

Participants: Executives who wish to develop personally as leaders and as people and maximise their managerial effectiveness

Frequency: Twice a year

Duration: 6 days

Cost: $4,400 incl accommodation, meals, materials

Aims: To help participants develop new strategies for maximising their leadership performance

Main topics: Leadership key success factors; foundations of leadership; the learning organisation; work, power and emotions; benchmarking your personal leadership skills; ethics and leadership; implementing a personal leadership plan

Kenan-Flagler Business School—University of North Carolina at Chapel Hill

■ **Leadership 2000**

Location: University of North Carolina, Chapel Hill, NC, US

Participants: Senior executives

Frequency: Once a year

Duration: 2 weeks

Cost: $10,500

Aims: To change perceptions of emergent and existing business reality to open the possibility for leadership

Main topics: Leadership in a changing environment; trends affecting corporate strategy; role of government; managing technology; building an effective global organisation

University of Michigan Business School

■ **Leading Change**

Location: Executive Education Center, Ann Arbor, MI, US

Participants: Senior executives responsible for large-scale change

Frequency: Twice a year

Duration: 5 days

Cost: $5,200 incl accommodation, meals, materials

Aims: To provide participants with the perspective and skills base necessary to lead change and conduct successful interventions

Main topics: Creating direction, commitment, capability, adaptability and sustainability

Notes: Each participant shares a description of the change initiative which they are planning their organisation. Using a personal action plan workbook, participants and teams will develop focused action for their own particular requirements

Owen Graduate School of Management—Vanderbilt University

■ The Leadership Development Program

Location: Owen Graduate School of Management, TN, US

Participants: Senior line managers responsible for the performance of their units

Frequency: Twice a year

Duration: 3 days

Cost: $1,395 incl most meals, materials

Aims: To enhance participants' ability to improve bottom-line results

Main topics: Current leadership issues; leader versus manager; leadership model; personal vision; Myers-Brigg and leadership implications; becoming a manager; leadership communication; vision statements; leadership courage; the four temperaments; mindfulness; integrity

The Mary Jean and Frank P Smeal College of Business Administration—Pennsylvania State University

■ Global Leadership Program

Location: Penn State University, PA, US

Participants: General and line managers with global responsibilities, managers preparing for international assignments

Frequency: Once a year

Duration: 1 week

Cost: $4,500 incl accommodation, meals, materials

Aims: To provide an overview of global business strategy development and global economics

Main topics: Strategy development; global economics; role of the general manager; international finance; cultural differences; impact of social economic and political environments on business strategy; conducting business internationally

■ Program for Strategic Leadership

Location: Penn State University, PA, US

Participants: Senior and upper-middle managers

Frequency: Twice a year

Duration: 2 weeks

Cost: $8,100 incl accommodation, meals, materials

Aims: To investigate how organisations function in a rapidly changing environment

Main topics: Leadership and the management process; corporate strategy; implementing change; executive team-building and reward systems; financial planning and control

Notes: This programme includes a 360-degree feedback instrument and computerised business simulation

University of South Carolina—Daniel Management Center

■ Leadership Competencies for the 21st Century

Location: Daniel Management Center, Columbia, SC, US

Participants: Senior and middle managers who want to achieve a higher degree of managerial effectiveness

Frequency: Twice a year

Duration: $4\frac{1}{2}$ days

Cost: $1,995

Aims: To use self-assessment and competency development to provide the skills necessary for effective leadership

Main topics: Effective leadership styles and organisational structures; leading strategically; coaching and empowering; putting leadership into action; individual and organisational change; perceptions of behaviour

Notes: This programme uses 360-degree feedback as well as individual coaching and group simulations

■ Leadership Through People Skills

Location: Daniel Management Center, Columbia, SC, US

Participants: Upper-level and middle managers who can manage subordinates and want to extend their skills to peers and superiors

Frequency: 3 times a year

Duration: $4\frac{1}{2}$ days

Cost: $1,595

Aims: To teach managers how to deal with people at all levels

Main topics: Managing peers, superiors and subordinates; coaching skills; self-awareness

Stanford Graduate School of Business—Stanford University

■ Leading and Managing Change

Location: Graduate School of Business, Stanford, CA, US

Participants: Senior managers

Frequency: Once a year

Duration: 2 weeks

Cost: $10,500 incl accommodation, meals, books, study materials

Aims: To help managers understand the key role that leadership plays in effecting change and in addressing the planning and activities required to move organisations in new directions

Main topics: The role of leadership in change (incl models of organisation, negotiation strategies, managing group conflict, empowering others); strategies and technologies of change (cross-cultural change, process redesign, building on core competencies, building visionary companies, overcoming resistance to change, implementing human resource change, creating innovative organisations)

Thunderbird—American Graduate School of International Management

■ Global Leadership Certificate

Location: Thunderbird, Glendale, AZ, US; Tempe, AZ, US

Participants: Middle managers with 3-10 years' experience, technical professionals making the transition to management, managers and team leaders about to take on more responsibilities

Frequency: Twice a year

Duration: 1 evening per week over 4 months

Cost: $1,950

Aims: To offer participants the broader knowledge they need to work cross-functionally and cross-culturally within their organisations

Main topics: Leadership challenges and opportunities; market relations in the global economy; customer service; competitive advantage through strategy; financial accounting; financial management; marketing management; production and operations management; organisational culture; management of IT; negotiating across cultures; managing change; leading change

Notes: At the end of the programme participants are awarded certificates of accomplishment

Wharton School—University of Pennsylvania—Aresty Institute of Executive Education

■ Executive Team Dynamics: When All the Members Are Leaders

Location: Wharton School, Philadelphia, PA, US

Participants: Senior managers

Frequency: Twice a year

Duration: 5 days

Cost: $5,950 incl accommodation, meals

Aims: To examine the common pitfalls of team dynamics and learn strategies for overcoming them

Main topics: Group development; performance and group processes; improving team performance; authority and leadership; intergroup relations

■ Leading Organizational Change

Location: Wharton School, Philadelphia, PA, US

Participants: Senior managers

Frequency: Twice a year

Duration: 5 days

Cost: $5,950 incl accommodation, meals

Aims: To help participants understand systems and current topics in organisational change

Main topics: The process of change; the role of leadership; change implementation; technology and change; globalisation; stress management; downsizing; paradoxes of change; growth management; strategic alliances; customer-driven change; teaming

University of Wisconsin-Madison—Graduate School of Business

■ Leadership Institute

Location: Management Institute, University of Wisconsin-Madison, WI, US

Participants: Executives, managers, team leaders

Frequency: Twice a year

Duration: 4½ days

Cost: n/a

Aims: To teach participants how to become more effective leaders

Main topics: Practice and theory of leadership; strategic thinking; self-management

UK

Ashridge Management College

■ Business Leadership for Women

Location: Ashridge Management College, Berkhamsted, UK

Participants: Woman executives responsible for leading, motivating and influencing others

Frequency: Twice a year

Duration: 5 days

Cost: £2,700 incl accommodation, meals

Aims: To enable participants to combine work on leadership skills with personal development

Main topics: Qualities of leadership; organisational analysis; leading groups and teams; leadership skills; strategy; power and influence; using and building networks

Notes: There are opportunities for personal counselling and one-to-one feedback

■ Leadership Development Programme

Location: Ashridge Management College, Berkhamsted, UK

Participants: Senior and middle managers wishing to review their personal impact and approach to leadership

Frequency: 11 times a year

Duration: 5 days

Cost: £3,990 incl accommodation, meals

Aims: To enable managers to explore their leadership skills, style and potential and to generate a personal action plan for future development

Main topics: Leadership models; utilising group resources; leadership and decision-making; leadership in different situations; leadership, learning and development; one-to-one professional and peer feedback; setting and achieving goals for personal development

Notes: This programme is presented under licence from the US Center for Creative Leadership and includes 360-degree pre-programme questionnaires. Participation in this programme can lead towards the Ashridge Diploma in General Management

University of Bradford Management Centre

■ Successfully Managing People

Location: Bradford Management Centre, Bradford, UK; Paris, France

Participants: Senior and middle managers

Frequency: Once a year

Duration: 5 days

Cost: £1,970 incl accommodation

Aims: To help managers identify and improve the key aspects of their leadership skills and their ability to manage people

Main topics: Leadership styles; managerial decisions; managing conflict; participating effectively in group decisions; leading meetings; improving personal management effectiveness

Notes: This programme is based on a successful Canadian course

Cranfield School of Management

■ The Director as Strategic Leader

Location: Cranfield School of Management, Cranfield, UK

Participants: Directors of all types of organisation

Frequency: 3 times a year

Duration: 5 days

Cost: £3,400 incl accommodation, meals

Aims: To enable participants to develop an effective strategy for their organisations and understand the personal actions needed to implement it effectively

Main topics: Strategic management; environmental, industry and competitive analysis; strategy formulation; implementing strategy; leadership to implement strategy; application of the concepts

Notes: This programme uses lectures, case studies, simulations, exercises, video feedback, profile questionnaires and guest speakers

- **High Performance Leadership**

  Location: Cranfield School of Management, Cranfield, UK

  Participants: Senior managers and directors

  Frequency: Twice a year

  Duration: 2 3-day modules

  Cost: £3,075 incl accommodation

  Aims: To provide participants with an overview of leadership and allow them to share experiences with other business leaders

  Main topics: Personality theory; personality variables; emotion and leadership; power and charisma; the nature of responsibility

Henley Management College

- **Corporate Leadership Programme**

  Location: Henley Management College, Henley-on-Thames, UK

  Participants: Directors, senior managers

  Frequency: Twice a year

  Duration: 5 days

  Cost: £2,800

  Aims: To provide an appreciation of the role of the chief executive

  Main topics: Each day a practising chief executive shares insights into the strategies and styles they have found successful; contributions on key issues from management specialists.

  Notes: Nominations for this programme are usually made by a chief executive or chairman

London Business School

■ Leadership for Change: Understanding and Action

Location: London Business School, London, UK

Participants: Chief executives, division heads, heads of functions

Frequency: Once a year

Duration: 5 days

Cost: £4,350

Aims: To enable participants to analyse the processes of change in organisations and to focus on the role of the leader

Main topics: Organisational change (exploring the analysis, envisioning, planning and management of change); personal change (giving feedback on participants' own change management and leadership skills)

Notes: Participants' strengths and weaknesses are evaluated with 360-degree surveys (using questionnaires completed by their bosses, peers and subordinates) and the results are compared with the school's databank on leaders

Roffey Park Management Institute

■ The Strategic Leadership Programme

Location: Roffey Park, Horsham, UK

Participants: Senior managers

Frequency: 3 times a year

Duration: 7 days (1 3-day session and 4 1-day sessions)

Cost: £3,100 incl accommodation, meals

Aims: To link leadership to strategic direction; identify relevant and appropriate patterns of leadership; integrate strategic management and organisational change; and to explore the concept of organisational cultures and develop strategies for working with them

Main topics: Leadership; strategy; organisational change; the link between strategy and leadership

Notes: Participants are asked to supply a personal history before attending so that topics covered can be tailored to their needs. During the programme they will identify and plan a personal learning package. The second part of the programme consists of 4 1-day meetings

Templeton College

■ The Oxford Strategic Leadership Programme

Location: Templeton College, Oxford, UK

Participants: Chief executives, managing directors, divisional and regional directors, corporate planners, economic advisers, heads of government departments

Frequency: Twice a year

Duration: 1 week

Cost: £6,000 incl accommodation, meals, books

Aims: To challenge preconceived and traditional thinking about leadership and enable participants to clarify their own thinking about their leadership roles

Main topics: Leading-edge frameworks for thinking about leadership; practical interventions open to leaders; the role and relevance of personal feedback

Notes: The programme (now in its 15th year) uses a mix of new ideas, experience and syndicate work to enable participants to define their current and future leadership roles. It makes extensive use of the traditional Oxford combination of tutorials and debate among peers

CMC Graduate School of Business

■ Executive Leadership

Location: CMC Graduate School of Business, Prague, Czech Republic

Participants: Experienced managers

Frequency: Once a year

Duration: 3 3-day modules

Cost: n/a

Aims: To teach participants how to manage themselves and their staff better for their own benefit and their organisation

Main topics: Managing ourselves; people in a group; people in an organisation

IMD—International Institute for Management Development

■ International Program for Board Members

Location: IMD, Lausanne, Switzerland

Participants: Experienced and newly appointed executive or non-executive directors

Frequency: Once a year

Duration: 3 days

Cost: Swfr8,000 incl some meals, materials

Aims: To contribute to the ongoing discussion of corporate governance

Main topics: The board proper; the role of the CEO and top management; the shareholders/stakeholders; the auditors

■ Job of the Chief Executive

Location: Singapore Institute of Management, Singapore

Participants: Top and senior managers of local companies and subsidiaries of multinational companies in Asia and the Pacific Rim

Frequency: Once a year

Duration: 6 days

Cost: S$5,500

Aims: To develop systematic ways of approaching the multifaceted job and challenges faced by senior executives in the growing markets of Asia and the Pacific Rim

Main topics: Overview of the job of the CEO; change; strategy and policy-making; structure and systems; marketing; finance; acquisitions; implementing strategy; negotiating; motivating

Notes: This programme has been offered by IMD for 18 consecutive years

■ Leading Corporate Renewal

Location: IMD, Lausanne, Switzerland

Participants: Senior and middle managers

Frequency: Once a year

Duration: 2 weeks

Cost: Swfr14,000 incl some meals, materials

Aims: To help managers develop viable change action plans, implement change and lead people to action

Main topics: Linking change to strategy; making change happen; learning to change relationships

■ Leading the Technology Enterprise

Location: Lausanne, Thun and Münchenwiler, Switzerland

Participants: High-potential, technically trained managers preparing for senior general management in technology-based enterprises

Frequency: Once a year

Duration: 2 3-week and 1 2-week module over 9 months

Cost: Swfr36,000

Aims: To help participants build the general management and leadership abilities required in a technology-intensive 21st century

Main topics: Core business competencies; technology, strategy and general management; global competitiveness and responsible progress

Notes: This programme is run in conjunction with the Center for Technology and Management (CTM), which was founded in 1994 by the two Swiss Federal Institutes of Technology, ETH Zürich and EPF Lausanne. CTM provides an organisational umbrella for executive development activities, interdisciplinary research and networking among industry and academic leaders

- ## Seminar for Senior Executives

Location: IMD, Lausanne, Switzerland

Participants: Senior managers

Frequency: Twice a year

Duration: 18 days

Cost: Swfr22,500 incl some meals, materials

Aims: To help senior managers redefine their priorities and agenda to reflect the new global challenge of leadership

Main topics: Setting direction and broadening strategic horizons; creating effective organisations and leading; future leadership challenges: global competitiveness and responsible progress; forces shaping the future global environment; redefining the senior executive's agenda

INSEAD—European Institute of Business Administration

- ## The Challenge of Leadership: Developing your Emotional Intelligence

Location: INSEAD, Fontainebleau, France

Participants: Chief executives, managing directors, general managers, executive directors

Frequency: Once a year

Duration: 3 1-week modules over 5 months

Cost: FFr104,000 incl some meals, materials

Aims: To improve leadership performance by increasing participants' understanding of how human behaviour affects the functioning of their organisations

Main topics: The executive life; organisational diagnosis and change; practical problem-solving and career planning

Notes: Intervals of around 8 weeks between modules allow participants to test classroom concepts in business situations

Rest of world

Australian Graduate School of Management— University of New South Wales

■ Leadership and Decision Making

Location: Australian Graduate School of Management, Sydney, Australia

Participants: Senior and middle operating and functional managers

Frequency: Once a year

Duration: 3 days

Cost: A$3,495 incl accommodation, meals, materials

Aims: To provide a range of opportunities for participants to build on their managerial experience and extend their skills

Main topics: Effective leadership; decision-making; communication with subordinates and colleagues

Notes: Information collected from participants and their subordinates before the programme is analysed by an AGSM computer program. Participants learn how to interpret and benefit from this audit of the strengths and weaknesses of their own management strategy

Curtin Business School

■ Facilitation Skills for Team Leaders

Location: QV1 Campus, Graduate School of Business, Perth, Australia

Participants: Managers who conduct team meetings; supervisors and leaders

Frequency: Once a year

Duration: 5½ days

Cost: A$1,400

Aims: To teach managers and team leaders key skills to facilitate teams and meetings

Main topics: Key skills for facilitators; conducting successful meetings; SAID and LENS techniques; brainstorming and decision-making groups; group process, ground rules and setting objectives; encouraging participation and dealing with resistance

Indian Institute of Management

■ Management of Excellence by Chief Executives

Location: IIM, Vastrapur, Ahmedabad, India

Participants: Chief executives, heads of divisions

Frequency: Once a year

Duration: 3 days

Cost: Rs33,000 ($1,700 for participants from outside India) incl accommodation, materials

Aims: To develop an awareness of what excellence means, different forms of excellence and ways of pursuing these forms

Main topics: Concept of management excellence; approaches to management excellence; the difference it can make to the effectiveness of the organisation; different types and models of management excellence; the chief executive as a change agent for corporate excellence

Macquarie Graduate School of Management— Macquarie University

■ The Director as a Strategic Leader

Location: Macquarie Graduate School, Sydney, Australia

Participants: Chief executives, general managers, functional directors

Frequency: Twice a year

Duration: 4 days

Cost: A$4,950

Aims: To provide a comprehensive and practical framework to challenge the long-term thinking of executives who have strategic responsibility within an organisation, emphasising the interchange of ideas and experiences among participants

Main topics: Strategic management; environmental, industry and competitive analysis; strategy formulation at the corporate and business unit levels and the relationship between them; implementing strategy

Notes: A particular feature is the high workshop content where participants in non-competing groups can dissect and discuss each other's strategic problems

■ Leadership in Senior Management

Location: Macquarie Graduate School, Sydney, Australia

Participants: Senior executives, functional managers

Frequency: Twice a year

Duration: 4 days residential; 5 days non-residential

Cost: A$3,950 (residential); A$3,600 (non-residential)

Aims: To challenge current thinking and question traditional approaches to the function of leadership

Main topics: Vision; leadership; quality; people and performance

Monash Mt Eliza Business School

■ Foundations of Leadership

Location: Mt Eliza, Australia

Participants: Middle managers, supervisors

Frequency: 3 times a year

Duration: 3 days

Cost: A$3,550

Aims: To introduce participants to the concepts of leadership

Main topics: Personal leadership skills and styles; conflict resolution; communication skills

Notes: This programme is conducted under licence from the Center for Creative Leadership, Greensboro, US

■ Leadership Development Programme

Location: Mt Eliza, Australia

Participants: Senior and middle managers

Frequency: 8 times a year

Duration: 6 days

Cost: A$5,950

Aims: To provide participants with an action plan to become more productive in their work and effective in leading others

Main topics: Contemporary leadership concepts; in-depth assessment of personal leadership styles through various feedback instruments by work colleagues including benchmarks

Notes: This programme is conducted under licence from the Center for Creative Leadership, Greensboro, US

■ Leadership in Action: the Looking Glass Experience

Location: Mt Eliza, Australia

Participants: Senior and middle managers

Frequency: 6 times a year

Duration: 5 days

Cost: A$5,450

Aims: To provide participants with an action plan for change

Main topics: A highly interactive simulation (Looking Glass) concentrating on the challenges of a company facing tough global competition

Notes: This programme is conducted under licence from the Center for Creative Leadership, Greensboro, US

■ Leading in Business

Location: Mt Eliza, Australia

Participants: Senior and middle managers

Frequency: 3 times a year

Duration: 5 days

Cost: A$4,550

Aims: To develop leadership skills and their application

Main topics: Gaining peak performance from staff; leading work teams; handling interpersonal relationships; developing management competencies in finance, strategy, marketing and human resource management

■ Leading High-Performance Teams

Location: Mt Eliza, Australia

Participants: Senior and middle managers involved in building and leading teams

Frequency: 3 times a year

Duration: 5 days

Cost: A$4,550

Aims: To enhance participants' knowledge of building and developing teams, interpersonal awareness and ability to provide accurate feedback

Main topics: The role of teams in organisations; the value of creativity and diversity in teams; the need for feedback in team development and functioning; conflict management; understanding team dynamics and facilitation skills

Notes: An in-depth analysis is made of participants' own work team dynamics through SYMLOG, a feedback instrument

Marketing programmes

Marketing programmes remain a fundamental part of executive education portfolios. It is notable that, over the last decade, such programmes have been targeted at more senior managers, and there has been a trend towards focusing on the more strategic elements of marketing. Strategic marketing programmes abound and they increasingly link marketing effectiveness to competitiveness. At a lower level there remains a wide variety of introductory and basic marketing programmes aimed at general managers, functional specialists and younger managers without a marketing background.

However, programmes that offer in-depth coverage of important issues, such as globalisation and the development of global brands, are scarce. Indeed, the two-week Marketing Leadership Forum (run by Duke's Fuqua School and London Business School) remains unique in its global coverage. Elsewhere, Thunderbird's Building Global Marketing Competitiveness is one of the few programmes which concentrates on international marketing.

Programmes are arranged alphabetically by provider in the following regions:

- North America (page 198)

- UK (page 210)

- Europe excluding UK (page 212)

- Rest of world (page 216)

North America

Amos Tuck School of Business

■ **Market-Driven Management Program**

Location: Amos Tuck School, Hanover, NH, US

Participants: Experienced marketing managers, general managers who must work closely with marketing managers

Frequency: Once a year

Duration: 5 days

Cost: $5,200 incl accommodation, meals, materials

Aims: To examine new concepts in delivering value to customers and developing customers as assets

Main topics: Creating customers as strategic assets; the potential of relationship marketing; how IT is redefining the key success factors in most industries; the vital role of a company's internal culture in its external focus on customer orientation

Berkeley Center for Executive Development—Haas School of Business

■ **Marketing 2001: Changing the Rules of the Game**

Location: Berkeley Centre for Executive Development, Berkeley, CA, US

Participants: Managers with operational responsibility for products and services, other managers who are concerned with the interface between the organisation and the market and are involved with customers and competitors

Frequency: Once a year

Duration: 4 days

Cost: $4,275 incl accommodation, meals, other social activities

Aims: To focus on the innovative concepts and techniques that leading-edge firms are employing to change the rules of the game and achieve superior performance

Main topics: A new framework for competition; developing market-driving strategies; designing and executing a winning value proposition; competing with information; information intensive strategies; building a knowledge portfolio; non-performance metrics; interactivity; rethinking organisational structure for competitive advantage

Carlson School of Management—University of Minnesota

■ Strategic Marketing Program

Location: Carlson School, Minneapolis, MN, US; West Bank Campus, Minneapolis, MN, US

Participants: Experienced managers with significant marketing responsibilities

Frequency: Once a year

Duration: 3 days

Cost: $2,200 incl meals, materials

Aims: To enhance the ability of experienced managers to develop and implement strategies that strengthen customer value and accelerate company growth

Main topics: Building a market orientation; achieving a strategic advantage; enhancing customer value; managing effective marketing partnerships; enhancing new product development success; managing mature brands for growth; effective marketing strategies

University of Chicago—Graduate School of Business

■ Strategic Marketing Planning

Location: Gleacher Center, University of Chicago Graduate School of Business, Chicago, IL, US

Participants: General managers, vice-presidents of marketing/sales, directors of marketing, product or brand managers, market analysts

Frequency: Twice a year

Duration: 5 days

Cost: $3,850 incl some meals, materials

Aims: To provide participants with the conceptual framework to develop, implement, evaluate and benchmark strategic marketing plans

Main topics: The strategic market planning process; industry and competitive analysis; creating competitive analysis; strategy implementation; analytical approaches to data-driven marketing

Columbia Business School

■ Competitive Marketing Strategy: Applications Workshop

Location: Arden House, Harriman, NY, US

Participants: Marketing vice-presidents and managers; product managers; business, product or marketing planners; directors and managers of market research/analysis; strategic planners

Frequency: Twice a year

Duration: 6 days

Cost: $5,200 incl accommodation, meals, materials

Aims: To teach participants how to make effective strategic marketing decisions by incorporating information on markets, customers and competitors

Main topics: Identifing and evaluating market opportunities; integrating market research analysis and market strategy; collecting and analysing customer data; analysing competitors; integration of marketing and technology; developing and implementing successful strategies

Notes: This programme is designed to integrate completely market research and market strategy

■ Marketing Management

Location: Arden House, Harriman, NY, US; Santa Barbara, CA, US

Participants: Managers responsible for the design and implementation of the marketing or product strategy; product, market or brand managers

Frequency: 6 times a year (once in Santa Barbara)

Duration: 1 week (Sunday pm-Friday pm)

Cost: $5,200 incl accommodation, meals, materials (Arden House); $4,500 excl accommodation, meals (Santa Barbara)

Aims: To help participants develop, execute and evaluate strategies for their products, services or markets

Main topics: The changing business environment and the need for market focus; achieving market focus; managing markets strategically; gaining a qualitative understanding of customer needs; developing market-focused strategies; designing and managing strong positioning platforms; pricing to value: strategies and tactics; analysing, predicting and managing competitors; integrated marketing: making strategy work; market 2000 and beyond

Notes: This programme has been running since 1963 and is updated annually

Darden Executive Education—University of Virginia

■ Strategic Marketing Management

Location: Darden School, Charlottesville, VA, US

Participants: Senior executives wishing to expand their marketing skills; marketing professionals with new roles

Frequency: Twice a year

Duration: 6 days

Cost: $5,200

Aims: To develop a knowledge of the concepts and skills necessary to create an integrated, comprehensive marketing strategy

Main topics: Consumer and buying process analysis; analytical techniques; segmentation and positioning; perceptual mapping; product/market evolution; cost and share leverage principles and relationships; marketing simulation

Fuqua School of Business—Duke University

■ Marketing Leadership Forum

Location: Fuqua School of Business, Durham, NC, US; London Business School, London, UK

Participants: Senior marketing executives

Frequency: Once a year

Duration: 2 weeks (2 1-week modules)

Cost: $11,900 incl accommodation, meals, materials, taxes

Aims: To provide a strong foundation for understanding forces that influence marketing executives' decision-making and offer insights into the crafting and implementation of effective strategies

Main topics: Strategies for global markets; trends and characteristics of the global environment; changes in the world economy; organisational structures capable of capitalising on local and global markets; key competencies for managers operating in a global company; global branding and creating customer value; implementation issues affecting market leadership; defending existing markets; growth topics; relationship marketing; new markets; price leadership; managing change and leadership

Notes: This programme is divided into 2 modules; the first is held at Fuqua, the second at London Business School

Goizueta Business School—Emory University

■ Marketing Strategies and Analysis for Competitive Advantage

Location: Goizueta Business School, Atlanta, GA, US

Participants: Marketing managers and directors, product managers, R&D managers, sales managers

Frequency: Twice a year

Duration: 1 week

Cost: $3,300 incl meals, materials

Aims: To teach participants the skills and concepts crucial to creating and implementing successful marketing strategies

Main topics: Marketing principles and strategy; competitor analysis; strategic options and market opportunities; understanding and using market research; market segmentation and targeting; resource allocation: tools and strategy; managing maturing markets; corporate financial decision-making; learning through diagnosis in contemporary organisations; globalisation for competitive advantage; evaluating market strategies

Notes: This programme uses a computer simulation

Harvard Business School

■ Strategic Marketing Management

Location: Harvard Business School, Boston, MA, US

Participants: General and senior managers in product management, marketing and customer services

Frequency: Once a year

Duration: 2 weeks

Cost: $9,500 incl accommodation, most meals, materials

Aims: To help participants understand the critical role of marketing in a corporation's overall success through discussions of advanced marketing concepts and provision of customer-oriented strategies

Main topics: Core marketing concepts and best contemporary practice; consumer-based track or business-to-business track; marketing and corporate strategy

Richard Ivey School of Business—University of Western Ontario

■ Marketing Management Program

Location: Spencer Hall, London, Ontario, Canada

Participants: Marketing managers with about 10 years' business experience; general managers, financial officers and operations managers who need to know more about the marketing function

Frequency: Twice a year

Duration: 2 weeks

Cost: C$9,350 incl accommodation, meals, materials

Aims: To strengthen participants' marketing and decision-making skills and improve their general management capabilities in an increasingly competitive global marketplace

Main topics: The marketplace and marketing issues; analysing the strengths, weaknesses, objectives and potential of the organisation; formulating marketing plans; corporate strategy

Johnson Graduate School of Management—Cornell University

■ Marketing Strategy

Location: Cornell University, Ithaca, NY, US

Participants: Marketing professionals, product and category managers, strategic planners, sales managers

Frequency: Once a year

Duration: 1 week

Cost: $4,300 incl accommodation, meals, materials

Aims: To help participants effectively analyse markets, identify future product and service markets, and formulate future marketing strategies

Main topics: Marketing strategy formulation process; finding unmet needs; strategic issues in new products; global markets; competitive positioning; market segmentation; analysing competitive strategies; developing customer-oriented strategies; advertising and brand equity strategies; allocating the marketing budget; pricing strategies

Jesse H Jones Graduate School of Management—Rice University

■ **Strategic Marketing of Products and Services**

Location: Rice University, Houston, TX, US

Participants: Owners and senior managers in smaller organisations; strategic planning, marketing and sales managers in medium-sized and larger organisations

Frequency: Twice a year

Duration: 4 days

Cost: n/a

Aims: To gain the tools necessary to develop a strategic marketing plan

Main topics: Creating and communicating superior customer value; analysing situations (including SWOT and PEST trends); strategy design (segmentation, targeting, positioning); strategy enactment (product, price, promotion, distribution)

Joseph M Katz Graduate School of Business— University of Pittsburgh

■ **Executive Course in Marketing Management**

Location: Katz Graduate School of Business, PA, US

Participants: Senior marketing managers

Frequency: Twice a year

Duration: 3 days

Cost: $745

Aims: To enable participants to conduct a marketing audit; develop new strategies; build customer focus and total quality; and segment markets and position products

Main topics: Conducting a marketing audit; customer satisfaction; organising the marketing function; developing new products; promotional programmes; positioning; competitive strategies; developing a marketing plan

Kenan-Flagler Business School—University of North Carolina at Chapel Hill

■ Marketing Strategy and Planning

Location: University of North Carolina, Chapel Hill, NC, US

Participants: Marketing managers

Frequency: 3 times a year

Duration: 3 days

Cost: $1,950

Aims: To review the fundamental principles of marketing strategy and planning

Main topics: Marketing-based management; the marketing environment; the basics of strategy development; planning marketing programmes; developing and implementing the marketing plan

McGill Executive Institute—McGill University

■ Basic Marketing Management

Location: McGill Executive Institute, Montreal, Canada

Participants: Marketing, product and sales managers; newcomers to marketing

Frequency: Twice a year

Duration: 4 days

Cost: C$1,595 incl lunches, materials

Aims: To enable participants to win market share and increase profits using the most effective current marketing strategies and techniques

Main topics: A marketing perspective; market segmentation; positioning strategy; market research; pricing strategies; consumer versus industrial markets; selling, selling, selling; the promotion decision; marketing communications for commercial clients; launching new products; customer service; marketing planning

■ Strategic Marketing

Location: McGill Executive Institute, Montreal, Canada; University of Toronto, Rotman School of Management, Toronto, Canada

Participants: Experienced marketing professionals; potential and newly appointed managers and supervisors

Frequency: 3 times a year

Duration: 3 days

Cost: C$1,595 incl lunches, materials

Aims: To acquire the training and skills necessary to increase profits and market share

Main topics: Placing an organisation in the commercial cycles of business; cross-industry sector commercial strategy; growth strategy; how to win competitive market wars; customer service strategy; consumer versus industrial marketing strategies; learning from the marketing crises of others

University of Michigan Business School

■ Marketing for the Non-Marketing Manager

Location: Executive Education Center, Ann Arbor, MI, US

Participants: Managers in corporate planning, engineering, finance, manufacturing, R&D, sales and general management who have no formal background in marketing

Frequency: Twice a year

Duration: 5 days

Cost: $5,100 incl accommodation, meals, materials

Aims: To provide participants with a clear understanding of the marketing function and enable them to work more effectively with the marketing team

Main topics: Orientation to marketing; the market planning process; the marketing information system in research and communication; marketing research; services marketing management; distribution

■ Strategic Marketing Planning

Location: Ann Arbor, US; Hong Kong; Singapore; Taipei, Taiwan; Bangkok, Thailand

Participants: Managers involved in the development of marketing plans

Frequency: 5 times a year (at Michigan)

Duration: 5 days

Cost: $5,200 incl accommodation, materials ($3,900 for programmes outside the US)

Aims: To help participants formulate and evaluate their marketing planning strategies

Main topics: Value-based market strategy; strategic market planning process; market research; segmentation and positioning; value creation and customer satisfaction; product development; brand equity; strategic marketing; communications

Owen Graduate School of Management—Vanderbilt University

■ Marketing Strategy

Location: Owen Graduate School of Management, TN, US

Participants: Senior and marketing managers

Frequency: Twice a year

Duration: 3 days

Cost: $1,395 incl most meals, materials

Aims: To help participants organise operations around customer needs, analyse sales and market trends, and plan strategies for growth

The Mary Jean and Frank P Smeal College of Business Administration—Pennsylvania State University

■ Marketing Strategy in Business Markets

Location: Penn State University, PA, US

Participants: Vice-presidents, directors and managers of marketing, sales, planning, new product development

Frequency: Twice a year

Duration: 1 week

Cost: $4,400 incl accommodation, meals, materials

Aims: To explore key issues in business-to-business marketing, develop a more strategic orientation and improve participants' ability to manage change

Main topics: Customer value definition and measurement; new product development; marketing strategy in business and corporate strategy; value pricing; market segmentation and positioning; integrated marketing communications; value chain marketing; globalisation

Stanford Graduate School of Business—Stanford University

■ **Marketing Management: A Strategic Perspective**

Location: Graduate School of Business, Stanford, CA, US

Participants: Senior executives in charge of marketing, executives whose work involves marketing

Frequency: Once a year

Duration: 2 weeks

Cost: $10,500 incl accommodation, meals, books, study materials

Aims: To help participants approach marketing as a strategic area reflecting the firm's overall business philosophy

Main topics: Relationship marketing; micromarketing; customer profitability and satisfaction; product development; channels of distribution; industry dynamics; competitor analysis; branding strategy; global marketing and the legal environment

Thunderbird—American Graduate School of International Management

■ **Building Global Marketing Competitiveness**

Location: Thunderbird, Glendale, AZ, US

Participants: Upper-level managers (business unit, division or subsidiary heads) with international responsibilities

Frequency: Twice a year

Duration: 1 week (Sunday pm-Friday noon)

Cost: $4,500 incl accommodation, meals

Aims: To broaden and strengthen global marketing competencies

Main topics: Dynamics of globalisation; market entry strategies; global brand management; financing international transactions; dynamics of emerging markets; market analysis; building relationships in a foreign environment

Wharton School—University of Pennsylvania—Aresty Institute of Executive Education

■ **Competitive Marketing Strategy**

Location: Wharton School, Philadelphia, PA, US

Participants: Senior and middle managers

Frequency: Twice a year

Duration: 5 days

Cost: $6,250 incl accommodation, meals

Aims: To develop an understanding of the competitive implications of marketing strategies

Main topics: Anticipating the competition's response; understanding the competition's strategies; strategy recognition; the simulation of competition; source of competitive advantage

University of Wisconsin-Madison—Graduate School of Business

■ **Competitive Strategy for Senior Executives**

Location: Management Institute, University of Wisconsin-Madison, WI, US

Participants: Executives, directors, managers

Frequency: Once a year

Duration: 3 days

Cost: n/a

Aims: To help participants focus on core competencies and new markets

Main topics: Competitive strategy and marketing; creating and delivering market-based value

UK

Ashridge Management College

■ **Brand Management Development Programme**

Location: Ashridge Management College, Berkhamsted, UK

Participants: High-potential managers

Frequency: Twice a year

Duration: 12 days

Cost: £5,050 incl accommodation, meals

Aims: To develop the ability to design and implement successful brand plans in the fast-moving, challenging environment of brand competition

Main topics: Key brand management issues; brand strategy; brand identity and the role of design; innovation and creativity; marketing finance; direct marketing; communicating the brand; managing relationships with agencies

■ **Business Development and Marketing Management**

Location: Ashridge Management College, Berkhamsted, UK

Participants: Managers who wish to improve their marketing effectiveness

Frequency: 3 times a year

Duration: 12 days

Cost: £5,400 incl accommodation, meals

Aims: To enable general managers and marketers to formulate integrated business strategies and plans in order to achieve a clearer market focus across the organisation

Main topics: Issues facing market-oriented companies; strategies for the elements of the marketing mix; options for business growth; marketing strategy; gaining competitive advantage; the impact of marketing decisions

Notes: Participation in this programme can lead to the Ashridge Diploma in General Management

Which executive programme? © The Economist Intelligence Unit Limited 1998

Cranfield School of Management

■ Strategic Marketing for Directors and Senior Managers

Location: Cranfield School of Management, Cranfield, UK

Participants: Directors, senior marketing managers

Frequency: 3 times a year

Duration: 3 days

Cost: £1,850 incl accommodation

Aims: To help participants understand the marketplace and develop and implement appropriate marketing strategies

Main topics: Strategic marketing management; relationship marketing; differentiation; managing innovation; achieving world-class marketing

London Business School

■ Marketing Leadership Forum

Location: Fuqua School of Business, Durham, NC, US; London Business School, London, UK

Participants: Marketing vice-presidents, marketing directors

Frequency: Once a year

Duration: 2 1-week modules

Cost: £7,000 incl accommodation, meals, taxes (but not travel)

Aims: To give senior marketing professionals an exclusive forum offering a chance for discussion and learning about key issues in marketing today

Main topics: The agenda for change in marketing (organisational design for global initiatives; being a global manager; the international business environment); the achievement of growth and market leadership (building and managing brands; creating customer value; international marketing); leading and managing change

Notes: This programme is divided into 2 modules; the first is at Fuqua, the second at London Business School

Europe excl UK

EAP—European School of Management

■ **Marketing D'Affaires Internationales**

Location: EAP International Executive Centre, Paris

Participants: Senior managers

Frequency: Once a year

Duration: 3 days

Cost: FFr10,000

Aims: To examine successful strategies in international marketing

Main topics: Project management; client relations; pricing

Notes: The open programme is taught in French. An in-company version of the programme can be taught in French or English

ESADE—Escuela Superior de Administración y Dirección de Empresas

■ **Marketing Management**

Location: ESADE, Barcelona, Spain; Madrid, Spain

Participants: Marketing managers

Frequency: Twice a year

Duration: 150 hours over 5 months (Mondays 9 am-6.45 pm)

Cost: Pta850,000

Aims: To provide participants with the tools to shape an overall vision of marketing-oriented management and design successful marketing strategies

Main topics: Threats, opportunities and changes affecting competitive environment; marketing strategies; results analysis to improve future business performance

HEC Executive Development Center

■ CESA Marketing

Location: HEC, Paris, France

Participants: Marketing, sales, advertising and brand managers

Frequency: Once a year

Duration: 15 days (3 5-day modules)

Cost: FFr42,000

Aims: To develop a global approach to the key areas of marketing and help participants define their own marketing strategy

Main topics: Marketing diagnosis, setting up marketing strategy, implementation of the marketing mix; evaluation of customer satisfaction; communication policies; brand management; distribution policies; the marketing function in relation to other functions in the organisation

Notes: The programme language is French

IMD—International Institute for Management Development

■ Managing for Marketing Success

Location: IMD, Lausanne, Switzerland

Participants: Marketing managers and managers in other functions involved in marketing

Frequency: Once a year

Duration: 2 weeks

Cost: Swfr12,000 incl some meals, materials

Aims: To focus on the overall marketing process and how to make it more market-driven

Main topics: Creating a market-focused organisation; building brand equity; exploiting new products; managing the distribution challenge; pricing for profit; industry analysis for advantage; differentiating through services; developing global marketing strategies; leading change in marketing; integrative problem-solving

INSEAD—European Institute of Business Administration

■ Advanced Industrial Marketing Strategy

Location: INSEAD, Fontainebleau, France

Participants: Managing directors, general managers, marketing vice-presidents, national sales and group product managers

Frequency: Twice a year

Duration: 2 weeks

Cost: FFr61,000 incl some meals, materials

Aims: To allow participants to experience the application and value of the concepts which underpin strategic market orientation

Main topics: Competitive dynamics; strategic market segmentation; strategic positioning; relationship marketing; allocation of strategic resources; negotiation strategy; pricing strategy; building and leveraging core competencies; managing product lines; marketing and cyberspace

Notes: This programme uses the INDUSTRAT strategic industrial marketing simulation

■ International Marketing Programme: Creating Customer Value

Location: INSEAD, Fontainebleau, France

Participants: Marketing, general, business development, technical and product managers

Frequency: Twice a year

Duration: 2 weeks

Cost: FFr55,000 incl some meals, materials

Aims: To help participants effectively create customer and shareholder value, and work in an international environment

Main topics: Value proposition; market and customer selection; market intelligence; delivering customer value; consumer marketing (optional); business-to-business marketing (optional)

Notes: This programme uses the Markstrat Services Simulation and was originally developed in 1968 as the European Marketing Programme

Maastricht School of Management

■ Marketing of Services

Location: Maastricht School of Management, Maastricht, Netherlands

Participants: Marketing executives at middle-management level in the services sector; marketing and general managers of non-governmental organisations

Frequency: Once a year

Duration: 14 weeks

Cost: G15,500 incl field-work expenses, materials

Aims: To help participants integrate services marketing and delivery to achieve competitive advantage and meet customer requirements

Main topics: Introduction to services; environmental developments; strategy design in services; globalisation of services; recent developments in selected service industries

Rotterdam School of Management—Erasmus Graduate School of Business

■ Marketing Management of New Products

Location: A conference centre in the Netherlands

Participants: Marketing directors, marketing managers

Frequency: Once a year

Duration: 6 days

Cost: G10,000 incl accommodation, meals, books

Aims: To help participants understand the conditions affecting the success rate of innovations

Main topics: Strategic and conceptual issues; recent developments in analytical tools; organisational conditions necessary for optimal new product processes

Notes: This programme is designed and run jointly by faculty from Rotterdam and Wharton School, University of Pennsylvania, US

Rest of world

Australian Graduate School of Management— University of New South Wales

■ Marketing Management

Location: Australian Graduate School of Management, Sydney, Australia

Participants: Marketing and sales managers, strategic planners

Frequency: Once a year

Duration: 5 days

Cost: A$5,585 incl accommodation, meals, materials

Aims: To provide participants with skills and methods for developing and implementing marketing plans

Main topics: Developing customer-driven strategies; basing strategies on core competencies and competitive advantage; integrating elements of the marketing mix; innovation; managing and defending brand equity; positioning products and services for maximum impact; the global market; monitoring the competitive environment

■ Marketing Tools for Marketing Managers

Location: Australian Graduate School of Management, Sydney, Australia

Participants: Marketing managers, consultants, researchers

Frequency: Once a year

Duration: 3 days

Cost: A$3,590 incl accommodation, meals, materials

Aims: To help participants understand the role of analytical approaches and computer-based tools in marketing decisions

Main topics: Marketing strategy development; segmentation, targeting and positioning; advertising and communications planning and development; salesforce sizing and allocation; promotional mix analysis; pricing and yield management; new product design and forecasting

■ Strategic Marketing of Consumer Products and Services

Location: Australian Graduate School of Management, Sydney, Australia

Participants: Senior brand managers, group product managers, marketing directors

Frequency: Once a year

Duration: 3 days

Cost: A$3,495 incl accommodation, meals, materials

Aims: To teach participants techniques for managing a range of products or services

Main topics: Portfolio management techniques; product line strategies; corporate fit and product roles; pricing; promotion; advertising; channel marketing and longer-term issues

University of Cape Town—Graduate School of Business

■ Marketing Management

Location: Graduate School of Business, Cape Town, South Africa

Participants: Managers new to a marketing position with some experience of other functional areas; managers in other functional areas who interact with marketing people

Frequency: Once a year

Duration: 6 days

Cost: R7,210 incl accommodation

Aims: To focus on how marketing and the role of the marketer are changing

Indian Institute of Management

■ Product Policy and New Product Management

Location: IIM, Vastrapur, Ahmedabad, India

Participants: Marketing directors and managers, product and group product managers, advertising managers, corporate planners

Frequency: Once a year

Duration: 6 days

Cost: Rs21,000 ($780 for participants' from outside India) incl accommodation, materials

Aims: To improve participants' understanding of and competence in making product-market choice, managing brands and managing new product introduction

Main topics: Product strategy; product line decisions and product mix analysis; market structuring and product positioning strategies; strategic management of brands and their equities; idea generation, concept development, evaluation and business analysis; testing products and other critical elements of marketing mix; test-market planning, evaluation and introduction strategies

Macquarie Graduate School of Management—Macquarie University

■ Marketing Management Programme

Location: Macquarie Graduate School, Sydney, Australia

Participants: Senior marketing executives

Frequency: Once a year

Duration: 6 days

Cost: A$5,995 incl accommodation, meals

Aims: To examine the application of current marketing concepts and techniques to secure competitive advantage

Main topics: Frameworks for marketing strategy; global competition and marketing management; marketing entrepreneurship and corporate strategy

Notes: This programme uses the Markstrat computer marketing simulation

Monash Mt Eliza Business School

■ Marketing: The Strategic Edge—Consumer Marketing

Location: Mt Eliza, Australia

Participants: Senior and middle managers

Frequency: Once a year

Duration: 5 days

Cost: A$5,950

Aims: To develop participants' strategic thinking and planning skills for making marketing decisions

Main topics: Creating and capturing value; managing brand equity

■ Marketing: The Strategic Edge—Business to Business

Location: Mt Eliza, Australia

Participants: Senior and middle managers

Frequency: Once a year

Duration: 5 days

Cost: A$5,950

Aims: To develop participants' strategic knowledge of marketing goods and services

Main topics: Market segmentation; managing the value proposition; relationships and processes; strategic pricing

National University of Singapore—Graduate School of Business Administration

■ Marketing Management Programme

Location: National University of Singapore

Participants: Marketing, sales, product and general managers

Frequency: Once a year

Duration: 2 weeks

Cost: $S4,000

Aims: To equip participants with an understanding of current marketing concepts and techniques

Main topics: Market-driven and market-driving organisations; market analysis; legal aspects of marketing in Asia-Pacific; economic and business trends in Asia-Pacific; strategic marketing planning; market segmentation, targeting and positioning; managing the marketing mix; customer satisfaction and value management; strategic marketing alliances; marketing in the 21st century

Wits Business School—University of the Witwatersrand

■ Product Strategy and Brand Management

Location: Wits Business School, Johannesburg, South Africa

Participants: Marketing directors and managers, product and brand managers, product development managers

Frequency: Once a year

Duration: 3 days

Cost: R4,950 incl materials, lunches, refreshments

Aims: To provide a systematic approach to analysing product policy and strategy in the South African context

Main topics: Role of the brand/product manager; developing the product plan; managing the product mix; the product life cycle; marketing new products; the product innovation process; measurement and forecasting of product sales; measurement of brand equity; developing brand equity; packaging decisions; controlling the product programme

■ Strategic Marketing Management

Location: Wits Business School, Johannesburg, South Africa

Participants: Marketing directors and managers, senior product managers, regional and area managers

Frequency: Once a year

Duration: 5 days

Cost: R7,350 incl materials, meals

Aims: To enhance the ability of participants to improve the effectiveness and efficiency of their organisation's marketing effort

Main topics: Overview of the strategic marketing process; marketing orientation improvement; customer analysis; segmentation and market development; competitive analysis; industry analysis; environmental analysis and scanning; performance analysis; obtaining a sustainable competitive advantage; global marketing strategy; the planning process; marketing implementation

Personal development programmes

Management is a human art as well as a practical science and greater emphasis is now being placed on personal development. Organisational development and personal development are increasingly regarded as mutually supportive rather than mutually exclusive. Indeed, organisations such as Roffey Park Management Institute in the UK have carved effective niches as experts in what was once dismissed as the softer side of business.

Some skills remain more elusive than others. Programmes on negotiating skills remain highly popular, and they often come in combination with the study of power and influence. There are also growing numbers of programmes on creativity, innovation and the skills required to work successfully in a team, as well as a selection of programmes on basic interpersonal skills, such as communicating.

Programmes are arranged alphabetically by provider in the following regions:

- North America (page 222)

- UK (page 230)

- Europe excluding UK (page 235)

- Rest of world (page 236)

North America

The Anderson School at UCLA—Executive Education Programs

■ Creativity and Innovation in the Organization

Location: The Anderson School at UCLA, Los Angeles, CA, US

Participants: Senior managers

Frequency: Once a year

Duration: 5 days

Cost: $4,950 incl accommodation, meals, books, materials

Aims: To provide organisational leaders with the tools to transform creative, innovative ideas into successful business solutions

Main topics: Making imaginative and rational decisions, developing the adaptive capacity to work creatively with change and uncertainty; exploring the process of creating a shared sense of purpose in the organisation; how employee networks operate; how networks and hierarchies interact; understanding action-based creativity

Columbia Business School

■ Negotiation Skills for Effective Management

Location: Arden House, Harriman, NY, US

Participants: Executives and managers who want to interact more effectively in negotiating situations

Frequency: Twice a year

Duration: 4 days

Cost: $3,200 incl accommodation, meals, materials

Aims: To teach participants how to use creativity to increase the effectiveness of their negotiating technique

Main topics: Understanding your style and how to be more effective; adapting your style to the situation; determining a negotiation goal and a range of options; developing an implementation plan for a negotiation

Notes: Data collected before the programme from those with whom participants negotiate are analysed to identify their style and develop feedback reports. Participants are taped in simulated negotiations which are then reviewed with faculty members

Darden Executive Education—University of Virginia

■ Bargaining and Negotiating: a Learning Laboratory

Location: Darden School, Charlottesville, VA, US

Participants: Senior and middle managers

Frequency: Twice a year

Duration: 4 days

Cost: $3,300

Aims: To understand, develop and implement effective negotiation techniques

Main topics: Key components of effective negotiation; role-play negotiations among participants

Jesse H Jones Graduate School of Management—Rice University

■ Successful Negotiation Skills

Location: Rice University, Houston, TX, US

Participants: Professionals who depend on negotiation for success, including managers of various disciplines, purchasing and sales professionals

Frequency: Twice a year

Duration: 5 Mondays over 2 months

Cost: n/a

Aims: To provide a conceptual framework for understanding what happens in the negotiation process and how to apply these concepts to strengthen negotiating skills

Main topics: Competencies for successful negotiations; competitive negotiation; criteria for collaborative negotiation; handling different negotiation situations; impact of context (culture, style, etc)

J L Kellogg Graduate School of Management— Northwestern University

■ Negotiation Strategies for Managers

Location: James L Allen Center, Evanston, IL, US

Participants: Merger and acquisition professionals; purchasing, sales, financial and HR managers; planning and development managers

Frequency: 4 times a year

Duration: 1 week

Cost: $2,950

Aims: To teach participants strategies and skills for managing the negotiation process

Main topics: Planning and implementing negotiation strategy, coalition formation, dispute resolution, cultural values and negotiation priorities

■ Team Building for Managers

Location: James L Allen Center, Evanston, IL, US

Participants: Entrepreneurs, sales and marketing managers, administrators of non-profit organisations, HR professionals

Frequency: Twice a year

Duration: 4 days

Cost: $2,950 incl accommodation, meals, materials

Aims: To help participants plan and implement more effective team-building and management strategies within their organisations

Main topics: Intra-team dynamics (conflict, selection, communication, leadership); inter-team dynamics (competition); the team within the organisation (compensation, networking, corporate team culture)

Notes: This programme is useful for both individuals and groups of workers from one organisation

Kenan-Flagler Business School—University of North Carolina at Chapel Hill

■ Management Effectiveness Workshop

Location: University of N Carolina, Chapel Hill, NC, US

Participants: Senior and middle managers

Frequency: Twice a year

Duration: 3 days

Cost: $1,950

Aims: To enhance participants' understanding of the role and relation of the management function to the organisation

Main topics: Leadership opportunities; power and influence; ethical dilemmas; personal and organisational renewal

McGill Executive Institute—McGill University

■ People Skills for Managers

Location: McGill Executive Institute, Montreal, Canada

Participants: Experienced managers wishing to renew their knowledge and skills; potential and newly appointed managers and supervisors

Frequency: 3 times a year

Duration: 3 days

Cost: C$1,395 incl lunches, materials

Aims: To enable participants to upgrade key communications skills, understand behaviour and improve their working relationships

Main topics: Understanding social styles; communicating effectively; managing teams; resolving conflict; coaching; from workshop to workplace

- ## Thinking Skills and Creative Problem-Solving

Location: McGill Executive Institute, Montreal, Canada

Participants: Finance, production, marketing, sales, HR and systems managers

Frequency: Times a year

Duration: 3 days

Cost: C$1,395 incl lunches, materials

Aims: To enhance participants' ability to find practical and profitable solutions to business challenges

Main topics: The basics of creative thinking: an "owner's manual for the mind"; improving thinking skills; methods for increasing thinking and creative ability; brainstorming; workable applications of creativity and thinking skills

- ## Win-Win Negotiations

Location: McGill Executive Institute, Montreal, Canada; University of Toronto, Rotman School of Management, Toronto, Canada

Participants: Managers, sales executives, project leaders

Frequency: 5 times a year

Duration: 3 days

Cost: C$1,395 incl lunches, materials

Aims: To provide participants with the skills and knowledge to succeed in negotiations

Main topics: Elements, tactics and stages of negotiation; dealing with difficult people

University of Michigan Business School

- ## Delegation and Team Effort: People and Performance

Location: Executive Education Center, Ann Arbor, MI, US

Participants: Managers who wish to enhance their managerial skills through effective delegation and team leadership

Frequency: 4 times a year

Duration: 5 days

Cost: $4,250 incl accommodation, meals, materials

Aims: To enable participants to develop further their managerial and leadership skills in creating and promoting high-performance teams

Main topics: Management in the new team environment; designing high-performing teams; creating a context for high-performing teams; delegation and high-performing teams; overcoming roadblocks to effective delegation

- ## Effective Managerial Coaching and Counselling

Location: Executive Education Center, Ann Arbor, MI, US

Participants: Senior and middle managers who have substantial responsibility for managing people.

Frequency: Twice a year

Duration: 3 days

Cost: $2,975 incl accommodation, meals, materials

Aims: To help participants distinguish between and develop strategies and skills in coaching and counselling

Main topics: When to coach and when to counsel; identifying and analysing people problems; structure and strategy of a counselling session; workshops in developing skills; evaluating a session; when not to counsel

Owen Graduate School of Management—Vanderbilt University

- ## Persuasion and Influencing Skills

Location: Owen Graduate School of Management, TN, US

Participants: Managers who utilise negotiating skills

Frequency: Twice a year

Duration: 3 days

Cost: $1,395 incl most meals, materials

Aims: To help participants identify their personal negotiation style and increase their influencing skills for maximum effectiveness

MIT Sloan School of Management—Massachusetts Institute of Technology

- ## Negotiation: Theory and Practice

Location: Sloan School of Management, Cambridge, MA, US

Participants: Senior managers

Frequency: Once a year

Duration: 5 days

Cost: $3,500 incl most meals, materials

Aims: To give participants a broad intellectual understanding of key negotiating concepts

Main topics: Individual negotiating styles; integrative bargaining and problem-solving; power; simulated negotiations

Rotman School of Management—University of Toronto

■ Negotiating for Success

Location: Rotman School of Management, Toronto, Canada

Participants: Senior and middle managers

Frequency: Once a year

Duration: 3 days

Cost: C$1,595 incl meals, materials

Aims: To provide participants with a variety of practical negotiating skills

Main topics: Competition in negotiation; win-win negotiation; multiparty, multi-issue negotiation; international and cross-cultural negotiation; personality and negotiation

Stanford Graduate School of Business—Stanford University

■ Managing Teams for Innovation and Success

Location: Graduate School of Business, Stanford, CA, US

Participants: Experienced team managers or teams of up to 6 people

Frequency: Once a year

Duration: 1 week

Cost: $5,700 incl accommodation, meals, books, study materials

Aims: To teach participants how to enhance organisational effectiveness through teams and groups

Main topics: When to use teams rather than individuals; team roles; obstacles to teamwork; motivational needs; working effectively with other teams

■ Negotiating and Influence Strategies

Location: Graduate School of Business, Stanford, CA, US

Participants: Senior managers who want to improve their negotiation skills

Frequency: Twice a year

Duration: 1 week

Cost: $5,700 incl accommodation, meals, books, study materials

Aims: To improve participants' negotiation skills and increase their influence

Wharton School—University of Pennsylvania—Aresty Institute of Executive Education

- ## Executive Negotiation Workshop: Bargaining for Advantage

   Location: Wharton School, Philadelphia, PA, US

   Participants: Senior and middle managers

   Frequency: 3 times a year

   Duration: 5 days

   Cost: $6,250 incl accommodation, meals

   Aims: To develop new strategies for addressing negotiations and explore the latest practice and theory

   Main topics: Power: what it is and how to use it; using agents effectively; relationship-building in negotiations; transforming competition into co-operation; personality strengths and weaknesses; culture, perception and international transactions; dealing with emotional and irrational situations; the firm as a negotiating environment

University of Wisconsin-Madison—Graduate School of Business

- ## How to Work More Effectively with People

   Location: Management Institute, University of Wisconsin-Madison, WI, US

   Participants: Executives, managers, team leaders

   Frequency: 4 times a year

   Duration: 3 days

   Cost: n/a

   Aims: To help participants improve their skills in the workplace

   Main topics: Interpersonal style and behaviour; managing and overcoming conflict

- ## Negotiating in the Pacific Rim

   Location: Management Institute, University of Wisconsin-Madison, WI, US

   Participants: Executives, directors, managers

   Frequency: Twice a year

   Duration: 3 days

   Cost: n/a

   Aims: To enable participants to take advantage of marketing and sourcing opportunities

   Main topics: Transnational planning; negotiations; business cultures

Ashridge Management College

■ Developing Skills for Management

Location: Ashridge Management College, Berkhamsted, UK

Participants: Managers wishing to develop their potential to handle further responsibility; specialists moving into broader roles in their organisations who wish to focus on personal skills

Frequency: 5 times a year

Duration: 12 days

Cost: £5,950 incl accommodation, meals

Aims: To provide accelerated personal development

Main topics: Self-awareness and self-managed development; managing relationships; teamworking; managing performance and business skills (participation in this programme can lead to the Ashridge Diploma in General Management)

■ Interpersonal Skills

Location: Ashridge Management College, Berkhamsted, UK

Participants: Managers wishing to expand their range of options when dealing with people

Frequency: 4 times a year

Duration: 5 days

Cost: £2,700 incl accommodation, meals

Aims: To explore practical approaches for using appropriate techniques in different situations

Main topics: Taking information in; giving information out; self-awareness and management style; skills practice (participation in this programme can lead to the Ashridge Diploma in General Management)

■ Performance through People

Location: Ashridge Management College, Berkhamsted, UK

Participants: Managers responsible for individual and team performance

Frequency: 6 times a year

Duration: 5 days

Cost: £2,700 incl accommodation, meals

Aims: To enable individuals to create an environment where performance will flourish

Main topics: Key issues in performance management; managing your own performance; achieving results; creating high-performance teams; organisational impact (participation in this programme can lead to the Ashridge Diploma in General Management)

University of Bradford Management Centre

■ Group and Personal Effectiveness

Location: Bradford Management Centre, Bradford, UK

Participants: Managers who spend a great deal of time with people or whose face-to-face contacts are vital to their success

Frequency: 3 times a year

Duration: 5 days

Cost: £1,970 incl accommodation

Aims: To give individuals help in managing and getting on with people

Main topics: Building and repairing relationships; working in groups; managing others; taking over a new group; planning behaviour before difficult encounters; listening, talking and influencing skills

Notes: This programme is also used by companies with bases in continental Europe as a means of rapidly absorbing UK business culture and style

Cranfield School of Management

■ Organisational and Interpersonal Skills in Management

Location: Cranfield School of Management, Cranfield, UK

Participants: Senior managers who aim to increase understanding of themselves and the ways in which they relate to others

Frequency: 4 times a year

Duration: 5 days (plus 2-day follow-up)

Cost: £3,750 incl accommodation, meals

Aims: To help people identify why and how they limit themselves and to experience ways of expressing themselves more effectively at work

Main topics: Organisational change and transition; boss-subordinate relationships; career planning; assessing and motivating others; balancing work and home life; being more sensitive to feelings; influencing others

Notes: The programme has 3 parts: a 5 day workshop, then approximately 8-10 weeks applying the new learning and a 2-day follow-up

London Business School

■ **Interpersonal Skills for Senior Managers**

Location: London Business School, London, UK

Participants: Chairmen, unit managing directors, general managers, managers of major functions

Frequency: 3 times a year

Duration: 5 days

Cost: £4,350

Aims: To improve skills in the areas of communicating, goal setting, motivating, building teams, promoting leadership, managing under uncertainty

Main topics: The employment process (recruitment, induction, coaching, goal setting, motivating, exiting); the control process (designing and maintaining structures, fact-finding, decision-making, evaluating and assessing performance); interaction (teamwork, assessing group behaviour, giving and receiving feedback, changing attitudes, managing diversity); the change process (planning, selling and implementing change)

Notes: The size of the participant group is deliberately restricted and the programme director reserves the right to accept only those applicants who could benefit

Roffey Park Management Institute

■ **Counselling Skills at Work**

Location: Roffey Park, Horsham, UK

Participants: Line managers, team leaders

Frequency: 3 times a year

Duration: 3 days

Cost: £1,360 incl meals, accommodation

Aims: To increase participants' personal awareness and develop their counselling skills

Main topics: The counselling process; developing personal awareness

Notes: The programme's final session is dedicated to transferring skills acquired into the workplace

■ **Effective Self-management**

Location: Roffey Park, Horsham, UK

Participants: Senior and middle managers

Frequency: 4 times a year

Duration: 4 days

Cost: £1,855 incl accommodation and meals

Aims: To improve the way in which participants manage themselves; help them prioritise and organise activities more effectively; and clarify their current role and its relation to others

Main topics: Self-management; personal domain mapping; role analysis; prioritisation; time management

Notes: The first 2 days concentrate on diagnostics; the last 2 days focus on individual strengths and development needs

■ Interpersonal Relationships in Organisations

Location: Roffey Park, Horsham, UK

Participants: All those whose work depends on effective relationships with others

Frequency: Monthly

Duration: 5 days

Cost: £2,500 incl accommodation, meals

Aims: To teach participants how to manage many types of relationship; increase their ability to become more influential in working relationships; enhance their ability to manage ambiguity and uncertainty; and develop effective working relationships

Main topics: Identifying learning needs; learning about relationships; integration

Notes: The programme uses one-to-one and group discussions. Learning objectives are discussed with a tutor before attending

■ Leading Effective Teams

Location: Roffey Park, Horsham, UK

Participants: Potential and current team leaders

Frequency: 7 times a year

Duration: 5 days (in 2 parts)

Cost: £2,350 incl meals, accommodation

Aims: To help participants understand the skills required to develop a high-performance team

Main topics: The role, make up and added value of teams; individual and team productivity; team leadership; removing the blocks to high-performance teams; vision, mission and culture in outstanding teams

Notes: The second 2-day session includes tailored workshops and production of individual action plans

■ The Manager as Developer

Location: Roffey Park, Horsham, UK

Participants: Managers, senior managers

Frequency: 3 times a year

Duration: 5 days (in 2 parts)

Cost: £2,350 incl meals, accommodation

Aims: To provide managers responsible for helping others to reach their full potential with technical and operational expertise

Main topics: The role of the line manager as a developer of others; how people learn and develop; the difference between coaching and counselling; guidelines for giving and receiving feedback

■ Meeting the Challenge of Change

Location: Roffey Park, Horsham, UK

Participants: Managers, senior managers

Frequency: Twice a year

Duration: 3 2-day modules

Cost: £2,800 incl meals, accommodation

Aims: To consider new ideas and ways of bringing about change, and to provide a supportive and challenging environment for understanding how different organisations deal with change

Main topics: The science of complexity and its application to organisations; organisational change; using the complexity approach in leadership, strategy and managing change; understanding and working with organisational dynamics

■ Personal Effectiveness and Power

Location: Roffey Park, Horsham, UK

Participants: Directors, senior and middle managers, analysts, consultants, engineers

Frequency: Monthly

Duration: 5 days

Cost: £2,500 incl accommodation, meals

Aims: To develop a wider range of choices in influencing others; improve assertion skills; practise skills; and explore sources of personal power and influence

Main topics: Influencing styles and strategies; influencing and self-esteem; influencing in groups; personal power

Notes: Participants complete a self-assessment instrument before starting the programme, which has a maximum of 12 participants

INSEAD—European Institute of Business Administration

■ AVIRA: Awareness, Vision, Imagination, Responsibility, Action

Location: INSEAD, Fontainebleau, France

Participants: Senior executives

Frequency: 3 times a year

Duration: 5 days

Cost: FFr55,000 incl some meals, materials

Aims: To encourage participants to take a broader assessment of their responsibility as a leader

Main topics: The leader in uncertain times; beyond the "economist's vision"; alternative competitive logic; accountability and responsibility

■ Negotiation Dynamics

Location: INSEAD, Fontainebleau, France

Participants: Managing, corporate purchasing, and marketing and sales directors; HR vice-presidents

Frequency: Twice a year

Duration: 3 days

Cost: FFr28,000 incl some meals, materials

Aims: To offer a pragmatic and analytical approach to making deals

Main topics: Negotiations within organisations; tender offers; pricing and procurement management; labour relations; mergers, acquisitions and joint ventures

Rest of world

Australian Graduate School of Management— University of New South Wales

■ Negotiation and Conflict Management in Organisations

Location: Australian Graduate School of Management, Sydney, Australia; Melbourne, Australia; Auckland, New Zealand

Participants: Senior, middle and functional managers

Frequency: 3 times a year

Duration: 3 days

Cost: A$3,395 (Sydney, Melbourne), A$3,195 (Auckland), incl accommodation, meals, materials

Aims: To provide participants with a theoretical and practical framework as well as experience in negotiating

Main topics: Negotiation strategies; power; personal style; constructive relationships; managerial dilemmas; group decision-making; ethical dilemmas; negotiation in a global arena

University of Cape Town—Graduate School of Business

■ Bargaining and Negotiating

Location: Graduate School of Business, Cape Town, South Africa

Participants: People who oversee business negotiations and those who conduct them

Frequency: Once a year

Duration: 6 days

Cost: R7,210 incl accommodation

Aims: To engage in a series of controlled experiences with measurable performance criteria

Main topics: Role and components of effective preparation and analysis; patterns of concession and opening offers; value of information, goals and predetermined walkways; conceptual structures of competitive and co-operative negotiations; mechanisms for identifying and creating value; formation of sustainable and effective coalitions; strategies for ensuring a good deal

Curtin Business School

■ Leading and Working in Teams

Location: QV1 Campus, Graduate School of Business, Perth, Australia

Participants: Team leaders, managers, professionals who participate in teams

Frequency: Once a year

Duration: 5 days

Cost: A$1,400

Aims: To provide leaders with the information and tools to lead teams effectively

Main topics: Effective teams; strategic change management; communications and managing conflict in teams; the learning organisation and learning team; leading teams; managing and leading team performance; integration of effective teams

Macquarie Graduate School of Management— Macquarie University

■ Personal and Managerial Effectiveness

Location: Macquarie Graduate School, Sydney, Australia

Participants: Managers from all industries and functions, especially those responsible for implementing workplace change programmes

Frequency: Twice a year

Duration: 3 days

Cost: A$2,450

Aims: To assist participants in effectively motivating people for performance and achieving results

Main topics: Using Myers-Brigg type indicator to understand yourself and your colleagues; effective conflict management and resolution; managerial skills building (communication, giving and receiving feedback, influencing without authority)

Notes: A 360-degree leadership instrument is completed by participants and several colleagues before the programme starts; the results are fully explored during the programme

Monash Mt Eliza Business School

■ Negotiating and Influencing Skills for Managers

Location: Mt Eliza, Australia

Participants: Senior and middle managers who deal with internal and external negotiations

Frequency: 3 times a year

Duration: 3 days

Cost: A$2,750

Aims: To provide a framework of ideas for effective negotiation and practical training through a series of specially designed simulations and exercises. Participants will leave with an enhanced ability to reach agreement in the workplace, to advance their full set of interests as managers and to lead change successfully

Notes: This programme is based on the Executive Program on Negotiation at Harvard University, US

Wits Business School—University of the Witwatersrand

■ Effective Interpersonal Skills

Location: Wits Business School, Johannesburg, South Africa

Participants: Executives, managers, HR development practitioners

Frequency: Twice a year

Duration: 5 days

Cost: R7,350 incl materials, meals

Aims: To help participants develop interpersonal effectiveness through understanding themselves in relation to others

Main topics: The business value of interpersonal skills; empathetic listening skills; understanding oneself in relation to others; models of interpersonal communication; solving problems created by ineffective interpersonal relations; theories of human behaviour; group dynamics and effective group performance; stereotyping and communication in a multicultural context; personal change and the challenge of continued improvement in interpersonal effectiveness

■ The Expert Negotiator

Location: Wits Business School, Johannesburg, South Africa

Participants: Managing directors, general and senior managers

Frequency: Twice a year

Duration: 4 days

Cost: R6,750 incl materials, refreshments

Aims: To provide the knowledge, techniques and skills necessary for successful negotiation

Main topics: Defining negotiation and setting the climate; preparation for negotiation; the bargaining model; the dynamics of groups and negotiation process variables; handling opinion change; putting it all together

Part 3

Directory of providers

Providers

Europe excluding UK

Rest of world

Which executive programme? © The Economist Intelligence Unit Limited 1998

Introduction

Part 3 of *Which executive programme?* is a comprehensive directory of leading business schools which offer executive programmes.

The growth of tailored programmes means that a number of business schools concentrate solely on tailored work and do not offer any open programmes. Their contact details are included as well as those of providers of open programmes. There are also comments on each business school, highlighting some courses that are not listed in the programme directory (because, for example, they may last less than three days or require many months of study, or they are highly specialised courses).

Providers are arranged alphabetically in the following regions:

- North America (page 246)

- UK (page 266)

- Europe excluding UK (page 277)

- Rest of world (page 287)

North America

Amos Tuck School of Business

Address
100 Tuck Hall
Hanover NH 03755-9050
US

Tel: +1 603 6462839
Fax: +1 603 6461308

E-mail:
tuck.exec.ed@dartmouth.edu

Website:
http://www.tuck.dartmouth.edu

Contact name
Marie T Eiter, director of
executive education

Status
Part of Dartmouth college;
founded 1900

Other offices
None

Teaching staff
Full-time 36

Comments
The world's first graduate school of management, Amos Tuck, was established in 1900. Located in leafy New Hampshire, the school retains a strong emphasis on open programmes; tailored work accounts for around 10% of its total executive programmes business. The number of participants has increased rapidly from 316 in 1991/92 to over 850 in 1996/97. Tuck is involved in an alliance with HEC Executive Development Center in Paris, France, and Templeton College in Oxford, UK, to use technology to support research and teaching. Open programmes cover four basic areas. Business strategy includes Strategic Revolution (five days) and Managing in Hypercompetitive Industries (three days). General management includes the four-week Tuck Executive Program, now in its 25th year, and Update 2000: A Senior Management Forum. Marketing is covered in the Market-Driven Management programme. Lastly, there are special focus programmes, one for entrepreneurs from minorities and another for healthcare professionals.

The Anderson School at UCLA—Executive Education Programs

Address
110 Westwood Plaza
Suite A101D
Los Angeles CA 90095-1464
US

Tel: +1 310 8252001
Fax: +1 310 8253340

E-mail: execed@agsm.ucla.edu

Website:
http://www.anderson.ucla.edu

Contact name
Alissa Brill, marketing director

Status
Part of UCLA; founded 1954

Other offices
None

Teaching staff
Full-time 120

Comments
The Anderson School at UCLA, situated near Beverly Hills, now has 120 faculty members. Its facilities include the state-of-the-art James A Collins Center, where executive programmes are delivered, and a sophisticated computer network serving its seven-building complex. Each of the buildings is interconnected and focuses on a specific aspect of management education. Anderson houses a variety of research centres and institutes offering specialised expertise. These include the UCLA-Anderson Business Forecasting Project, the Center for Corporate Renewal and the Price Center for Entrepreneurial Studies. It offers more than 40 open and tailored programmes (although its emphasis remains on the former). Over 2,000 executives, nearly 25% of whom came from outside the US, attended its programmes during 1997. These include the ten-week Management Development Program for Entrepreneurs, run twice a year, and the flagship Anderson Executive Program.

Arthur D Little School of Management

Address
194 Beacon Street
Chestnut Hill MA 02167-3835
US

Tel: +1 617 5522877
Fax: +1 617 5522051

E-mail:
adlschool.mgmt@adlittle.com

Website:
http://www.arthurdlittle.com

Contact names
Karlin B Jessen, Will Marris

Status
Private, non-profit

Other offices
US: Cambridge, MA

Teaching staff
Consultants and professors 25

Comments

The Arthur D Little School of Management's origins lie in the early 1960s when the first management education programme focusing on training managers from developing countries was launched. The Management Education Institute, located in Boston, was modelled on MIT's Sloan Program and, in 1976, was the first corporate university to be accredited. It was renamed the Arthur D Little School and is now an independent non-profit organisation closely aligned with the consulting firm. As such the school is unique: it is the only corporate university offering degrees in the US and Arthur D Little is the only consultancy with its own business school. It offers a combination of tailored and open programmes. Its tailored programmes have included such topics as the learning organisation, managing change, strategic planning and project management. Its newest programme is entitled Managing Virtual Teams.

Babson College—School of Executive Education

Address
Wellesley MA 02157
US

Tel: +1 781 2394354
Fax: +1 781 2395266

E-mail: exec@babson.edu

Website:
http://www.babson.edu/see

Contact name
Maureen Perlmutter, business development manager

Status
Private college; School of Executive Education founded 1973

Other offices
None

Teaching staff
Full-time 2; part-time 42

Comments

Founded by a financier, Roger Babson, in 1919, Babson College is located in Wellesley, Massachusetts, just 30 minutes' drive from Boston. It emphasises its entrepreneurial origins and aspirations, saying its mission is "to educate innovative leaders capable of anticipating, initiating and managing change". Babson has a purpose-built Center for Executive Education in its 450-acre wooded campus from where it offers both open and tailored programmes. It also offers the Consortium for Executive Development, a corporate membership programme for global companies with common educational goals. Tailored programmes form an increasingly important part of its activities. Recent clients include Atlantic Data Services, with which it developed a Professional Leadership Program, and Pitney Bowes, with which it developed a four-module Executive Development Program. Babson has also worked closely with Digital Equipment over a lengthy period. Despite its small size, the school has established a distinguished niche. It is notably international in outlook, with over 50% of its programme participants coming from outside the US.

Berkeley Center for Executive Development—Haas School of Business

Address
University of California
Berkeley CA 94720-1900
US

Tel: +1 510 6424735
Fax: +1 510 6422388

E-mail: bced@haas.berkeley.edu

Website:
http://www.haas.berkeley.edu

Contact name
Claudia Welss, director

Status
Part of Haas School of Business,
University of California at
Berkeley; Berkeley Executive
Program founded 1958

Other offices
None

Teaching staff
Haas School: 90 lecturers

Comments
The Berkeley Center for Executive Development (BCED) is part of the Haas School, the oldest centre for management studies at a US public university. Situated close to the San Francisco Bay area, Haas is home to the Lester Center for Entrepreneurship and Innovation and the Fisher Center for Management and Information Technology. BCED's activities are fairly evenly split between open and tailored programmes. It now offers over 20 open programmes, which are divided into general management programmes and executive seminars (including Strategic Sales Management, Strategic Planning Under Uncertainty and Implementing Strategy). BCED's programmes are strongly multinational. The four-week Executive Program features the Berkeley Leader Lab (personal examination of the leadership styles of participants), use of a scenario-based planning framework and a spouse's programme. The three-week Advanced Management Program examines a range of issues including macroeconomics and financial markets, the market-focused organisation and negotiation as a strategic tool.

Carlson School of Management—University of Minnesota

Address
Executive Development Center
321 19th Avenue S
Minneapolis MN 55455, US

Tel: +1 612 6242545
Fax: +1 612 6269264

E-mail: edc@csom.umn.edu

Website:
http://www.csom.umn.edu/edc

Contact name
Bill Scheurer, director

Status
Part of university; founded 1970

Other offices
None

Teaching staff
n/a

Comments
The Carlson School in Minneapolis has over 25 years of experience in offering executive programmes. Open programmes remain the core of its activities, but tailored programmes now account for around 25% of its work. Among its 12 courses are the four-week Minnesota Executive Program, delivered in four separate one-week modules and aimed at experienced senior managers, and "an MBA alternative", the three-week Minnesota Management Institute, covering broad-based management concepts in the major functional areas. It also offers an Advanced Management Program for Healthcare Executives (six days), an Advantage Program to update skills and Strategic Excellence: A Decision-Focused Approach.

Carnegie Mellon University—Graduate School of Industrial Administration

Address
Executive Education Center
Posner Hall, Suite 150
5000 Forbes Avenue
Pittsburgh PA 15213-3890
US

Tel: +1 412 2682304
Fax: +1 412 2682485

E-mail:
ccjordan@andrew.cmu.edu

Website:
http://www.gsia.cmu.edu

Contact name
C Clark Jordan, director,
executive education

Status
University graduate school;
founded 1949

Other offices
US: New York

Teaching staff
Full-time 62

Comments
Carnegie Mellon's Graduate School of Industrial Administration (GSIA) is based just outside Pittsburgh in a 103-acre campus next to Schenley Park. Founded in 1949 by William Larimer Mellon, the GSIA's reputation is built on research into the scientific principles underlying business management. GSIA faculty have won three Nobel Prizes and its research has most notably covered organisational theory, artificial intelligence, operations research and corporate finance. It has also been at the forefront of usage of computer simulations, and the FAST laboratory continues its work in experiential learning. Executive programmes, now numbering over 30, are delivered at Posner Hall in Pittsburgh. Many have a technical slant, including Green Engineering and Management and Management in Technology Organizations. More specific programmes on new technology cover such areas as wireless networks and networked multimedia. Some programmes are also offered in New York City. Tailored programmes now form over half of the GSIA's executive programmes.

University of Chicago—Graduate School of Business

Address
1101 East 58th Street
Chicago IL 60637
US

Tel: +1 773 7027369
Fax: +1 773 7029085

Website:
http://www-gsb.uchicago.edu

Contact name
Don Martin

Status
Private; founded 1898

Other offices
None

Teaching staff
Full-time 95; part-time 44

Comments
Executive programmes at the University of Chicago are delivered at the Gleacher Center, situated on the Chicago River in the heart of the city's Magnificent Mile. The Graduate School of Business has a formidable intellectual pedigree. The university as a whole boasts 67 Nobel laureates. However, Chicago was a late entrant in the executive education market with programmes starting as recently as 1996. Tailored programmes account for over 33% of its executive education revenue. Open programmes include the five-day Executive Program in Corporate Strategy, which provides an intensive introduction to industry analysis and positioning, competitive advantage, corporate-level strategy, strategy implementation, competitive dynamics, technology strategy and strategic thinking. The school also offers an innovative programme entitled Enhancing Leadership Performance: the Leader as Teacher, which involves Barbara Lanebrown, a playwright, director and actress.

Columbia Business School

Address
Executive Education
480 Armstrong Hall
2880 Broadway
New York NY 10025
US

Tel: +1 212 8543395
0800 6923932 (US only)
Fax: +1 212 3161473

E-mail:
exec@claven.gsb.columbia.edu

Website:
http://www.columbia.edu

Contact name
Mary Banks, Columbia executive education

Status
Part of Columbia University

Other offices
US: Harriman, NY

Teaching staff
Full-time 100; part-time 85

Comments

Columbia Business School has been in the executive education market since 1952. Most of its programmes are held at Arden House, a mountain-top conference centre 50 miles north of New York. The four-week Senior Executive Program celebrates its 100th session in October 1998. First offered in 1952, the programme attracts over 60% of its participants from outside the US. Among the school's other popular open programmes is The Learning Organization: Driving Superior Performance (four days), launched in 1997. Columbia has offered tailored programmes since 1984 and they constitute around half of its executive education business. It highlights its use of account managers and its commitment to "tangible and measurable results": Clients for tailored programmes include Sony, BOC Group and Deloitte & Touche. The school also runs the Gulf Executive Program with the Bahrain Institute of Banking and Finance.

Edwin L Cox School of Business—Southern Methodist University

Address
PO Box 750333
Dallas TX 75275-0333
US

Tel: +1 214 7682630
Fax: +1 214 7683956

E-mail:
mbainfo@mail.cox.smu.edu

Website:
http://www.cox.smu.edu

Contact name
Donna Lau Smith

Status
Private

Other offices
None

Teaching staff
Full-time 69; part-time 23

Comments

The Edwin L Cox School of Business at Southern Methodist University in Dallas, Texas, is one of the largest providers of executive education in the US. During 1997 it ran over 50 programmes with nearly 7,000 participants. Established for over 75 years, it offers open and tailored programmes. Open programmes include Management of Managers, Leading the High-Performance Sales Organization, the Mid-Management Program (a 12-week certificate programme) and the First-Line Management Program. Cox also offers a range of shorter programmes covering sales and marketing and accounting and finance. Among its new offerings is the Advanced Management Program for Telecommunications Executives. Cox runs a number of residential programmes, including some covering issues relevant to the energy industry, such as financial planning and strategic leadership in the oil and gas industry. In 1998 the Strategic Leadership Program is also delivered in London, UK. Cox offers tailored programmes which follow a five-step approach: definition, analysis, design, implementation and evaluation. All of its open programmes can be delivered in-house.

Darden Executive Education—University of Virginia

Address
PO Box 6550
Charlottesville VA 22906-6550
US

Tel: +1 804 9243000
Fax: +1 804 9822833

E-mail:
Darden.Exed@Virginia.edu

Website:
http://www.darden.virginia.edu

Contact name
Diana P Pickral, director,
executive education

Status
Part of University of Virginia;
founded 1954

Other offices
None

Teaching staff
Full-time 70

Comments

Part of the University of Virginia, Darden's reputation in the field of executive education has been steadily enhanced in recent years. Founded in 1954 and located in Charlottesville, Darden Executive Education offers an extensive range of over 50 programmes, with consortium and tailored programmes forming a growing part of its business. Its major open programmes include the six-week Executive Program and the three-week Developing Managerial Excellence, targeted at high-potential managers. Darden also offers a variety of short programmes on more specialist subjects. These include Managing the Corporate Aviation Function (sponsored with the National Business Aircraft Association) and Evaluation of Capital Projects. Among its newest programmes are Strategic Evolution and Revolution in the Americas (held in Mexico and Canada), Managing in the Global Business Environment and the Darden Minority Business Executive Program (run in co-operation with the Office of Minority Procurement Programs). The school has recently opened a $30m five-building complex, Darden Grounds.

Fisher College of Business—The Ohio State University

Address
10 Page Hall
1810 College Road
Columbus OH 43210-1310
US

Tel: +1 614 2929300
Fax: +1 614 2926644

E-mail: Stenner.1@osu.edu

Website:
http://www.cob.ohio-state.edu

Contact name
Steve Stenner, program manager

Status
Executive Education, founded
1945, is a department within the
Fisher College of Business, The
Ohio State University

Other offices
None

Teaching staff
Full-time 80; part-time 20

Comments

The Ohio State University's College of Business was boosted by a $20m donation from an industrialist, Max M Fisher, and is now called the Fisher College of Business. Tailored programmes, offered since the early 1960s, constitute the bulk of its activities. The school also offers a range of open programmes. These include Business to Business Marketing, the Academy for Financial Executives, Project Management, the Logistics Management Program and Customer-Driven Manufacturing. A number of specialised programmes are offered for participants in the nursing home industry. Among the school's most innovative programmes is the Korean R&D Management Program, aimed at R&D managers in South Korean organisations and co-ordinated by Chungnam University in South Korea. Fisher also offers a four-part Executive Development Program.

Fuqua School of Business—Duke University

Address
Box 90116
Durham NC 27708-0116
US

Tel: +1 919 6608011
(0800 372 3932 US only)
Fax: +1 919 6817761

E-mail:
fuqua-execed@mail.duke.edu

Website:
http://www.fuqua.duke.edu

Contact name
Registration co-ordinator

Status
Part of Duke University; Fuqua
School of Business founded 1969

Other offices
Belgium: Brussels

Teaching staff
Full-time 117

Comments

Tailored programmes (offered only since 1985) now constitute the majority of executive education programmes at Duke University's Fuqua School of Business in Durham, North Carolina. Executive programmes are based in the purpose-built R David Thomas Conference Center. One of Fuqua's most prestigious open programmes is the six-week Global Executive Program, made up of three two-week sessions and delivered at Fuqua as well as in Asia and Europe. "We try to get firms to boldly go where no firms have gone before," says Peter Frews, the academic programme director. "We provide a concise but deep exposure to the challenges of managing global organisations and the differences encountered in managing in economies at varying stages of maturation." Over 40% of the senior managers on the programme are typically from outside the US. Among Fuqua's other longer programmes are the Advanced Management Program (four weeks) and the two-week Program for Manager Development.

Goizueta Business School—Emory University

Address
Office of Executive Programs
1300 Clifton Road
Suite 215
Atlanta GA 30322-2710
US

Tel: +1 404 7272200
Fax: +1 404 7273072

E-mail: oep@bus.emory.edu

Website:
http://www.emory.edu/BUS

Contact name
Candy Tate, marketing manager

Status
Part of Emory University; business
school founded 1959

Other offices
None

Teaching staff
Part-time 20

Comments

Named after the late Coca-Cola chief, Roberto Goizueta, Emory University's Goizueta Business School is a mere five miles from downtown Atlanta. Tailored programmes form 65% of the school's executive programmes and it has over 30 years' experience in tailoring programmes. Clients include the Federal Reserve Bank, United Parcel Service and Lockheed-Martin. Among Goizueta's open programmes is the three-week Executive Development Consortium Program for Senior Managers, delivered over five months, which now features an action-learning project. Developing Leaders in High-Potential Managers features a computer-based business simulation which divides participants into teams charged with guiding their "companies" through decision-making in areas such as resource allocation, marketing strategy, new product development and increasing bottom-line profitability.

Harvard Business School

Address
Soldiers Field
Boston MA 02163
US

Tel: +1 617 4956555
Fax: +1 617 4956999

E-mail:
executive_education@hbs.edu

Website:
http://www.exed.hbs.edu

Contact name
Bob Fogel, executive director,
executive education

Status
Part of Harvard University

Other offices
None

Teaching staff
Full-time 185

Comments
Harvard, the best-known business school in the world, has managed to stay ahead because of its high-calibre faculty and willingness to change with the times. It was the top-ranked school in *Business Week's* 1997 survey of executive education. The dean, Kim Clark, has brought the school up to speed with technology, and the first electronic case study was used for instruction in 1996. Its executive programmes attracted over 4,500 participants during 1997. New offerings include the Program for Global Leadership, which delivers one module in Singapore and one through distance learning. Its leading programmes remain among the most renowned in the world and are priced accordingly: the two-month Advanced Management Program costs $40,500. Harvard's faculty contains some leading management thinkers, such as Rosabeth Moss Kanter, Michael Porter and Chris Argyris. However, the school has not yet boarded the tailored programmes bandwagon with unbridled enthusiasm. These still account for only a small percentage (around 15%) of its executive programmes.

University of Illinois at Urbana-Champaign—Executive Development Center

Address
205 David Kinley Hall
1407 W Gregory Drive
Urbana IL 61801
US

Tel: +1 217 3334552
Fax: +1 217 2448537

E-mail: edc@uiuc.edu

Website:
http://www.cba.uiuc.edu/edc/

Contact name
Carolyn M Pribble, acting director

Status
Division of university; founded
1957

Other offices
None

Teaching staff
Full-time 150

Comments
The Executive Development Center at the University of Illinois, based on the Illinois prairie in the twin cities of Urbana and Champaign, was established in 1957. It is home to the Center for Supercomputing Research and Development and the Beckman Institute for Advanced Science and Technology. Illinois offers three main executive programmes: the Executive Development Program (three weeks); the Program for International Managers (one year); and the Specialized Program for International Managers (18 weeks). The last two are geared towards executives whose first language is not English. The Program for International Managers includes English tuition at the university's Intensive English Institute. Illinois has over 40 years' experience in tailored programmes. These form the bulk of its activities and all its open programmes can be tailored.

Richard Ivey School of Business—University of Western Ontario

Address
London
Ontario N6A 3K7
Canada

Tel: +1 519 6613272
Fax: +1 519 6613411

E-mail: execdev@ivey.uwo.ca

Website:
http://www.ivey.uwo.ca/executiv

Contact name
Beverley Lennox, director of marketing, executive development programs

Status
Faculty of university; business school founded 1923

Other offices
None

Teaching staff
Full-time 45

Comments

The Richard Ivey School of Business at the University of Western Ontario has been offering executive education programmes for over 40 years. One of Canada's leading business schools, it was previously known as Western Business School but changed its name to reflect growing global aspirations. Among Ivey's programmes are the Western Executive Program, a four-week development programme for general managers and senior functional managers. It also runs an Executive Marketing Program with the American Electronics Association. This five-day programme is designed to help executives in high-tech companies create and implement successful market plans for technology-intensive products and services. Ivey offers tailored programmes and has worked with a small number of multinational corporations, including National Semiconductor and Groupe Schneider.

Johnson Graduate School of Management—Cornell University

Address
Executive Education
Sage Hall
Ithaca NY 14853-6201
US

Tel: +1 607 2554251
Fax: +1 607 2550018

E-mail: execed@cornell.edu

Website:
http://www.gsm.cornell.edu

Contact name
Ann Sampson Poe, marketing manager for executive education

Status
Part of Cornell University; Johnson School founded 1946

Other offices
None

Teaching staff
Full-time 60

Comments

Situated in up-state New York, Cornell dominates the town of Ithaca. It is one of the largest and most comprehensive universities in the Ivy League and big-name management alumni include Tom Peters, Kenneth Blanchard and John Naisbitt. Cornell's faculty includes an exceptional sprinkling of Nobel laureates and Pulitzer Prize winners. The Johnson School delivers an almost equal split of open and tailored programmes. Among the more interesting of its 13 open programmes is the one-week Executive Program for Midsized Companies, which covers everything from a 360-degree appraisal of an individual's leadership style to the development of a strategic plan. Johnson also offers Strategic Leadership in an Uncertain World, held in Ithaca, NY, and New York City. This is one of the few programmes to have grasped the nettle of dealing with the uncertainty and ambiguity now prevalent in the corporate world. Johnson's tailored programme customers include Glaxo Wellcome and Hyundai.

Jesse H Jones Graduate School of Management—Rice University

Address
Office of Executive Education
6100 Main Street MS 531
Houston TX 77005
US

Tel: +1 713 5276060
Fax: +1 713 2855131

Website:
http://www.ruf.rice.edu/~jgs

Contact name
Kelley Ennis, registrations
co-ordinator

Status
Part of university; founded 1983

Other offices
None

Teaching staff
Full-time 8; part-time 5

Comments

By US standards Rice is a small and intimate university. Despite being close to downtown Houston, it prides itself on the small ratio of students to faculty. The Office of Executive Development at the university's Jesse H Jones Graduate School of Business offers an almost equal split of open and tailored programmes. Content is broadly divided into seven areas: general management; finance and accounting; marketing and sales; operations management; individual and group behaviour; communications; and special programmes. Tailored programmes have been delivered to over 50 organisations and vary in length from half a day to 15 days or more. Executives attending programmes at the Jones School are generally North American, with less than 5% coming from elsewhere.

Joseph M Katz Graduate School of Business— University of Pittsburgh

Address
276 Mervis Hall
Pittsburgh PA 15260
US

Tel: +1 412 6481700
Fax: +1 412 6481656

E-mail: mba-admissions
@katz.business.pitt.edu

Website:
http://www.pitt.edu/~business/

Contact name
Carol J Swanberg

Status
Affiliated to University of
Pittsburgh

Other offices
None

Teaching staff
Full-time 64; part-time 25

Comments

The showpiece of the Joseph M Katz Graduate School of Business at the University of Pittsburgh is the Management Program for Executives (MPE). Founded in 1949, the four-week MPE is one of the three oldest executive programmes in the US. It is an unashamedly traditional general management programme focusing on strategic planning and implementation. Among the features of the MPE are a team project, a management simulation and the involvement of a global business panel of outside speakers. Katz also runs tailored programmes, which now form the bulk of its business, and offers a wide variety of seminars lasting 1-3 days. These are generally specialised and include activity-based costing, purchasing control and writing marketing plans.

Kelley School of Business—Indiana University

Address
Executive Education
IU Research Park, Suite 106
501 N Morton Street
Bloomington IN 47404-3730
US

Tel: +1 812 8550229
Fax: +1 812 8556216

E-mail: bocastel@indiana.edu

Website:
http://www.kelley.iu.edu/ee

Contact name
Bob Costello

Status
Public; affiliated to Indiana
University

Other offices
US: New York

Teaching staff
Full-time 111; part-time 20

Comments
At the end of 1997 the business school at Indiana University, in Bloomington, was renamed the Kelley School of Business following a donation of $18m from E W Kelley to fund scholarships for undergraduates. Executive education at Indiana includes open, tailored and consortium programmes. During 1997 over 1,300 participants took part in its executive programmes. It currently offers two series of open programmes: the Professional Development Series; and the Personal Development Series. Consortium programmes, in which the school has over ten years' experience, are "structured as a strategic alliance of companies to pursue common educational objectives". They include the Global Partnership for Executive Development, the Indiana Partnership for Management Development, the Indiana Forum for Management Development and the International Service Partnership. Tailored programmes have been offered at Indiana since 1968.

J L Kellogg Graduate School of Management—Northwestern University

Address
James L Allen Center
2169 N Sheridan Road
Evanston IL 60208-2800
US

Tel: +1 847 4677000
Fax: +1 847 4914323

E-mail: execed@nwu.edu

Website:
http://www.kellogg.nwu.edu

Contact name
Kate B Mohr, director of
marketing, executive programs

Status
Part of Northwestern University

Other offices
None

Teaching staff
150

Comments
The J L Kellogg Graduate School of Management at Northwestern University is one of the highest-ranked and best-known business schools in the world. In the most recent *Business Week* survey it came third, but as a consolation it was ranked first for marketing. Its executive programmes began in 1951 and are now based at the James L Allen Center on the Evanston campus. The Allen Center, 30 minutes' drive from downtown Chicago, overlooks Lake Michigan and has 150 bedrooms among other resources. New programmes include a number of alliances with other institutions, such as Direccão 2000, a general management programme tailored for senior executives from Brazil and Latin America run in conjunction with Brazil's Fundação Dom Cabral. Among its 60 programmes, Kellogg also offers the six-day Frontiers of Business Practices in alliance with French and Dutch organisations. Tailored programmes, which have been offered for over 25 years, account for around 50% of Kellogg's executive programmes. Sessions last from several days to several weeks and may be modular in format.

Kenan-Flagler Business School—University of North Carolina at Chapel Hill

Address
Campus Box 3490
McColl Building, Chapel Hill
NC 27599-3490, US

Tel: +1 919 9623236
Fax: +1 919 9620898

E-mail: mba-info@unc.edu

Website:
http://www.bschool.unc.edu

Contact name
Shannon M Dahill

Status
A division of public University of
North Carolina; founded 1953

Other offices
None

Teaching staff
Full-time 73; part-time 15

Comments

Kenan-Flagler was one of the first business schools to offer executive education when it started up in 1953. More than 4,000 executives attend its programmes each year and its facilities are being greatly expanded. The new $44m McColl Building provides a sizeable extension, and work is now under way on the Paul J Rizzo Conference Center at Meadowmount. This state-of-the-art residential executive education complex will include additional classrooms and seminar rooms, offices, 56 guest rooms and a health club. Kenan-Flagler offers open and tailored programmes from its Chapel Hill base. In 1997 *Business Week* rated it the top provider of tailored programmes.

Krannert Executive Education Programs—Purdue University

Address
1310 Krannert Center for
Executive Education & Research
West Lafayette IN 47907-1310
US

Tel: +1 765 4947700
Fax: +1 765 4963483

E-mail:
sheahan@mgmt.purdue.edu

Website:
http://www2.mgmt.purdue.edu

Contact name
Michael Sheahan, associate
director

Status
Part of Krannert Graduate School
of Management at Purdue
University; founded 1983

Other offices
None (but joint programmes
conducted with institutions
worldwide)

Teaching staff
Full-time 8; part-time 50

Comments

Purdue University's Krannert Graduate School of Management at West Lafayette, Indiana, offers a range of open and tailored programmes. Its open programmes are "designed to offer a quality, mini-MBA learning experience for mid-career professionals". Krannert's most prestigious programme is the intensive one-week residential Engineering/Management Program. Launched in 1986, it covers state-of-the-art developments in technical areas of current importance and provides appropriate managerial tools. Tailored programmes include the 12-month Owens-Brockway Technical Training and Development Program. Designed for technical and management staff, it consists of three three-day modules addressing issues such as managing new product innovation and developing critical human resources. Krannert also offers sponsored programmes which are tailored to meet the needs of a co-sponsoring professional society or association.

McGill Executive Institute—McGill University

Address
1001 Sherbrooke Street West,
Room 401
Montreal
Quebec H3A 1G5
Canada

Tel: +1 514 3983970
Fax: +1 514 3987443

E-mail:
executive@management.mcgill.ca

Website:
http://www.management.mcgill.ca

Contact name
Dora Koop, associate director

Status
Part of McGill University; founded 1950

Other offices
None

Teaching staff
Part-time 45

Comments

The McGill Executive Institute, part of McGill University in Montreal, offers short courses covering a variety of skills and a range of functionally based programmes. About 25% of the programmes it offers are tailored. New programmes include Marketing in the Information Age and Performance Management, both lasting three days. McGill also offers an Advanced Management Course and an Executive Development Course which run for 13 week-day evenings and three weekends. In keeping with its reputation as Canada's only Ivy League university, its faculty includes a leading thinker, Henry Mintzberg. He has developed the International Master's Program in Practising Management, part of which is delivered by McGill. This 16-month programme also involves France's INSEAD, the Indian Institute of Management, Japan's Hitosubashi University and the UK's Lancaster Business School. All McGill's open programmes are available for in-house delivery.

University of Michigan Business School

Address
Executive Education Center
Ann Arbor MI 48109-1234
US

Tel: +1 734 7631003
Fax: +1 734 7639467

E-mail: um.exec.ed@umich.edu

Website:
http://www.bus.umich.edu

Contact name
Charles Ferguson, director of marketing

Status
University-based business school

Other offices
Hong Kong

Teaching staff
Full-time 130

Comments

Michigan Business School, based in the college town of Ann Arbor (25 miles from Detroit Airport), is a major force in executive education and has been in the business for nearly 50 years. The school annually attracts over 5,000 participants to 54 different executive programmes (residential, ranging in length from three days to four weeks). Its programmes are increasingly innovative and international. One of Michigan's most interesting ventures is the Global Program for Management Development held in Bangalore, India, Shanghai, China, and Barcelona, Spain. Over recent years the school has greatly developed its international presence. It now runs programmes throughout the world including, in Asia, Bangalore, Bangkok, Shanghai, Singapore and Taipei. It is particularly active in China. In Europe programmes are run in Geneva and Barcelona. Michigan's tailored programmes are mostly in the area of organisational change and the school has developed a well-tested approach for collaborating with companies.

MIT Sloan School of Management—Massachusetts Institute of Technology

Address
50 Memorial Drive E52-101
Cambridge MA 02142
US

Tel: +1 617 2537166
Fax: +1 617 2521200

E-mail: sloanexeced@mit.edu

Website:
http://web.mit.edu/sloan/www

Contact name
Robert Russman Halperin,
director, executive education

Status
Part of Massachusetts Institute of
Technology; founded 1931

Other offices
None

Teaching staff
100

Comments
The Sloan School of Management at the Massachusetts Institute of Technology (MIT) was founded in 1931 and has a formidable track record. In *Business Week*'s 1997 executive education survey it was the top-ranked school in information systems, R&D and manufacturing. Sloan's faculty includes pioneers such as Jay Forrester and Ed Schein, as well as contemporary gurus such as Peter Senge. The school offers a small number of intensive, high-calibre programmes. These include System Dynamics: Modeling for Organizational Learning, a one-week introduction to a subject which MIT originated and continues to dominate. It also runs Managing the IT Infrastructure for Global Competitiveness led by faculty from the MIT Center for Information Systems Research. This covers IT infrastructure in the next century, leveraging the public network infrastructure, developing and managing a distributed computing environment and strategic choices in infrastructure management. Tailored programmes are also offered, although so far these form only a small part of Sloan's executive education activities.

Owen Graduate School of Management—Vanderbilt University

Address
401 South 21st Avenue
Nashville TN 37203
US

Tel: +1 615 3226469
Fax: +1 615 3431175

E-mail:
tonya.hobbs@owen.vanderbilt.edu

Website:
http://mba.vanderbilt.edu

Contact name
Tonya Hobbs

Status
Private, part of Vanderbilt
University; founded 1969

Other offices
None

Teaching staff
Full-time 43; part-time 17

Comments
The Owen Graduate School of Management at Vanderbilt University in Nashville, Tennessee, was founded in 1969 and offers both open and tailored programmes. Its open programmes usually last three days and concentrate on management tools and techniques. They include Successful Sales Management, Finance and Accounting for Non-Financial Managers, Coaching and Counselling, Persuasion and Influencing Skills and Marketing Strategy. Owen also offers a one-week Executive Leadership Program delivered in Santa Fe, New Mexico, and a three-day Leadership Development Program. Its latest programme is aimed at fund-raisers, board members and managers of charitable organisations and is presented in association with the National Society of Fund Raising. In 1997 *Business Week* ranked Owen's Executive MBA among the top 20.

Rotman School of Management—University of Toronto

Address
105 St George Street
Toronto
Ontario M5S 3E6
Canada

Tel: +1 416 9784441
Fax: +1 416 9712866

E-mail:
execed@mgmt.utoronto.ca

Website:
http://www.mgmt.utoronto.ca

Contact name
Richard E Kurovsky, assistant dean

Status
Part of University of Toronto

Other offices
Montreal; Ottawa; Hong Kong

Teaching staff
Full-time 60; part-time 45

Comments

The Joseph L Rotman School of Management at the University of Toronto, founded in 1978, offers a small number of open and tailored executive programmes. Tailored programmes dominate the school's output. New programmes include the Advanced Program in Managing Strategic Change and the forthcoming Global Management Program. Rotman's best-established programme is the Advanced Program in Human Resources Management, now in its tenth year. This is a joint venture with the Human Resources Professionals Association of Ontario. It covers eight subject areas in four one-week learning modules, which are held every two months.

Simmons Graduate School of Management

Address
409 Commonwealth Avenue
Boston MA 02215
US

Tel: +1 617 5213835
Fax: +1 617 5213870

E-mail:
mdp@vmsvax.simmons.edu

Website:
http://www.simmons.edu

Contact name
Joan Kelly, director of marketing

Status
Part of Simmons College

Other offices
None

Teaching staff
Full-time 12; part-time 4

Comments

Simmons Graduate School of Business, a women-only establishment, was founded in 1973 by the authors of *The Managerial Woman*, Margaret Hennig and Anne Jardim. Based in Boston's historic Back Bay area, the school runs two residential executive programmes. The four-week Program for Developing Managers covers functional understanding, behavioural insight and current issues. The one-week Managing for Results programme has a more personal approach, allowing participants to assess their management styles and make changes to improve effectiveness. Simmons' programmes can be tailored for use by a single organisation.

William E Simon Graduate School of Business Administration—University of Rochester

Address
Schlegel Hall, Box 270107
University of Rochester
Rochester NY 14627-0107
US

Tel: +1 716 2753439
Fax: +1 716 2443612

E-mail: edp@ssb.rochester.edu

Website:
http://www.ssb.rochester.edu

Contact name
Richard M Popovic

Status
Private; part of University of Rochester

Other offices
None

Teaching staff
Full-time 50; part-time 11

Comments

The Simon School of Business is based in the University of Rochester's campus near the banks of the Genesee River, three miles from downtown Rochester. It concentrates on open programmes, most of which last five days. These include: Corporate Strategy; Management of Change in Complex Organizations; Managing the IT Infrastructure for Global Competitiveness; Negotiation: Theory and Practice; Product Design, Development and Management; and System Dynamics. The school is also involved in the Greater Boston Executive Program, a consortium of local companies and business schools. Simon has close associations with Nijenrode University in the Netherlands and the University of Bern in Switzerland, offering Executive MBA programmes in association with each of them.

The Mary Jean and Frank P Smeal College of Business Administration—Pennsylvania State University

Address
Penn State Executive Programs
310 Business Administration Building
University Park PA 16802
US

Tel: +1 814 8653435
Fax: +1 814 8653372

E-mail: pjs17@psu.edu

Website:
http://www.smeal.psu.edu/psep

Contact name
Peter Steinberg, client development manager

Status
Public; part of Pennsylvania State University

Other offices
None

Teaching staff
n/a

Comments

Smeal College is located on the Penn State campus in Nittany Valley. It is one of the most rapidly growing providers of executive education in the US, and the number of participants has doubled over the last five years. Smeal offers seven general management executive programmes ranging in length from one to four weeks. These include an Executive Management Program as well as the more unusual Engineer/Scientist as Manager Program and the Agribusiness Executive Program. Three operations programmes cover manufacturing strategy and technology, logistics and supply management and purchasing. The school also offers two human resource management programmes. Tailored programmes now account for almost half of Smeal's executive education business. Recent clients include Daimler-Benz, Armstrong World Industries and the US Army.

University of South Carolina—Daniel Management Center

Address
1705 College Street
Columbia SC 29208
US

Tel: +1 800 EXEC DMC
Fax: +1 803 7774447

E-mail:
PeterT@darla.badm.sc.edu

Website:
http://www.uscdmc.org

Contact name
Peter Topping, director, Daniel
Management Center

Status
Part of the Darla Moore School
of Business

Other offices
None

Teaching staff
Faculty 110; consultants &
practitioners as needed

Comments
The Daniel Management Center, founded in 1960, is based in Columbia and offers a range of open and tailored programmes. Open programmes cover professional management, managerial excellence, finance and accounting, teams and teamwork, front-line management, communications and interpersonal skills and international business. The school also runs a number of annual conferences and seminars. Tailored programmes account for over half of the centre's activities, and most of its open programmes can be adapted. The subjects covered by tailored programmes have included customer-focused management, finance for non-financial managers, time and priority management and international business training. The number of foreign participants has increased over recent years.

Stanford Graduate School of Business—Stanford University

Address
Executive Education
Graduate School of Business
Stanford CA 94305-5015
US

Tel: +1 650 7233341
Fax: +1 650 7233950

E-mail: executive_education
@gsb.stanford.edu

Website:
http://www-gsb.stanford.edu/eep

Contact name
Alice Sheehan, assistant director
for administration

Status
Part of Stanford University

Other offices
None

Teaching staff
Approximately 60 business school
faculty cover executive education

Comments
Stanford has long been established as one of the world's leading business schools. It now boasts the new Schwab Residential Center on its 8,000-acre campus, 35 miles south of San Francisco. Stanford's faculty includes authors Jerry Porras and James Collins, Jeffrey Pfeffer and Paul Romer. At other times it calls on Intel's Andy Grove and a former secretary of state, George Shultz. Programmes include a comprehensive 6½-week general management programme (established in 1952), a general management programme for smaller companies, a variety of one- and two-week programmes and two overseas programmes offered in conjunction with the National University of Singapore. Among its new programmes is the one-week Managing Technology and Strategic Innovation for managers in high-tech industries. It also runs the topical Store Wars programme on the packaged goods industry and Strategic Uses of Information Technology. A small number of tailored programmes is available.

Leonard N Stern School of Business—New York University

Address
44 West 4th Street
New York NY 10012-1126
US

Tel: +1 212 9980273
Fax: +1 212 9954502

E-mail: sternmba@stern.nyu.edu

Website:
http://www.stern.nyu.edu

Contact name
Diane Belville

Status
Private

Other offices
None

Teaching staff
Full-time 206; part-time 110

Comments

The Stern School of Business is based on New York University's historic Greenwich Village campus, sandwiched between Wall Street and Manhattan. There is a strong financial element to its open programmes and its excellent reputation in this field is one of the school's main attractions. Such programmes include Frameworks for Measuring the Credit Risk of Credit Asset Portfolios, Frontiers in Corporate Valuation and Understanding the Basis and Consequences of Managerial Financial Decisions. The school's Salomon Center is a research centre focusing on the global financial services industry and its principal institutions. Stern also offers tailored programmes. Under the dean, George Daly, the emphasis at Stern is moving away from strictly finance-related topics to a broader range of programmes . "If I were God and I had a business school, this is where I'd put it," says Mr Daly.

University of Texas at Austin—Graduate School of Business

Address
Executive Education
PO Box 7337
Austin TX 78713-7337
US

Tel: +1 512 4715893
Fax: +1 512 4710853

E-mail: edp@uts.cc.utexas.edu

Website:
http://www.bus.utexas.edu

Contact name
Ken Graham, associate dean

Status
Part of the University of Texas at Austin; founded 1955

Other offices
None

Teaching staff
About 170 full-time faculty teach part-time in executive education

Comments

The Graduate School of Business at the University of Texas at Austin has offered executive education since the mid-1950s. It currently runs 11 executive programmes. These include two new programmes: Enhancing Your Selling Skills for Success and Expanding the Strategic Role of the Accounting and Finance Profession. The longest programme is the nine-month Competitive Business Leadership Institute, which is a series of monthly meetings designed for middle and senior managers who need to build up their knowledge of business strategies in order to progress to leadership positions. The school also runs the Institute for Management Leadership for technical managers who need to cover important business issues at a faster rate. More than half of its executive programmes are tailored and these form a growing part of the school's activities. Although it is one of the larger providers of executive education with over 2,500 participants annually, only a small percentage of these come from outside the US.

Thunderbird—American Graduate School of International Management

Address
Thunderbird Executive Education
15249 North 59th Avenue
Glendale AZ 85306-6004
US

Tel: +1 602 9787925
Fax: +1 602 4394851

E-mail: executiv@t-bird.edu

Website:
http://www.t-bird.edu/execed

Contact name
Frank Lloyd, vice-president for
executive education

Status
Department of Graduate School
of Business; founded 1946

Other offices
France: Archamps; Japan: Tokyo

Teaching staff
Full-time (whole school) 103

Comments
Thunderbird has long been the most internationally oriented US business school. Typically, one-third or more of programme participants come from outside North America. The faculty is similarly multinational. The school offers a range of open and tailored programmes. Not surprisingly, given its avowed internationalism, Thunderbird delivers a strong global message. The Global Leadership Certificate, for example, surveys 14 global management topics. Among its other programmes are Financial Issues in Global Competition, Building Global Marketing Competitiveness and Globalisation: Merging Strategy with Action. Thunderbird also has expertise in the oil and gas industry. As part of its international commitment, Thunderbird has a Language and Culture Center. Tailored programmes dominate at Thunderbird. It also operates a number of international consortia of companies.

Wharton School—University of Pennsylvania—Aresty Institute of Executive Education

Address
Steinberg Conference Center
255 S 38th Street
Philadelphia PA 19104-6359
US

Tel: +1 215 8981776
Fax: +1 215 3864304

E-mail:
execed@wharton.upenn.edu

Website:
http://www.wharton.upenn.edu

Contact name
Course consultant, Aresty
Institute of Executive Education

Status
Part of university; Wharton
School founded 1881

Other offices
None

Teaching staff
Full-time 186; part-time 40

Comments
Over 9,000 executives annually pass through Wharton programmes at its Aresty Institute in Philadelphia. In *Business Week*'s 1997 survey of executive education providers Wharton was ranked fourth, but it was ranked first for finance. Among its leading programmes is the five-week Advanced Management Program for senior line or functional executives. The class size is limited to 45 and, typically, two-thirds of participants come from outside the US. Several of Wharton's programmes offer on-line forums for discussion. Among its more unusual offerings is the Wharton/Spencer Stuart Directors Institute, a living case with participants serving on the board of MegaMicro Inc. A number of Wharton's programmes are offered in Asia: Managing Strategic Change in Taiwan; a Banking and Risk Management Program with the National University of Singapore; and a programme with the Nomura School of Advanced Management in Japan. More of these are anticipated. The school also offers tailored and industry-specific programmes.

University of Wisconsin-Madison—Graduate School of Business

Address
975 University Avenue
Madison WI 53706-1323
US

Tel: +1 608 2621556
Fax: +1 608 2654192

E-mail:
uwmadmba@bus.wisc.edu

Website:
http://www.wisc.edu/bschool/

Contact name
Randall Dunham

Status
Public university

Other offices
None

Teaching staff
Full-time 82; part-time 1

Comments

The University of Wisconsin's Graduate School of Business in Madison offers more than 250 open programmes. These fall into four categories: executive development, leadership development, human resource management and marketing. Executive development programmes include Project Management Success, Economic Outlook 1999-2000 and Building and Empowering High Performance Teams. Wisconsin offers a particularly wide variety of leadership-related programmes, ranging from Managing Negative Thinking and Behavior to Full-Range Leadership. It also offers tailored programmes, although they make up only a small part of its executive education activities.

Yale School of Management

Address
135 Prospect Street
New Haven CT 06520
US

Tel: +1 203 4325932
Fax: +1 203 4329991

E-mail: som.admissions@yale.edu

Website:
http://www.yale.edu/som

Contact name
Jeffrey E Garten

Status
Private; part of Yale University

Other offices
None

Teaching staff
Full-time 39; part-time 43

Comments

Yale, located in New Haven, Connecticut, is one of the quintessential Ivy League universities. The School of Management was founded in 1976 and provides a variety of tailored programmes for organisations, ranging from short seminars to more integrative programmes lasting several months. Some programmes focus on a particular discipline, such as finance or operations management, while others embrace a broader, multidisciplinary approach. Yale's faculty includes Victor Vroom, who delivers programmes on Leadership and Team Effectiveness.

UK

Ashridge Management College

Address
Berkhamsted
Hertfordshire HP4 1NS
UK

Tel: +44 1442 841000
Fax: +44 1442 841036

E-mail: info@ashridge.org.uk

Website:
http://www.ashridge.org.uk

Contact name
Christine Brown, client
development manager

Status
Independent self-financing
educational trust; founded 1959

Other offices
Representatives in UK: London;
Czech Republic: Prague;
Germany: Erfstadt; Spain: Madrid

Teaching staff
Full-time 71; associates 85

Comments
Ashridge Management College is set in a large country estate 50 km from London. It combines neo-gothic architecture with state-of-the-art facilities, including an excellent Learning Resource Centre and the innovative Ashridge On-Line network. Ashridge has an extensive track record in executive education. Over recent years it has built an international network of associate institutions, practising managers and consultants whose expertise is drawn upon. Unusually, Ashridge has its own consulting firm, Ashridge Consulting, as well as the London-based Strategic Management Centre, a world leader in this subject. Its open programmes fall into eight categories: strategic management; leadership; performance management; personal skills; internal consultancy skills; market-driven business development; financial management; and general management. Many of its offerings are five-day programmes, although the Strategic Management Programme takes three weeks. Tailored work now forms a substantial part of Ashridge's business.

Aston Business School—Aston University

Address
Postgraduate Office
Aston Business School
Birmingham B4 7ET
UK

Tel: +44 121 3335940
Fax: +44 121 3334731

E-mail: abspg@aston.ac.uk

Contact name
Lorraine Croker

Status
Part of Aston University

Other offices
None

Teaching staff
Full-time 78; part-time 25

Comments
Aston Business School is part of Birmingham's Aston University, and its origins lie in the creation of one of the UK's first industrial administration departments in 1947. John Saunders, a leading marketing academic, became head of the school in October 1997. Aston's Management Development Centre delivers a range of programmes tailored to the needs of clients. The number of participants on Aston programmes has grown fivefold since 1993 and clients include Lloyds TSB, Tarmac and Powergen. Aston's conference centre has recently been refurbished and has 20 purpose-built training rooms, a lecture theatre and the Multimedia Decision Support Centre. The business school has a link with EAP (European School of Management) in France, which enables some of its international business students to study there.

University of Bradford Management Centre

Address
Heaton Mount
Keighley Road
Bradford
West Yorkshire BD9 4JU
UK

Tel: +44 1274 234440
Fax: +44 1274 234444

E-mail:
mcclements@bradford.ac.uk

Website:
http://www.brad.ac.uk/edp/

Contact name
Robert McClements, chairman,
Executive Development
Programme

Status
Part of the University of Bradford;
founded 1962

Other offices
None

Teaching staff
Full-time 60; support 80

Comments

The Bradford Management Centre, founded in 1962, is located at Heaton Mount, a self-contained facility in parklands on the outskirts of the city. The majority of Bradford's work is the delivery of tailored programmes. In particular, it has an extensive track record in developing and delivering Executive MBA programmes tailored for particular organisations. Bradford also offers open programmes. These include Skills for Managing Strategically, Profitable Negotiation, Finance for Managers, Employee Relations Negotiation, Principles and Practices of Marketing, Managing People in Organisations, Strategic Marketing and Best Practice Management. Bradford has strong international links with France, Germany, Israel, the Netherlands and Singapore and a good reputation for research.

University of Cambridge—The Judge Institute of Management Studies

Address
Trumpington Street
Cambridge CB2 1AG
UK

Tel: +44 1223 766185
Fax: +44 1223 339701

E-mail: ahw20@cam.ac.uk

Website:
http://www.jims.cam.ac.uk

Contact names
Andy Neely, director of executive
programmes
Angela Walters, research assistant

Status
Department of the University of
Cambridge

Other offices
None

Teaching staff
Full-time 45; part-time 20

Comments

The Judge Institute is the centre of management teaching and research at the University of Cambridge, itself a late convert to business education. The institute is in its fledgling years but has obvious advantages in a globally recognised brand and executive resources. Judge "aims to provide practitioners with a forum for discussion, debate and learning about management and business issues". It offers both open and tailored programmes. Programmes that can be tailored include: Corporate Leadership and Accountability; Business Performance Measurement; and High Performance Manufacturing. It also runs one-day workshops on doing business in China led by a renowned China expert, John Child. These deal with human-resource management issues and new laws and regulations affecting business with and in China. Tailored programmes can be arranged directly or through the Cambridge University Programme for Industry.

City University Business School

Address
Executive Development
24 Chiswell Street
London EC1Y 4TY
UK

Tel: +44 171 4778710
Fax: +44 171 4778882

E-mail: execdevelop@city.ac.uk

Website:
http://www.city.ac.uk/cubs/ed

Contact name
Mike Lewis

Status
Part of City University; founded 1965

Other offices
None

Teaching staff
Full-time 82; part-time 120

Comments

City University Business School has been based in the Barbican Centre in the City of London since 1981 and this location has many advantages. Not surprisingly, City's expertise generally lies in finance-related areas. It has a Centre of Internal Auditing which contributes to programmes covering such topics, which include operational auditing and internal auditing in banks. The school also offers a range of management-skills training programmes including Understanding Company Accounts, Advanced Business Communication and Negotiation Skills. Tailored programmes are offered in specific functional or technical areas, or as full executive development programmes.

Cranfield School of Management

Address
Cranfield
Bedford MK43 0AL
UK

Tel: +44 1234 751122
Fax: +44 1234 751806

Website:
http://www.cranfield.ac.uk/som

Contact name
Fiona Sparkes, marketing manager

Status
Faculty of Cranfield University; founded 1967

Other offices
None

Teaching staff
Full-time 120; part-time 61

Comments

Cranfield School of Management, located about 75 km from London, is one of Europe's leading university management schools. Part of Cranfield University, it has been involved in management education and development since the late 1940s. The School of Management was established in 1967 and has around 120 full-time faculty. Its centres of excellence include the Strategy Network, the Institute for Advanced Research in Marketing, the Human Resource Network, the Centre for Logistics and Transportation, the Operations Management Research Centre and the Information Systems Research Centre. Over 6,000 executives take part in programmes each year, with over 1,000 coming from outside the UK. Its open programmes are extensive (over 100 are offered) and tailored programmes have been run for 110 client organisations. Cranfield is also involved in The European Management Programme Organisation (TEMPO), which allows it to draw on the resources of network members in Germany, France and Spain.

Durham University Business School

Address
Mill Hill Lane
Durham City DH1 3LB
UK

Tel: +44 191 3742211
Fax: +44 191 3743748

Website:
http://www.dur.ac.uk/dubs

Contact name
Mary Urwin, marketing officer

Status
Department of the University of
Durham; founded 1965

Other offices
None

Teaching staff
Full-time 58; network of
associates and visiting professors

Comments

Durham University Business School is part of the UK's third oldest university. Although it has close links with the university, it is largely financially independent. Durham offers both open and tailored programmes. Its emphasis, however, is on tailored programmes, usually delivered in a modular format to minimise time away from the workplace. Open programmes include the one-week Durham Senior Management Programme; it also offers the Institute of Directors' Diploma in Company Direction. Durham is perhaps best known for its Small Business Centre. This works with over 1,000 enterprises as well as local business support networks and offers a number of small business-oriented programmes. These include Maximising Overseas Sales and International Competitiveness, made up of six one-day workshops over 18 weeks, and Managing Innovation which helps owner-managers and key individuals in small businesses to improve competitiveness through the use of innovative ideas and approaches.

Edinburgh Business School—Heriot-Watt University

Address
Edinburgh EH14 4AS
UK

Tel: +44 131 4513090
Fax: +44 131 4513002

E-mail: enquiries@ebs.hw.ac.uk

Website: http://www.ebs.ac.uk

Contact name
Gillian Steele

Status
Part of Heriot-Watt University

Other offices
None

Teaching staff
Full-time 22; part-time 28

Comments

Edinburgh Business School is the Graduate School of Business of Heriot-Watt University. It is located to the west of Edinburgh, close to the airport. The school was launched in 1995, amalgamating Heriot-Watt University Business School and the Esmée Fairbairn Research Centre. The research centre is noted for its work on the development of innovative teaching approaches. Edinburgh is a notable exponent of distance learning and specialises in the design and delivery of tailored programmes. It believes that companies and individuals require "short, sharp workshops addressing specific management training needs", which are then put to use on returning to the workplace.

University of Glasgow Business School

Address
53 Southpark Avenue
Glasgow G12 8LF
UK

Tel: +44 141 3305040
Fax: +44 141 3304939

E-mail: r.paton@mgt.gla.ac.uk

Contact name
Robert Paton

Status
Part of University of Glasgow

Other offices
None

Teaching staff
Full-time 80; part-time 9

Comments
The University of Glasgow counts Adam Smith among its alumni and boasts extensive facilities, including a library with over 1m volumes. The university is particularly proud of its research and the practical application of its ideas. It holds over 100 patents, is involved in 12 joint-venture companies and has over 20 licensing agreements. Glasgow Business School provides tailored and open programmes. Its Department of Management Studies delivers programmes either in-house or on company premises. Programmes can be tailored to allow accreditation of modules against Executive MBA programme subjects. Through its Healthcare Management Centre, the Department of Management Studies plans, manages, delivers and maintains the Accelerated Management Development Programme, Leadership 2000, on behalf of the National Health Service in Scotland.

Henley Management College

Address
Greenlands
Henley-on-Thames
Oxon RG9 3AU
UK

Tel: +44 1491 571454
Fax: +44 1491 571635

E-mail: execed@henleymc.ac.uk

Website:
http://www.henleymc.ac.uk

Contact name
Loraine Isherwood, business
development manager

Status
Independent; founded 1945

Other offices
Hong Kong; Netherlands

Teaching staff
Full-time 50; part-time 50

Comments
Founded in 1945, Henley is the oldest independent management college in Europe. It is located on the banks of the Thames and is renowned for its use of technology. Its executive programmes emphasise group work through the syndicate method, although more personal support is given through regular one-to-one meetings with faculty. Henley's open programmes include general management programmes, programmes for directors, shorter programmes and two language programmes. Its directors' programmes provide more specialised subjects for senior executives and include the Executive Survival Programme, designed by an Olympic athlete and his team, as well as the five-day Corporate Leadership Programme. Henley's tailored programmes are typically 1-2 weeks long and involve 15-24 participants. They may be designed to support major changes in strategic direction or culture or focus on specific skills enhancement. The college is also involved in consortium programmes and company qualification programmes. In 1997 Henley opened premises at Regent's College in Regent's Park, London, and plans to expand this site.

Imperial College Management School

Address
53 Prince's Gate
Exhibition Road
London SW7 2PG

Tel: +1 44 171 5949149
Fax: +1 44 171 8237685

E-mail: m.school@ic.ac.uk

Website: http://www.ic.ac.uk

Contact name
Debbie Johnson, admissions
administrator

Status
College of University of London;
founded 1987

Other offices
None

Teaching staff
Full-time 40; part-time 4

Comments

Imperial College is one of the largest colleges of the University of London. Its Management School was created in 1987 as an interface for management, technology and innovation. Imperial has the advantage of being based in the heart of London and, under the guidance of its director, David Norburn, has quickly cemented a good reputation. Imperial's emphasis is on tailored rather than open programmes. In particular, its clients come from technology-based industries, the oil industry (Imperial has links with the International Petrol Marketing Association) and the health sector. Imperial also provides country-specific programmes for executives from a cross-section of sectors who wish to learn more about British industry as well as requiring functional training. Imperial has hosted delegations from Japan, Thailand and Eastern Europe and organises industrial visits to complement its teaching.

Lancaster University—The Management School

Address
Lancaster LA1 4YX
UK

Tel: +44 1524 594031
Fax: +44 1524 381454

E-mail:
v.goulding@lancaster.ac.uk

Website: http://www.lancs.ac.uk

Contact name
Val Goulding, executive
programmes administrator

Status
Part of university; founded 1964

Other offices
None

Teaching staff
Full-time 88; part-time 22

Comments

Situated on a distinctive 1960s campus just outside the city, the Management School is one of Lancaster University's six faculties. The Management Development Division specialises in designing and implementing programmes tailored to corporate needs, although it also runs open programmes. Lancaster has long-established links with a number of client companies. It has run an MBA programme in partnership with British Airways since 1988 and other clients include Nuclear Electric, Royal Mail and British Aerospace. Programmes make use of the nearby Lancaster House Hotel and Training Centre, which include 14 meeting rooms and links to the university's mainframe computer. Lancaster is also involved in the International Master's Programme in Management, an innovative programme for senior executives involving McGill University, Montreal; the Indian Institute of Management, Ahmedabad; INSEAD, Paris; and Hitosubashi University, Tokyo. Lancaster is one of only three UK business schools to have achieved both the maximum ranking for research and the excellent rating for teaching awarded by the Higher Education Funding Council.

London Business School

Address
Sussex Place
Regent's Park
London NW1 4SA
UK

Tel: +44 171 7066836
Fax: +44 171 7246051

E-mail: execinfo@lbs.ac.uk

Website: http://www.lbs.ac.uk

Contact names
Karen Nisbet or Praful Patel,
client services

Status
Postgraduate school of business
with trust status; founded 1965

Other offices
None

Teaching staff
Full-time 72 teaching (34
research); part-time 13; visiting 44

Comments
In rankings of European schools, London Business School (LBS) usually fights for top place with INSEAD and IMD. Under the leadership of George Bain, LBS cemented its leading place among global schools. Mr Bain's successor, John Quelch, inherits in 1998 a school with growing resources and a high-class faculty, including Sumantra Ghoshal, John Stopford, John Hunt and Gary Hamel, who is a visiting professor and runs an annual open programme. LBS offers a small, but high-quality, number of open programmes, as well as a growing number of tailored programmes. Among the most international is the two-week Marketing Leadership Forum, a modular programme run with Duke University's Fuqua School of Business in Durham, North Carolina. It also runs a Senior Executive Programme which aims to turn senior executives into more effective leaders. LBS's Centre for Management Development works on the development of its tailored programmes, which are limited in order to sustain quality.

Manchester Business School

Address
Booth Street West
Manchester M15 6PB
UK

Tel: +44 161 2756333
Fax: +44 161 2756489

E-mail: p.ogden@fs2.mbs.ac.uk

Website: http://www.mbs.ac.uk.

Contact name
P Ogden, administrative officer

Status
Faculty of The University of
Manchester; founded 1965

Other offices
None

Teaching staff
Full-time 60; visiting 45

Comments
The project-based approach of Manchester Business School (MBS) is labelled the Manchester method. Situated in the heart of the city, MBS's Executive Centre provides a variety of open and tailored programmes. Among the most imaginative are its Service Quality programmes. These are study tours of organisations which are at the leading edge of delivering quality service and include a seven-day tour of North American companies. MBS has a Business Development Centre which provides general management programmes for small and medium-sized companies. Among its activities, the Centre offers company strategy workshops to enable smaller companies to review and re-establish their business strategy. MBS has offered tailored programmes since it first opened its doors in 1965 and is now part of the Manchester Federal School of Business and Management. This gives it access to a much larger number of faculty and resources through the University of Manchester Institute of Technology and the University of Manchester.

The Open University Business School

Address
Course Reservations and Sales
Centre
Walton Hall
Milton Keynes MK7 6AA
UK

Tel: +44 1908 658585
Fax: +44 1908 654320

E-mail: crel-gen@open.ac.uk

Website:
http://www.oubs.open.ac.uk

Contact name
Jenny Lewis

Status
University

Other offices
Belgium: Brussels; Ireland: Dublin

Teaching staff
Full-time 200; part-time associate
lecturers 800

Comments

The Open University Business School (OUBS) was founded in 1983 and has grown rapidly to become a major provider of management development with an annual turnover of over £20m and 25,000 current students. Its distance-learning and modular-based approach has clearly struck a chord. OUBS does not deliver executive programmes in the conventional sense. Individual courses can be built into the Professional Certificate in Management, the Professional Diploma in Management and the MBA. However, electives within the MBA programme may be usefully taken as one-offs to enhance specific areas of management skills. These include Managing Human Resources, International Enterprise, Managing Knowledge, Creative Management and Performance Measurement and Evaluation. A number of companies, such as Price Waterhouse, Whitbread and IBM, have put large numbers of managers through OUBS programmes.

Roffey Park Management Institute

Address
Forest Road
Horsham
West Sussex RH12 4TD
UK

Tel: +44 1293 851644
Fax: +44 1293 851565

E-mail: info@roffey-park.co.uk

Contact name
Catherine Bailey, marketing
assistant

Status
Registered charity; founded 1946

Other offices
None

Teaching staff
Full-time 15; part-time 30

Comments

Roffey Park Management Institute, located near Gatwick Airport, delivered its first programme in 1946. Since then it has developed a reputation for innovative programmes which challenge mainstream thought. Its open programmes are built around personal development, active learning, flexibility, and learning to see things differently and more completely. Two new programmes have been added to its portfolio: the three-day International Leader Series and the two-day Harnessing the Positive Power of Conflict. Three other established programmes (Groups that Work, Improving Self Management and Leading Effective Teams) have been updated. Among programmes being developed are Power, Politics and Principles and Strategic HR Issues. Roffey Park also delivers tailored programmes anywhere in the world. Its 15 faculty are backed by an impressive list of visiting fellows and speakers, among whom are Fons Trompenaars and Ralph Stacey.

Sheffield University Management School

Address
9 Mappin Street
Sheffield S1 4DT
UK

Tel: +44 114 2223379
Fax: +44 114 2223348

E-mail: sums@sheffield.ac.uk

Website: http://www.sums.ac.uk

Contact name
Mandy Robertson, manager,
executive MBA programme

Status
Part of university; formed 1970

Other offices
None

Teaching staff
Full-time 45; part-time 10

Comments
Sheffield University Management School is now based in spacious new accommodation in the city's St George's Square. The £2.5m purpose-built building was opened in 1993. The school was founded in 1970 and offers a small number of open and tailored programmes. Its open programmes include Developing the International Manager, a programme for young executives from outside the UK delivered in four three-month modules. This unusual programme aims to give delegates experience of practical management and in-company training in an international environment, as well as the cultural and language skills necessary to work and manage themselves in a global business environment.

University of Stirling—Faculty of Management

Address
Stirling FK9 4LA
UK

Tel: +44 1786 467415
Fax: +44 1786 450776

E-mail: mba@stir.ac.uk

Website: http://www.stir.ac.uk

Contact name
Peter Rosa

Status
Part of University of Stirling

Other offices
None

Teaching staff
Full-time Faculty of
Management 120

Comments
The Faculty of Management at Stirling University, located in the heart of Scotland, provides facilities for residential or one-day open programmes. The university, founded in 1967, has particular expertise in the start-up and development of small and medium-sized enterprises. Stirling's Management Development Unit also develops and delivers tailored programmes for a diverse client base. Stirling has recently established the Stirling University Consultancy Initiative (SUCi), a consulting and training company. Its remit is wide with interests ranging from helping organisations survive change to modules addressing the need to be commercially aware. Stirling University is also home to a School of Management, which is one of the largest and most highly regarded in Scotland.

Strathclyde Graduate Business School

Address
199 Cathedral Street
Glasgow G4 0QU
UK

Tel: +44 141 5536167
Fax: +44 141 5528851/2501

E-mail: melissa@sgbs.strath.ac.uk

Website:
http://www.strath.ac.uk

Contact name
Melissa McCrindle, business
development manager

Status
Part of the University of
Strathclyde; founded 1947

Other offices
None

Teaching staff
Full-time 15

Comments

Glasgow's Strathclyde Graduate Business School (SGBS) concentrates entirely on tailored executive programmes and is one of the largest business schools of its kind in Europe. Its philosophy is "to integrate executive development with corporate strategy" through an approach which "encompasses research, consultancy and pedagogy in close collaboration with the client organisation". SGBS's research and education have been highly ranked in recent years, reflecting its growing reputation. Its tailored programmes draw from the university's 230-strong faculty. Even so, SGBS is distinct from the university and funded the development of its own building, including a purpose-built residential management facility.

Templeton College

Address
Templeton College
Oxford OX1 5NY
UK

Tel: +44 1865 422500
Fax: +44 1865 422501

E-mail:
enquiries@coll.temp.ox.ac.uk

Website:
http://www.templeton.ox.ac.uk

Contact name
Stephanie Parsons, business
support manager

Status
Graduate college of Oxford
University; founded 1965

Other offices
None

Teaching staff
Full-time 22; part-time 32

Comments

Templeton College had an interesting year in 1997 as Oxford's new Said Business School moved forward towards full operation. Although the two schools are independent, two-thirds of their faculty will be shared. Currently, 1,500 executives pass through Templeton programmes each year. Its central programmes aimed at senior executives are the Advanced Management Programme, the Strategic Leadership Programme and the Senior Executive Finance Programme. Templeton has the advantage of access to the expertise of Oxford University; its Oxford Briefings look at developments in science, technology and society. It also has an extensive track record in tailored programmes. Over 40 organisations have commissioned programmes over the last five years. These include programmes to increase general knowledge of business strategy and operations, contextual programmes examining particular topics, such as the environment, and advanced programmes "to broaden perceptions, foster strategic thinking and develop leadership abilities". Templeton emphasises individual development and claims to have adapted Oxford's traditional tutorial system for modern ends.

Warwick Business School

Address
University of Warwick
Coventry CV4 7AL
UK

Tel: +44 1203 572547
Fax: +44 1203 523719

E-mail:
inquiries@wbs.warwick.ac.uk

Contact name
Deborah Watson, client manager,
Executive Short Course
Programme

Status
Department of Warwick
University; established 1967

Other offices
None

Teaching staff
Full-time 170

Comments
Warwick Business School is part of the University of Warwick and has produced over 12,000 graduates since its creation in 1967. Warwick now has over 3,100 students from around 70 countries worldwide on 17 major study programmes. It has a wide range of areas of expertise and its research is highly rated, with centres covering such subjects as corporate strategy and change, local government and small and medium-sized enterprises. It describes its emphasis as being on impact, partnerships, internationalisation and integration. The majority of Warwick's executive programmes are tailored, with a four-stage process of analysis, design, delivery and evaluation. It also runs the Warwick Masterclass series, comprising one-day seminars on key management issues. Warwick's executive programmes take place at its conference centres in the city, Radcliffe and Scarman House.

AESE—Escola de Direcção e Negócios

Address
Av Sidónio Pais, 20 r/c Dto
1050 Lisbon
Portugal

Tel: +351 1 3154247
Fax: +351 1 3154250

E-mail: aese@mail.telepac.pt

Website:
http://www.cidadevirtual.pt/aese

Contact name
Armando Galhardo

Status
Private; founded 1980

Other offices
Portugal: Oporto

Teaching staff
Full-time 5; part-time 28

Comments
Portugal's leading business school, AESE, was founded in 1980 with the aim of offering "professional formation to executives, within a Christian perspective of man and society". It collaborates closely with IESE, the International Graduate School in Barcelona (itself part of the University of Navarra in Pamplona). AESE offers Advanced Management Programmes and Management Development Programmes. It has run some 20 Advanced Management Programmes in Lisbon and Oporto, involving over 830 business people from a range of organisations. It also runs Follow-up Programmes aimed at executives who have taken part in other programmes and want to keep their skills up to date. AESE offers tailored programmes, but these account for only a small part of its activities.

SDA Bocconi

Address
Via Bocconi 8
20136 Milan
Italy

Tel: +39 2 58363075
Fax: +39 2 58363071

E-mail:
daniela.ballabio@sda.uni-bocconi.i

Website:
http://www.sda.uni-bocconi.it

Contact name
Daniela Ballabio, marketing
services

Status
Founded 1971

Other offices
None

Teaching staff
Full-time 302; part-time 180

Comments
In 1971 Bocconi University set up its own business school. Now SDA (Scuola di Direzione Aziendale) Bocconi, based in Milan, has over 300 faculty and 9,000 executives participate in its executive programmes each year. Commonly regarded as Italy's leading business school, Bocconi offers open and tailored programmes. The latter form a growing part of its business and clients include IBM Europe, for which it designed a General Management Programme. SDA Bocconi is one of the six partners in the five-week Programme for International Managers in Europe (PRIME). Among its facilities is a large economics and business library with nearly 500,000 volumes.

CMC Graduate School of Business

Address
Namesti 5, Kvetna 2
250 88 Celakovice
Czech Republic

Tel: +420 202 899152
Fax: +420 202 892150

E-mail: info@cmc.cz

Website:
http://www.Centraleurope.com

Contact name
Stephen Schackwitz, International
Executive MBA

Status
Non-profit organisation;
established 1990

Other offices
None

Teaching staff
Full-time 6; part-time about 30

Comments
CMC Graduate School of Business aims "to provide management education to strengthen business and enrich society". Situated about 25 km north-east of Prague, it was established in 1990 as a result of co-operation between the University of Pittsburgh's Katz School and the Czech Ministry of Industry. In 1993 CMC was awarded the Center of Excellence designation by the US Agency for International Development. Executive programmes are offered in Czech and English and are delivered in the Czech Republic and other countries in the region. Faculty members are multinational and all are fluent in English. The school also offers tailored programmes and clients include Skoda and Coca-Cola Amatil. A range of international programmes make up a significant part of CMC's activities. These are run for students from visiting schools and include relevant local issues such as forming strategic alliances with the Czech Republic and cross-culture marketing.

EAP—European School of Management

Address
6 avenue de la Porte de
Champerret
75838 Paris Cedex 17
France

Tel: +33 1 44093331
Fax: +33 1 44093335

E-mail: mba@eap.net

Website: http://www.eap.net

Contact name
Farhad Rad-Serecht

Status
Owned by the Paris Chamber of
Commerce and Industry

Other offices
Germany: Berlin; Spain: Madrid;
UK: Oxford

Teaching staff
Full-time 35; part-time 15

Comments
EAP's International Management Development Centre has facilities in France, Germany, Spain and the UK, making it one of the most convincingly international programme providers. Founded in 1973 by the Paris Chamber of Commerce, the faculty of EAP (Ecole Européenne des Affaires) is backed up by a network of over 60 visiting academics and consultants. The majority (around 80%) of its executive programmes are tailored. EAP identifies its main areas of expertise as building crossborder teams; developing effective international collaborative structures; preparing to operate in new business environments; developing international projects; managing technology and innovation across borders; and developing country-to-country interpersonal skills. The school also offers specialised language training in Paris and recently moved its Berlin campus to larger premises in Charlottenburg to cope with rising demand.

ESADE—Escuela Superior de Administración y Dirección de Empresas

Address
Centro de Desarollo Directivo (CDD)
Avenida de Esplugues 92-96
08034 Barcelona
Spain

Tel: +34 3 2804008
Fax: +34 3 2048105

E-mail: cdd@esade.es

Website:
http://www.esade.es/escsup

Contact name
Ceferí Soler

Status
Private business school promoted by ESADE foundation

Other offices
Spain: Madrid

Teaching staff
Full-time 102; part-time 248

Comments

Escuela Superior de Administración y Dirección de Empresas (ESADE), established in 1958 and based in Barcelona, is a private business school which prides itself on the closeness of its relationships with industry. It combines a tradition of internationalism with a commitment to social responsibility and business ethics. Executive development programmes are delivered through the Centro de Desarrollo Directivo. ESADE offers open and tailored programmes in Barcelona and Madrid. Its first Senior Management Programme was taught in 1960. Open programmes are generally quite long; among its shorter programmes are the two-week Entrepreneurship Programme and the 16-hour Process Management, Benchmarking and Re-engineering Programme.

ESSEC Executive Programs

Address
CNIT BP 230
2 Place de la Défense
92053 Paris La Défense
France

Tel: +33 1 46924922
Fax: +33 1 46924990

E-mail: laffaille@edu.essec.fr

Contact name
David Manson, executive programmes director

Status
Executive education branch of Essec University

Other offices
None

Teaching staff
Full-time 80; part-time 50

Comments

The Ecole Supérieure des Sciences Economiques et Commerciales (ESSEC) university was founded in 1907 to offer a two-year programme in industrial, commerce and finance studies. It has established a reputation for innovative approaches to management development. The executive education centre, founded in 1968, is located in the CNIT building next to the World Trade Centre in central Paris. ESSEC now operates as ESSEC IMD and offers over 100 open programmes which can be taken in French and English. These include the General Management Programme, a senior management, French-language programme for executives who wish to "develop their skills and become motors of change for their businesses". Tailored programmes include the Advanced Management Programme for Bull Europe. A number of language programmes are also offered.

Groupe CPA

Address
6-14 avenue de la Porte de
Champerret
75838 Paris Cedex 17
France

Tel: +33 1 44093434
Fax: +33 1 44093499

E-mail:
mcdrumar@schamp.ccip.fr

Contact name
Marie-Christine Drumare,
commercial department

Status
Part of Paris Chamber of
Commerce; founded 1930

Other offices
France: Jouy-en-Josas, Nice, Lille,
Lyon, Toulouse; Spain: Madrid

Teaching staff
Full-time 40; part-time 200

Comments
Groupe CPA (Centre de Perfectionnement aux Affaires) was founded in 1931 by the Paris Chamber of
Commerce with support from Harvard Business School. Its initial aim was "to respond during a time of crisis
to the necessary mobility of executives and to their promotion into senior management positions". One of
the few schools dedicated solely to executive education, its motto today is "Managers training managers",
and its programmes and ethos emphasise the practical application of business theories. Groupe CPA
concentrates on open programmes but it also offers tailored programmes, varying in length from 25 to 40
days. Its major programmes are the one-year General Management Programme (attended by 300 executives
each year) and the one-week European Management Programme, a joint venture with three other providers.
The first CPA campus outside France opened in 1993.

HEC Executive Development Center

Address
1 rue de la Libération
78351 Jouy-en-Josas, Cedex
France

Tel: +33 1 39677018
Fax: +33 1 39677430

E-mail: seyfried@hec.fr

Website: http://www.hec.fr

Contact names
Bertrand Moingeon, associate
dean for executive education
Marie-Pierre Seyfried,
international project manager

Status
Supported by Paris Chamber of
Commerce and Industry

Other offices
None

Teaching staff
Full-time 100;
adjunct lecturers 450

Comments
HEC (the Ecole des Hautes Etudes Commerciales) is a *grande école* which was founded by the Paris Chamber
of Commerce in 1881 as an acknowledgement that management was a profession requiring specific training.
It is located in Jouy-en-Josas just outside Paris. HEC's programmes include PRIME (Programme for
International Managers in Europe—it is one of the six partners), Strategies for Competitive Success and
Business Strategies for Emerging Countries. One of HEC's highest-profile open programmes is the two-day
Annual HEC-Michigan Conference for Top Executives. It also offers tailored programmes in French or English
covering a range of subjects from general management to operations management. HEC's MBA programme
is delivered by the Institut Supérieur des Affaires (ISA).

IE—Instituto de Empresa

Address
María de Molina 11, 13, 15
28006 Madrid
Spain

Tel: +34 91 5689600
Fax: +34 91 4115503

E-mail: admissions@ie.ucm.es

Website: http://www.ie.ucm.es

Contact name
Julian Trigo

Status
Private

Other offices
Colegio de Dirección IE

Teaching staff
Full-time 72; part-time 219

Comments

Instituto de Empresa (IE) was founded in 1973 and is one of the most prominent Spanish providers of executive education. Its Colegio de Dirección offers a range of executive programmes from its Madrid base. Among the areas IE identifies as central to the needs of modern senior executives are: understanding of customer satisfaction and loyalty; leadership through participation and motivation; quality and innovation in products and services; maximisation of value for shareholders; attention towards emerging markets; a cultural base for strategic initiatives; and efficient use of global market resources. Its open programmes are divided into seminars (2-3 days), executive development programmes (covering issues such as logistics and taxation), advanced programmes (for senior executives) and sectoral programmes for particular industries. IE also offers tailored programmes and has recently established the Department of Knowledge Technologies to keep abreast of technological advances and to maximise the use of technology in teaching.

IESE—International Graduate School of Management—University of Navarra

Address
Avenida Pearson 21
08034 Barcelona
Spain

Tel: +34 3 2534200
Fax: +34 3 2534343

E-mail: simpson@iese.edu

Website: http://www.iese.es/

Contact name
Rory Simpson, director of
international corporate relations

Status
Faculty of the University of
Navarra, founded 1958

Other offices
Spain: Madrid

Teaching staff
Full-time 74; part-time 36

Comments

IESE, one of the largest and best-connected business schools in Spain, based in Barcelona, is a member of TEMPO (The European Management Programme Organisation). It offers international senior executive programmes, executive programmes, seminars, a continuous education programme and tailored programmes. The most eye-catching of IESE's activities is a series of international programmes in collaboration with major business schools from North and South America. These include Achieving Breakthrough Service with Harvard and Argentina's Instituto de Altos Estudios Empresariales; Management in the Information Age with MIT's Sloan School; Strategic Management of Technology-Based Companies with Stanford; and the Global Program for Management Development with Michigan and the China Europe International Business School. IESE's new director of international corporate relations is Rory Simpson, formerly with Disneyland in Paris. One of his aims is to develop the executive programme range still further.

IMD—International Institute for Management Development

Address
PO Box 915
1001 Lausanne
Switzerland

Tel: +41 21 6180342
Fax: +41 21 6180715

E-mail: info@imd.ch

Website: http://www.imd.ch

Contact name
Karen Lindquist, information officer

Status
Independent, non-profit organisation; founded 1946

Other offices
None

Teaching staff
Full-time 31; part-time 12

Comments

IMD in Lausanne was the result of a merger in 1992 of two international management centres created respectively by Alcan and Nestlé: IMI Geneva and IMEDE Lausanne. Today IMD is routinely ranked among the top business schools in Europe and the world. It continues to champion connections with business and has over 120 partner and business associate companies. It is also truly international: its full-time faculty are drawn from 17 countries and as many as 91 countries are represented by the 3,600 executives attending IMD programmes in a single year. In 1997 IMD offered 22 open programmes and delivered around 35 tailored ("partnership") programmes. Its flagship Program for Executive Development is a ten-week programme delivered in two modules (Leading the Business and Leading the Multi-Business Enterprise). In alliance with the Center for Technology and Management in Zürich, IMD runs the nine-week modular Leadership Competences Programme, which is delivered in Lausanne, Thun and Münchenwiler.

INSEAD—European Institute of Business Administration

Address
Boulevard de Constance
77300 Fontainebleau Cedex
France

Tel: +33 1 60724290
Fax: +33 1 60745513

E-mail: execed@insead.fr

Website: http://www.insead.fr

Contact name
Janet Burdillat, information co-ordinator

Status
Private business school; founded 1957

Other offices
None

Teaching staff
Full-time 90; part-time 45

Comments

INSEAD is one of the world's leading business schools with a high-calibre faculty, impressive resources and an abiding commitment to internationalism. In 1997 4,500 executives participated in its programmes. INSEAD's campus, situated 65 km south of Paris, continues to expand. The latest addition, a new west wing, provides more teaching space, offices, a restaurant and recreational facilities. The school's open programmes include the 30-year-old Advanced Management Programme (AMP), which focuses on five areas: strategic perspective, world view, managing people, functional disciplines and their interface and self-renewal. The growth of the AMP is symptomatic of the growth of INSEAD. Starting as an annual programme with 25 executives from seven countries, the AMP is now run three times a year with two separate cohorts of 50 participants from over 20 countries. INSEAD also offers consortium and tailored programmes.

EM Lyon

Address
23 Avenue Guy de Collongue
BP 174
69130 Ecully Cedex
France

Tel: +33 4 78337800
Fax: +33 4 78337866

E-mail: entreprise@em-lyon.com

Contact name
Paul-André Faure, director of
executive programmes

Status
Private business school affiliated
to the Chamber of Commerce &
Industry of Lyon; founded 1872

Other offices
France: Paris

Teaching staff
Full-time 85

Comments
The Management Development Centre of EM Lyon (previously Groupe ESC Lyon) was established in 1960.
Its campus is close to the centre of Lyon and it also has an office in Paris. EM Lyon offers around 50 open
programmes but tailored programmes form the bulk of its activities. Clients include Alcatel, IBM and
Rhône-Poulenc. Programmes are delivered in Spanish, German and English as well as in French. EM Lyon was
involved in the creation of The European Management Programme Organisation (TEMPO) with Cranfield in
the UK, IESE in Spain and USW in Germany. TEMPO delivers pan-European executive programmes. The
school also has a Management Research Institute which keeps it abreast of the latest developments in
management tools and techniques.

Maastricht School of Management

Address
PO Box 1203
6201 BE Maastricht
Netherlands

Tel: +31 43 3618318
Fax: +31 43 3618330

E-mail: information@msm.nl

Website: http://www.msm.nl

Contact name
Jerry L Huxell

Status
Private

Other offices
None

Teaching staff
20 full-time, 25 part-time;
70% foreign

Comments
Maastricht School of Management (MSM), founded in 1952, is a management training and consulting
institute located in the town's new mini-campus. One of the leading schools in the Netherlands, MSM
benefits from its location close to both Amsterdam and Brussels. A number of international institutions are
based in the town including the European Centre for Development Policy Management, a branch of the
United Nations University and the State University of Limburg. MSM specialises in developing executives "in
the context of industrial development and economic transition". It offers both open and tailored
programmes. Regular open programmes include Advanced Consultancy Skills, Marketing Management and
Physical Distribution, and Management of the Environment. One of its longer programmes is the two-week
Business to Business Programme aimed at senior executives from companies in emerging economies and
senior Dutch executives.

Nijenrode University—The Netherlands Business School

Address
Nijenrode Executive and
Management Development
Centre
Straatweg 25
3621 BG Breukelen
Netherlands

Tel: +31 346 291413
Fax: +31 346 291300

E-mail: info@nijenrode.nl

Website:
http://www.nijenrode.nl

Contact name
Koen Hazewinkel

Status
Private university

Other offices
None

Teaching staff
n/a

Comments
Nijenrode is a private university which was established by Dutch businessmen in 1946. Located just outside Amsterdam, it aims to develop "reflective practitioners". Nijenrode offers executive programmes in three forms: tailored programmes (an area in which it has over ten years' experience); longer-running general management programmes; and short, intensive programmes and seminars. It has a portfolio of around ten open programmes including the intensive Advanced Management Programme (delivered in Dutch) and the General Management Programme (a ten-week programme sometimes used as a precursor to studying for an MBA). Nijenrode's MBA programmes are highly rated and it has strong links with the University of Rochester in the US.

NIMBAS Graduate School of Management

Address
PO Box 2040
3500 GA Utrecht
Netherlands

Tel: +31 30 2314323
Fax: +31 30 2367320

E-mail:
nimbas@compuserve.com

Website:
http://www.nimbas.com

Contact name
Dirk Ilsink

Status
Independent; affiliated to
University of Bradford
Management Centre

Other offices
Germany: Bonn, Mainz

Teaching staff
Part-time, visiting 67

Comments
NIMBAS Graduate School of Management, with campuses in Utrecht, Bonn and Mainz, is best known for the MBA programmes it offers in conjunction with the UK's University of Bradford Management Centre. The school runs tailored executive programmes ranging from short, board-level diagnostic sessions or workshops to one- or two-day programmes covering selected major areas of interest. It also offers longer, three- or four-week skills courses in management. NIMBAS's corporate clients include British Petroleum, Allied Breweries, ICI and Coca-Cola.

Rotterdam School of Management—Erasmus Graduate School of Business

Address
PO Box 1738
3000 DR Rotterdam
Netherlands

Tel: +31 10 4082222
Fax: +31 10 4529509

E-mail: rsm@fac.rsm.eur.nl

Website: http://www.rsm.nl

Contact name
Klaas Wassens, director, executive programmes

Status
Private, affiliated to Erasmus University

Other offices
None

Teaching staff
n/a

Comments

Rotterdam School of Management (RSM) is the business school of Erasmus University. It started life in 1970 as a co-operative venture between Delft University of Technology and Erasmus. The school offers open and tailored programmes, and the executive programmes are closely linked to its MBA programmes. It also offers in-company executive MBA programmes. Open programmes include Marketing Management of New Products, Risk Management and Business Valuation. (Some programmes are taught in Dutch.) Rotterdam also organises one-day management seminars with a leading Dutch financial newspaper, *Het Financieele Dagblad*. It has healthy international links with, among others, Michigan Business School, and is consistently highly rated in business school rankings.

The Michael Smurfit Graduate School of Business—University College Dublin

Address
Blackrock
Co Dublin
Ireland

Tel: +353 1 7068934
Fax: +353 1 2831911

E-mail: padmin@blackrock.ucd.ie

Website: http://www.ucd.ie/gsb

Contact name
Ann Naughton

Status
Part of National University of Ireland

Other offices
None

Teaching staff
Full-time 77; part-time 25

Comments

The Michael Smurfit Graduate School of Business at Dublin's University College is the largest school of its kind in Ireland. Its 20-acre campus is near Blackrock, five miles south of Dublin. The school was set up in 1989, incorporating the college's previous Faculty of Commerce, following a founding endowment from one of Ireland's leading businessmen, Michael Smurfit. The Advanced Management Programmes Division was set up in the early 1990s and is based in Management House on the Blackrock campus. It offers open and tailored programmes of various lengths with an emphasis on action-centred learning.

Theseus Institute

Address
Rue Albert Einstein BP 169
06903 Sophia Antipolis
France

Tel: +33 4 92945100
Fax: +33 4 93653837

E-mail: info@theseus.fr

Website: http://www.theseus.fr

Contact name
Yury Boshyk, director, executive
education programmes

Status
Founded 1989

Other offices
None

Teaching staff
Full-time 6; associate 10;
visiting 40-50

Comments
Theseus Institute, based in the Sophia Antipolis technology park in the south of France, offers open and tailored programmes. In particular, it emphasises the importance of partnership. Among its open programmes is a new two-week Global Change Leadership Programme designed for "leaders who are, or will be, managing important changes within their organisations and for change agents who must see beyond today and understand tomorrow's impacts". Other programmes include the new Programme for Energising People which uses "Dynamic Action Groups" and the High-Potential Professionals Programme (a consortium programme). The latter is built around three residential modules of seven days and two distance-learning modules spread over two months.

Rest of world

Australian Graduate School of Management—University of New South Wales

Address
Sydney NSW 2052
Australia

Tel: +61 2 99319333
Fax: +61 2 96628862

E-mail: executive.programs
@agsm.unsw.edu.au

Website:
http://www.agsm.unsw.edu.au/

Contact name
Ernie Waldstein, director,
executive programmes

Status
Part of the University of New
South Wales; founded 1976

Other offices
None

Teaching staff
Full-time 40; part-time 12

Comments

The Australian Graduate School of Management (AGSM), located on the campus of the University of New South Wales in Sydney, has an international reputation as one of Australia's top-rated business schools. It offers executive programmes for senior and middle managers which include some tailored programmes. Its 80 open programmes are usually residential and last from two days to four weeks. Among the subjects covered are effective sales management, industrial relations, investment evaluation and strategic human resource management. The AGSM also runs a six-day General Manager Programme and a three-week Accelerated Development Programme. As this directory was being prepared, the AGSM announced a proposed merger with the University of Sydney Graduate School of Management.

University of Cape Town—Graduate School of Business

Address
Breakwater Campus
Portswood Road, Green Point
8001 Cape Town
South Africa

Tel: +27 21 4061339
Fax: +27 21 215693

E-mail:
mbaenqry@gsb2.uct.ac.za

Website:
http://www.gsb.uct.ac.za

Contact name
Robert Macdonald

Status
Part of University of Cape Town

Other offices
None

Teaching staff
Full-time 16; part-time 15

Comments

The University of Cape Town's Graduate School of Business began life in 1964 and is now consistently rated as one of the best business schools in South Africa. More than 1,200 participants pass through its executive programmes each year. The school currently runs 29 open programmes. Its premier general management programme, the Programme for Management Development, was first offered in 1967. Among its other programmes are the Accelerated Development Programme (four one-week sessions), Information Technology Management (six days) and Manufacturing Management (six days). The school runs the Achieving Breakthrough Service programme as a joint venture with Harvard Business School. It also offers tailored programmes.

Chinese University of Hong Kong

Address
MBA Programmes
The Chinese University of Hong
Kong
Shatin, NT
Hong Kong

Tel: +852 26097786
Fax: +852 26036289

E-mail: laurenlee@cuhk.edu.hk

Website:
http://www.cuhk.edu.hk

Contact name
Lauren Lee, admissions
co-ordinator

Status
Part of the Chinese University of
Hong Kong

Other offices
None

Teaching staff
Full-time 104; part-time 7

Comments
Following the handover of Hong Kong to China, the Chinese University of Hong Kong occupies an intriguing position on the border between Western and Eastern cultures. The University's Faculty of Business Administration runs both open and tailored programmes, as well as MBA programmes which are rated among the best in Asia by *Asia Inc* magazine. Its senior executive programmes aim to help senior managers set strategic directions, establish priorities and objectives, formulate business plans, tighten decision-making processes and develop procedures for efficient follow-through. The faculty's tailored programmes can target a company's entire operations in Asia and Australasia or specific countries in the region. In 1990 the Asia-Pacific Institute of Business was established as the external arm of the Faculty of Business Administration. The institute aims to provide educational programmes, research and consultancy services to assist managers and companies in meeting business challenges in Hong Kong and elsewhere in Asia and Australasia.

Curtin Business School

Address
30th Floor, QV1 Building
250 St George's Terrace
Perth WA 6000
Australia

Tel: +61 8 92667773
Fax: +61 8 92662808

E-mail: cbc@cbs.curtin.edu.au

Website:
http://www.cbs.curtin.edu.au/cbc

Contact name
Shelley Acham

Status
Part of Curtin University of
Technology

Other offices
None

Teaching staff
Full-time 12; part-time 11

Comments
Curtin Business School in Perth, Western Australia, is one of the largest business schools in Asia and Australasia. It focuses strongly on South-east Asia and is highly cosmopolitan. Executive development programmes, both open and tailored, are delivered by Curtin Business Centre. It offers a range of practical programmes covering such areas as computer skills, business skills and legal issues. Curtin University has a unique Strategic Planning and Decisions Unit, dedicated to helping organisations address difficult problems and policy issues. Programmes usually involve senior executives working with Curtin facilitators. In 1998 Curtin launched its Master of International Business programme, a pan-Asian qualification for experienced managers. It has also recently opened a Small Business Unit.

The Hong Kong University of Science and Technology—School of Business and Management

Address
Dean's Office
School of Business and
Management
HKUST
Clear Water Bay, Kowloon
Hong Kong

Tel: +852 23587547
Fax: +852 23581467

E-mail: bmkitty@ust.hk

Website: http://www.bi.ust.hk

Contact name
Kitty Chan, associate director,
executive programmes

Status
Part of The Hong Kong University
of Science and Technology;
founded 1991

Other offices
None

Teaching staff
140

Comments

The School of Business and Management at The Hong Kong University of Science and Technology, founded in 1991, is one of the newest in the Asia and Australasia region. It emphasises the quality of its research and teaching and its ability to attract academics from all over the world. Open programmes form the majority of the school's work. Some of these are offered in conjunction with The Anderson School at UCLA and include Managing the Information Resource, International Financial Risk Management, Finance for Non-Financial Managers and Corporate Financial Strategies. The school also offers a range of workshops and seminars including a number on more specialised finance-oriented subjects. Its tailored programmes (usually lasting two weeks) are geared to the public and quasi-government sectors in Hong Kong and China. The school has been involved in co-operative projects in support of economic developments in China and the region.

Indian Institute of Management

Address
Vastrapur
Ahmedabad 380 015
India

Tel: +91 79 407241
Fax: +91 79 6423352

E-mail:
mdp@mdplan.iimahd.ernet.in

Website:
http://www.iimahd.ernet.in

Contact name
Ravi Acharya, manager, MDA

Status
Autonomous; founded 1961

Other offices
None

Teaching staff
Full-time 74; visiting 11;
fellows 4; other 16

Comments

The Indian Institute of Management (IIM) at Ahmedabad is generally considered to be the highest-ranking business school in the subcontinent. (There are other IIMs at various locations around India.) The IIM was founded in 1961 and in its formative years collaborated with Harvard Business School. As a result, the IIM pioneered the case method of teaching in India. The Institute regards itself as a school of management rather than a business school. Its management development programmes have been running for 33 years and have attracted 26,000 participants from over 3,000 organisations. The IIM operates in both the public and private sectors offering general management and functional programmes, some of which cover issues concerning business in India. It also offers tailored (or sponsored) programmes. These are supported by national and international agencies which nominate participants and, typically, are concerned with specifically Indian or emerging economy issues.

Macquarie Graduate School of Management—Macquarie University

Address
99 Talavera Road
North Ryde
Sydney NSW 2109
Australia

Tel: +61 2 98509044
Fax: +61 2 98508630

E-mail: sue.selden@mq.edu.au

Website:
http://www.gsm.mq.edu.au/

Contact name
Sue Selden, client relationship
executive

Status
Wholly-owned company of
Macquarie University

Other offices
Strategic alliances in Singapore
and Hong Kong

Teaching staff
Full-time 38; part-time 48

Comments

Sydney's Macquarie Graduate School of Management, founded in 1969, is now acknowledged as one of the leading schools in Asia and Australasia. It offers a variety of executive development programmes designed for small, interactive groups of senior executives, ranging in length from a few days to a week or longer. Its open programmes include the three-week Macquarie Advanced Management Programme, which aims to provide participants with a "comprehensive perspective of the key issues of contemporary management". It also offers programmes ranging from Creative Business Development to Logistics Management and functionally based programmes such as Marketing Management and Finance for Managers. As well as open programmes, Macquarie can arrange one- and two-day facilitated workshops for individual organisations.

Melbourne Business School—University of Melbourne

Address
200 Leicester Street
Carlton Vic 3053
Australia

Tel: +61 3 93498400
Fax: +61 3 93498404

E-mail:
v.turnbull@mbs.unimelb.edu.au

Website:
http://www.mbs.unimelb.edu.au

Contact name
Val Turnbull, manager, executive
courses

Status
Affiliated to University of
Melbourne; founded 1956

Other offices
Singapore; Hong Kong

Teaching staff
Full-time 40; visiting 20

Comments

Melbourne Business School began life in 1956 when the University of Melbourne offered Australia's first residential executive programme. Over the last decade the school has grown rapidly and now offers world-class facilities in its own four-storey building. The Australian government has awarded it the status of a national management school. It has a number of research centres covering international finance, international trade, finance, retailing and marketing, management of IT and manufacturing management. The school offers a comprehensive range of open programmes including a four-week Executive Development Programme (run twice a year) and a number of shorter programmes including Manufacturing Management (four days) and Leveraging Information Technology for Business Value (two days). It also runs one- and two-day seminars covering topical issues. Melbourne Business School has developed tailored programmes for many large corporations.

Monash Mt Eliza Business School

Address
4th floor
27 Sir John Monash Drive
Caulfield Vic 3161
Australia

Tel: +61 3 92151100
Fax: +61 3 95723691

E-mail:
klindsey@monashmteliza.edu.au

Website:
http://www.mteliza.edu.au

Contact name
Kate Lindsey, manager, corporate
marketing

Status
Aligned with Monash University,
but operates as a separate entity;
founded 1957

Other offices
Australia: Brisbane, Sydney;
China: Guangzhou; Fiji: Suva;
Indonesia: Jakarta

Teaching staff
Full-time 110; part-time 30

Comments

Monash Mt Eliza Business School, founded in 1957 and located south of Melbourne, is a substantial provider of executive development programmes in Asia and Australasia. With some 110 full-time faculty and 7,200 individuals participating in its programmes each year, the school is highly influential. It offers a wide range of residential executive programmes. Its open programmes cover the areas of general management, internal performance management, strategy, leadership and marketing. These include a range of government- and industry-specific programmes. The emphasis is on practical implementation and experience through field visits. It also offers tailored programmes. Monash Mt Eliza is active throughout Asia and Australasia, with almost half of its students taking part in programmes outside Australia.

National University of Singapore—Graduate School of Business

Address
10 Kent Ridge Crescent
Singapore 119260

Tel: +65 8743191
Fax: +65 8720041

E-mail: fbakuopj@nus.eud.sg

Website:
http://www.fba.nus.edu.sg/edp

Contact name
Kuo Pey Juan, administrative
officer

Status
Part of university; founded 1965

Other offices
None

Teaching staff
186 (full-time, part-time,
associate)

Comments

More than 7,500 individuals from 77 countries have taken part in executive programmes offered by the National University of Singapore (NUS) since it entered the executive education market in 1980. Its open programmes (all delivered in English) are divided into four areas: management programmes; collaborative programmes; special interest programmes; and Asia programmes. The school also delivers tailored programmes (over one-third of the total) and programmes in Mandarin. The NUS is notable particularly for its collaborative programmes with four US schools. These are the Stanford-NUS Executive Program, the Cornell-NUS Hospitality Management Program, the Wharton-NUS Banking & Risk Management Program and the Pennsylvania State-NUS Logistics Management Program. Its Asia programmes cover strategic marketing and managing technological innovation.

The University of Sydney—The Graduate School of Business

Address
Locked Bag 20
Newtown NSW 2042
Australia

Tel: +61 2 93510000
Fax: +61 2 93510099

E-mail: gsbinfo@gsb.usyd.edu.au

Website:
http://www.usyd.edu.au/su/gsb/

Contact name
Vanessa Munro, marketing
manager

Status
Part of the University of Sydney

Other offices
None

Teaching staff
Full-time 9; part-time 16

Comments

The Graduate School of Business originated in the University of Sydney in 1987 and moved into its own building in 1988. The university is Australia's oldest, with over 30,000 students and more than 2,000 faculty. The school offers tailored programmes for a minimum of 20 participants. Potential contents are described by the school as accelerated development, industry-specific knowledge, group learning and help in moving a project from theory to application. It is proposed that the University of Sydney's Graduate School of Business is to merge with the University of New South Wales's Australian Graduate School of Management. The planned joint venture will create a larger school able to compete more effectively with international business schools. (In March 1998 the merger received approval in principle from the governing bodies of both universities.)

Wits Business School—University of the Witwatersrand

Address
PO Box 98
Wits 2050
South Africa

Tel: +27 11 4885600
Fax: +27 11 6432336

E-mail:
reg@zeus.mgmt.wits.ac.za

Website: http://www.wits.ac.za

Contact name
Mike Ward

Status
Part of the University of the
Witwatersrand

Other offices
None

Teaching staff
Full-time 20; part-time 15

Comments

Wits Business School, at the University of the Witwatersrand in Johannesburg, was founded in 1968. It has grown rapidly since then into one of South Africa's leading business schools. It has a number of centres of expertise, including the Centre for Business Studies and the Centre for Developing Business. Wits offers a wide range of open programmes. These include Product Strategy and Brand Management (three days), Strategic Industrial Relations (three days), Project Management (four days), The Expert Negotiator (four days), Global Business Strategy (five days) and Effective Interpersonal Skills (five days). It also offers a four-week Executive Development Programme.

University of the West Indies—Institute of Business

Address
Royal Caribbean Building
109-109A St Vincent Street
Port of Spain
Trinidad & Tobago

Tel: +1 868 6274415/23/27
Fax: +1 868 6235678

E-mail: iob@trinidad.net

Contact name
Denise Dumas Koylass, manager
training and consultancy

Status
Established 1989 as affiliate
business school of University of
the West Indies

Other offices
Trinidad: St Augustine (university
campus)

Teaching staff
Full-time 15; part-time 30

Comments

The University of the West Indies Institute of Business was established in 1989 as a collaborative venture
between the local business communities and the university. Its executive programmes aim to share
knowledge with the business communities and to create learning organisations as well as learning managers
and leaders. The institute hopes to play an important role in the transformation of Caribbean-based
businesses into globally competitive, export-driven, international enterprises. It tailors programmes for a
variety of clients usually lasting three-six days and can include multiweek presentations and/or residential
programmes. The institute also offers in-company consultancy as well as diagnostic studies. Open
programmes are geared towards gaining certificates in operational skills and it also offers a five- or
seven-module Executive Development Programme.